PATRICIAN
DEMOCRAT

Charles Cowper, colonial secretary and premier of New South Wales, 1865
By courtesy of the Council of the State Library of N.S.W.)

PATRICIAN
DEMOCRAT

The Political Life
of Charles Cowper
1843–1870

ALAN POWELL

Senior Lecturer in History
Darwin Community College

MELBOURNE UNIVERSITY PRESS

1977

First published 1977

Printed in Hong Kong by
Silex Enterprise & Printing Co. for
Melbourne University Press, Carlton, Victoria 3053
U.S.A. and Canada: International Scholarly Book Services, Inc.,
Box 555, Forest Grove, Oregon 97116
Great Britain, Europe, the Middle East, Africa and the Caribbean:
International Book Distributors Ltd (Prentice-Hall International),
66 Wood Lane End, Hemel Hempstead,
Hertfordshire HP2 4RG, England

National Library of Australia Cataloguing in Publication data

Powell, Alan Walter, 1936 — .

Patrician democrat.

Index.

Bibliography.
ISBN 0 522 84132 5.

1. Cowper, Sir Charles, 1807-1875. 2. Statesman — New
South Wales — Biography. I. Title.

320.994403

Contents

Illustrations

Acknowledgements

The help of two people was indispensable to the production of this book. Since the beginning of the project five years ago Allan Martin has been mentor to it. To his scholarship, perception, enduring patience and timely wit I owe a very great deal. My wife Wendy has spent many hours in typing various manuscripts, and in the countless ways that a wife can find she has encouraged me in every aspect of the work.

I owe thanks to Bede Nairn for first putting me on Cowper's track; and like all who have spent much research time in the Mitchell Library, the Archives Office of New South Wales and the La Trobe Library I am most appreciative of the knowledge and helpfulness shown by the staff of those institutions. Sue Summerhayes provided most effective help in the preparation of the final draft.

To Sir Norman Cowper I express my special thanks for his very kindly and practical interest in this book.

A.P.

Conversion Factors
(to two decimal places)

1 inch	2·54 centimetres
1 foot	0·30 metre
1 mile	1·61 kilometres
1 acre	0·40 hectare
1 ounce	28·35 grams
1 ton	1·02 tonnes
£1	A$2
1s	10c
1d	0.83c

Introduction

Occasionally it happens that a man is remembered for some quirk of character, real or apocryphal, rather than his genuine worth. Charles Cowper, first 'liberal' premier of New South Wales under responsible government, is such a man. His political career spanned twenty-seven vital years in the evolution of democratic government within Australia. He played a leading part in almost every momentous political issue which arose during that time and he headed the government of New South Wales for nine of its most formative years. Australian democracy owes him no small debt; yet he is remembered, if remembered at all, principally as 'Slippery Charlie', politician of remarkable flexibility and few firm principles. 'Slippery' he certainly was at times; I hope this book will show that he was a good deal more than that.

Cowper lived and worked in the relatively small society of mid-nineteenth-century New South Wales, a society which took considerable interest in the public actions of its leading men. Thus many aspects of his political career are well documented from public sources and to a lesser extent from the private papers of his contemporaries. Regrettably, the same is not true of his private life. Australians of the Victorian era probably knew more about the personal lives of their public men than we know of ours: it was a gossipy society. But such things were seldom written of. Victorian mores (and litigiousness) precluded the publication of intimate glimpses into personal lives luckily for their standards of journalism, unluckily for modern-day biographers; and Cowper's letters to his family have not survived. Of necessity, then, this book is mainly concerned with the politician rather than the whole man.

A great deal of work remains to be done on the events and institutions in which Cowper was closely involved. Much of the material presented here relates to the form and functioning of political organizations and government administration in New South Wales between 1843 and 1870, but this book does not pretend to provide complete studies of, for instance, the Australian anti-transportation movement, the Legislative

1

Council of 1843–56, the Cowper governments as a whole or the functioning of the Colonial Secretary's Department which Cowper headed for nine years. Historians will recognize my debt to Buckley, Baker and Dyster on the land problem; to Cleverley, Turney, Austin, Fogarty and Barcan on education; to Walker, Barrett, Roe and Turner on state aid and the churches; to Irving on the development of liberal politics prior to 1856; and to Loveday and Martin on faction politics under responsible government. It is to be hoped that the building upon their work which I have done and my attempts to concentrate upon Cowper's personal involvement in politics rather than upon the overall development of political organization and administration will enable readers to make a reasonable assessment of both the man and the value of his work.

1

The Shaping of a Colonial Conservative

Charles Cowper was born a Yorkshireman. In 1807, the year of his birth, his father held a curacy in the village of Drypool, a few miles from the seaport of Hull. But the Reverend William Cowper sought a deeper commitment to his Lord than he could find in rural England. In 1808 he met Samual Marsden who, putting aside the cares of his colonial chaplaincy and his prospering properties in New South Wales, had returned to England, partly in the hope of recruiting clergy for the young penal colony. His task was unrewarding. The fastidious products of Oxford and Cambridge who manned the pulpits of the Church of England saw little glory and less comfort in ministering to the sinners of New South Wales. William Cowper was of sterner mould and Marsden soon secured him as his first recruit. William and Hannah Cowper bundled up their meagre belongings and prepared to sail for New South Wales with baby Charles and his elder brothers, Harry and Thomas. At the last moment Hannah Cowper died and it seemed that the new colonial chaplain might not sail, but Cowper was a resourceful man. He is said to have appealed from the pulpit for some dedicated member of the fair sex to help him with his missionary work in New South Wales and when a zealous (or at least enterprising) young woman rose in response, he lost no time in marrying her. Within a few months the newly-weds and their ready-made family took passage for Sydney in the brig *Indispensable*. Charles was barely two years old when the ship cast anchor in Sydney Cove on 19 August 1809. He could not have remembered England. Like so many of the free settlers of nineteenth-century Australia he took pride in his British heritage, but in his own eyes and those of his contemporaries he was an Australian and he saw no more of his birthplace until he was an old man.

Until Marsden's return to New South Wales in 1810, William Cowper was the only ordained and practising Anglican clergyman in the colony. With Marsden back, Cowper took up the living at St Phillip's Church in Bridge Street, Sydney, with a parish extending around Sydney Cove and back into the business area of the straggling little town. There

he remained until his death forty-eight years later, when his son William
Macquarie Cowper succeeded him and served the city until 1902 — surely
a remarkable family record.

Macquarie Cowper, born in 1810, retained vivid memories of Sydney
as it was while he and his half-brother Charles spent their early years
under the rule of Governor Macquarie who had followed them within
a few months to New South Wales and who became parishioner,
friend and benefactor to their father. For three years the Cowpers
occupied the low, verandahed cottage built in Bent Street for the
colonial chaplain of the first fleet, Richard Johnson. Macquarie Cowper
recalled the two orange trees which flanked the path from the dusty
street and the flourishing orchard behind, where, no doubt, he and his
brothers scrambled and gorged themselves as small boys do. [1] But the
cottage was small and the Cowper family moved to 'a more commodious
dwelling', which boasted a balcony as well as a verandah, around the
corner in Macquarie Place [2] — not the most salubrious part of the town,
for the Cowpers were bordered by the stone mansion and stores of
wealthy emancipist Simeon Lord and a beaver hat factory on one side
and by Brown's counting-house, the 'Reiby Cottage' and a blacksmith
on the other. On the western side of Sydney Cove were King's Wharf,
the commissariat store, the Custom House and the premises of leading
merchant Robert Campbell. In front of the Cowper house and sweeping
right around to the eastern point of the Cove, the grey-green native
scrub remained untouched. So, too, was the triangle of land at the
corner of Bent Street and Macquarie Place, where the Cowper boys
saw Port Jackson blacks gather to hold corroboree, reminding the
whites that they yet clung only to the fringe of a vast land they did
not understand.

M. H. Ellis has called old St Phillip's 'the ugliest church in Chris-
tendom' [3] and certainly its combination of a warehouse-like building
with a Crusader's tower at one end and a structure resembling a covered
water-tank at the other, was not pleasing to the eye, but William Cowper
made it the centre of a vigorous parish life. He was a man of great
energy and firm adherence to his personal concept of Christian ethics.
In his youth, prospects of a commercial career had been abruptly ended
when he refused his employer's demand that he work on a Sunday.
In 1842 his bishop W. G. Broughton remarked that Cowper had never
been afraid to speak the truth openly 'in a place where it required some
fortitude to use plain language. [4] Broughton valued highly the honesty,
zeal and vigour shown by Cowper, but he feared that, having been
'brought up among very low churchmen, if not dissenters, of the
Calvinistic school', he needed 'a grain or two of warmer preference

for Church principles over those of the Bible Society'. [5] Broughton's
judgement was influenced by his own High Church leanings. Cowper's
sincerity, practical kindliness and willingness to co-operate with other
sects in charitable works brought him wide respect.

The parishioners of St Phillip's ranged from the governor to the
denizens of the town gaol, and few failed to recognize Cowper's worth
even though, as Macquarie Cowper wryly remarked, 'they might not
act as he taught them'. [6] On Sundays the convicts, gathered at the
old gaol yard in lower George Street, heard him first. The fashionable
morning service at St Phillip's followed. Macquarie and his aides in
full uniform clanked their way to the front pews with their ladies,
followed by the great traders and mercantile families of the town,
Campbells, Joneses, Rileys. The afternoon service catered for the lower
classes. Cowper's own family and servants down to the nursemaid with
the latest babe in arms had to attend without fail each Sunday, for
William Cowper believed that all should be exposed to the word of
God. He was one of the few Anglican clergymen in early New South
Wales who declined to engage in temporal pursuits, refusing Macquarie's
repeated requests that he enter the magistracy. He served his God
full-time.

Believing strongly that education without religion was 'inadequate to
the nature of man', [7] he took a close interest in church schools, founding
one himself at St Phillip's and playing a leading part in organizing the
Protestant agitation of 1836 and 1839 which compelled successive
governors, Bourke and Gipps, to forego their plans for a system of
secular education. He spent an hour or two each day teaching his own
children and, according to Macquarie Cowper, was responsible for the
entire education of young Charles. [8] Not surprisingly, Charles came to
share the fervent evangelical faith of his father and the plainness of
his speech and writings reflected the instruction of a largely self-taught
man. Charles grew into a slight, delicate youth of bright face and
pleasing manner, sharing his father's equable temperament and capacity
for hard work. As the son of an Anglican clergyman he joined the
families of the greater landowners and government officials in the ranks
of the colonial upper class, but, reared in the complex society of his
father's parish, he lacked the arrogant exclusiveness of his peers. Robert
Campbell, son of the great merchant of the same name, was his
boyhood friend and later his closest political ally, and Cowper's wide
contacts amongst city men were to form a vital base for his political
career.

In 1825, as William Cowper considered the prospects for his son's
future, the thought of a political career would not have occurred to

him. The autocratic Macquarie had gone, leaving his legacy of roads, fine buildings and the vision of new lands beyond the coastal ranges, but his successor, Brisbane, carried a commission which gave him the same sweeping powers, hardly diminished by the formation of a hand-picked Legislative Council in 1823. William Charles Wentworth had barely begun his campaign for leadership of the emancipist and small free settler group, and the upper-class Exclusives quarrelled pettishly with one another and with the governor. Just before he was recalled, Brisbane graciously solved the problem of a career for Charles Cowper by appointing him a clerk in the Commissariat Department, where his diligence and natural charm soon led Deputy Commissary-General Wemyss to think him indispensable. In the same year Archdeacon Thomas Hobbes Scott arrived in New South Wales to head the Church of England and to inaugurate his brain-child, the Clergy and School Lands Corporation. Coming to Australia as secretary to Commissioner J. T. Bigge in 1819, Scott wrote his own supplementary reports on religion and education, gained the ear of Lord Bathurst at the Colonial Office, took Holy Orders and returned to the colony with a sweeping educational mandate. The corporation was to be endowed with one-seventh of the colony's Crown lands, and the revenues were meant to provide for the upkeep of the Anglican clergy and for all education in New South Wales. Scott struck up a friendship with William Cowper and appointed him one of the trustees to the corporation. Since a degree of nepotism was not unusual in the making of public service appointments, no one showed surprise when nineteen-year-old Charles Cowper became secretary to the corporation in June 1826, at the princely salary of £450 a year. Thus fortunately launched in life, Cowper made the most of his chance. In 1829 Scott told Governor Darling of 'the tried talent and integrity of Mr. Charles Cowper...I have had the most convincing proof, during a close and daily intercourse of three years; and to him I left the detail of almost every matter connected with the Temporalities of the Church and through whose [sic] hands and very accurate circumspection the Annual Expenditure of £20,000 has passed. In no one else, should I feel disposed to place...[such] implicit Confidence'. [9] Scott had faith enough in the young man to give him sole management of his personal lands in New South Wales when he left the colony in 1830, and modern researchers have borne out Scott's high opinion of Cowper's administrative efficiency as secretary to the corporation. [10]

In earning such commendation Cowper wore himself out. The affairs of the Clergy and School Lands Corporation were an adminis-trator's nightmare. The undermanned Survey Department could not select and survey more than a minute fraction of the corporation's lands, and the promised revenues never materialized. Dependent on parsimonious grants from a reluctant government, the corporation was permanently understaffed. Dissenters and Catholics, fearing the corporation as an organ of Anglican supremacy, opposed it bitterly. So did many others, even Anglicans, who considered the colony's progress or their own ambitions endangered by the encroachment of the Church on the unused Crown lands of the colony. By 1828 the British government had begun to repent the scheme it had so easily approved three years before, and the corporation was replaced with a temporary commission. Cowper stayed on as secretary to this body. Desperate under the continuing burden of overwork and consequent ill-health, he almost resigned in 1829, but hung on until the demise of the commission in 1833. Scott, back in England, had not forgotten him. He pressed the Colonial Office to help Cowper, and they in turn urged the new governor, Sir Richard Bourke, to find the young secretary an equivalent position. For once, Cowper's charm and eminent sponsors failed him. Bourke offered only a post worth less than half his previous salary, and Cowper declined. 'This gentleman's health was much impaired' explained Bourke, 'and, having enjoyed a salary of £400 a year under the Corporation, he was not inclined to accept the inferior Salary which I thought it right to offer him.' [11]

Cowper's forethought during the years when he drew an official salary allowed him to reject Bourke's offer with impunity. His personality, which had so charmed Wemyss and Scott, impressed Darling and the officials of the land board too. In 1827 the board endorsed his application for a land grant with the notation, 'a very respectable young man and worthy of encouragement'. [12] The governor granted him 1250 acres of land in the County of Argyle plus a similar amount in 1830. According to disgruntled fellow-officers, he was one of only two public servants below the rank of department head who gained land grants from the irascible Darling. [13]

In 1828 Cowper began to buy land. In that year, financial stringency forced the Clergy and School Lands Corporation to sell most of the glebe lands belonging to St Phillip's. Cowper bought 25 acres. Thus by 1833 he was a small landholder and he spent much of the next ten years in becoming a large one. In 1836 he bought Scott's 2560-acre grant, Chatsbury, a few miles from the straggling hamlet of Goulburn and adjacent to his grants from Darling. By 1840 further purchases had expanded the property to more than 12 000 acres. In addition he held Crown land leases in the same area amounting by 1857 to nearly 20 000 acres. The land was good, well watered, only 130 miles from Sydney and it formed the basis of Cowper's fortunes. There his manager ran sheep and grew wheat for the Sydney market, but Cowper never lived on the property himself, for he had gained a wife and family and felt their home should offer greater comfort and a more gracious social life than could be had in the wind-swept, sparsely settled Goulburn highlands.

Cowper's wife, Eliza, was a daughter of Daniel Sutton, town clerk of the small Essex city of Colchester. The Cowpers married in 1831 and had six children, one of whom died in infancy, but apart from the oldest, Charles, who followed his father into politics, little is known of them. They always remained shadowy figures in the background of his political career. Eliza Cowper seems to have been a good Victorian wife, loyal, self-effacing and uncomplaining. No scandal ever touched the Cowpers' marriage and there is no reason to doubt the assessment of the *Town and Country Journal* that Charles Cowper was always 'a dutiful son, a kind father [and] a good husband'. [14] In 1836, Cowper's increasing prosperity enabled him to build a substantial mansion on 900 acres of agricultural land, most of it originally a grant from Macquarie to his father, in the Camden district. This property, Wivenhoe, became his permanent home. It still stands as part of a Catholic orphanage. Here Cowper was comfortably at home amongst the estates of his friends: the Hassalls at Denbigh, the Macleays at Brownlow Hill, James and William Macarthur at Camden Park. Like them, he played the country squire, patronizing the labourers who tilled his land, endowing the church in the neighbouring hamlet of Cobbitty, exchanging social calls and baskets of produce with his neighbours and exhibiting his home-grown wines before the New South Wales Vineyard Society.

This was not enough to absorb his restless energy. The fine wool markets of England were booming and the demand for colonial wool seemed to be insatiable. Cowper joined the rush of men and stock to the vast lands beyond the nineteen counties, the now useless bounds of settlement prescribed by the government. In 1836 settlement of the rolling lands between the eastern highlands and the present site of Albury began and Cowper, following in 1838, laid claim to 12 000 acres of timber and kangaroo-grass south of the Murray River and in the shadow of the high alps. The station, Corryong, has given its name to a modern town on part of the site. There Cowper ran fine shorthorn cattle for the beef markets of Sydney and the fast-growing town of Melbourne. Two years later he took up a larger station a few miles further west to carry his surplus young stock. Appropriately, it was known as Cowper's Heifer Run. In 1842 Cowper turned westward, towards the western plains, and by 1857 his two sheep stations in the Lachlan district, Narraba and Grogan Creek, covered 47 000 acres.

Cowper took little interest in the political strife of the 1830s. The Legislative Council, expanded in membership and powers in 1828, was still a nominee body controlled by the upper-class Exclusive faction under the leadership of James Macarthur. The Macarthurs were Cowper's friends, but friendship did not tempt him to join Exclusive opposition to Wentworth, the Australian Patriotic Association and the mass of lower-class settlers they purported to represent, in their efforts to bring more widely responsible government to New South Wales. No doubt Cowper, busy in building up his landholdings, had little time for politics. In view of his city upbringing it is also likely that he was not fully in sympathy with Exclusive conservatism. Yet, ironically, a stigma of Exclusivism clung to him in the early years of his political career. His social position as a large landholder and member of an 'old' family probably contributed to this image, but as the *Port Phillip Patriot* pointed out in 1843.[15] the main factor was his close connection with the church of the Exclusives.

As secretary to the Clergy and School Lands Commission, Cowper had worked closely with Scott's successor, Archdeacon W.G. Broughton, later (1836) to be created bishop of Australia. Broughton took a liking to the young man and Cowper served his church well during the 1830s. He belonged to the Society for Promoting Christian Knowledge and, when that body merged with the Society for the Propagation of the Gospel in 1836, joined James and William Macarthur and local clergymen on the Camden district committee of the combined societies. Almost their first task was the organization of committees to aid Broughton in his battle to prevent the introduction of Bourke's plan for secular education. Broughton won and Bourke could only reply by passing the Church Act of 1836, giving state aid to the four main Christian denominations in proportion to their numbers in the colony. Anglicans grumbled at what they saw as government support of ecclesiastical error as well as truth, but most realized that as the sect with the largest number of nominal adherents, theirs was the greatest gain. Cowper went on to become the main force behind the building of St Paul's Church, Cobbitty. Broughton came up to open it in April 1840.

By this time the exhilaration of the first great squatting rush was over and ever-growing problems beset the new holders of the lands. Rural labour was scarce. Free immigrants poured into New South Wales in the late 1830s, but few would face the harsh loneliness of station life, and assigned convicts filled the gap. While Cowper, like

many another good churchman, viewed the transportation system as
a moral evil, his need for labour was great and, not for the last time
in his life, expediency overcame principle: convicts were assigned to
his properties. But the current of penal reform ran strongly in Britain.
In 1838, assignment ceased and two years later came the ending of
transportation to New South Wales. At the same time, signs of the
first great commercial depression in Australia's history began to appear.
Business slackened and wool prices slowly declined. Caught between the
rising cost and scarcity of free labour and the decline in profits, often
financially over-extended in their search for quick fortunes, the landholders were further undermined •by a fierce drought which seared
most of New South Wales from 1837 to 1843. It was, said Charles
MacAlister, neighbour to Cowper's Goulburn property, 'impossible to
find water enough to drown a rabbit in'. [16] Even the snow-fed streams
which ran by Corryong dried up and men walked across the Murray
River at Albury, where they never had before and never have since.

Cowper's economic position worsened rapidly after 1837. His land
purchases alone between 1835 and 1837 had cost him £2000 and in
1841 he was unable to pay the interest on the debt he owed to Scott
for the purchase of Chatsbury. In trying to alleviate his problems, he
joined nearly seven hundred other stockholders in petitioning Bourke's
successor, Sir George Gipps, for the importation of cheap labour from
India at government expense. [17] In doing so, Cowper and many of
the other signatories had to overcome their own antipathy to coloured
labour. They justified themselves by contending that, desirable as it
was to retain the British character of the colony, it was even more
necessary to keep alive the vital grazing interest they represented. All the
same, many a conscience must have been uneasy, and little protest
followed Gipps's refusal to spend government money on shipping
coolies to New South Wales.

As the colony slid deeper into depression Wentworth and other
great landholders looked towards political solutions for their economic
problems. Probably this hope prompted Cowper to take his first interest
in politics. By the beginning of 1842 it was generally expected that a
new constitution, giving electoral rights to the citizens of New South
Wales, was imminent. The pervasive hope that the coming new order
would allow the colonists to control their own revenues and run their
own internal affairs caused ambitious men to think of a political career.
Cowper was amongst them. In March, he appeared at a Sydney meeting
held to petition for a representative legislature, securing election to the
managing committee which drew up the petition and produced a plan
for the division of the colony into electorates. He seemed well placed

to enter the new political scene. His term with the Clergy and School Lands Corporation, while almost ruining his health, had proved his capacity for administration and given him a sound knowledge of the workings of government. The social elite of the colony considered him one of themselves, yet he was not tainted by previous involvement in Exclusive politics, as were the Macarthurs. Charles Kemp, co-proprietor of the colony's leading newspaper, the *Sydney Morning Herald,* was his friend. His pleasant manner and natural courtesy made him popular with those who knew him, at least with those of his own class. Sir Norman Cowper, great-grandson of Charles, recalls that he once asked an old man who had worked on Cowper's Chatsbury property what he remembered of his employer and was told that Charles was 'a stuck-up old bugger', which probably reflected rather the general attitude of the lower class to the landed gentry than any particular sins on Cowper's part. His popularity was enhanced by his exemplary conduct on the bench after Gipps appointed him a justice of the peace. Against these advantages, he lacked political experience (but so did most other potential candidates for office) and his connection with the Clergy and School Lands Corporation gave rise to a lingering suspicion of High Church intolerance and some jealousy of the favour shown him by the unpopular Darling regime.

Cowper's background and economic interests suggested that he would be numbered amongst the more conservative elements in colonial politics. Even before the ship *Aden* delivered the new Constitution Act to New South Wales in November 1842, there were ominous signs that the wealthy and conservative would not have it all their own way in colonial politics. In October, Sydney's first municipal council elections took place and the voting franchise (£25 paid in annual rental or £100 in freehold property) did not protect the social elite. 'The gentlemen most conspicuous for their wealth and station were not those on whom the choice of their fellow citizens fell', reported Gipps to Lord Stanley, [18] with considerable understatement. His appended list of 24 councillors included merchants, publicans, tanners, a miller and a cabinetmaker, but only one 'esquire'.

The new Constitution Act suffered the common fate of compromise: it satisfied no one. The colonists were to elect two-thirds of the thirty-six members to the Legislative Council, but the governor kept his full executive powers. He also had the sole right to originate money bills and he could reasonably expect support for his policies from the six colonial officials and six unofficial nominees who were to make up the balance of the legislature. The provision for an 'enormous' civil list of £81 600 yearly [19] was bound to be unpopular, since it meant that a hostile majority in the Council could not halt the basic operations of government. As Gipps well knew, his concept of local government, approved by the act, was anathema to landowners. [20] What colonist, being part of a finely drawn thread of settlement in a vast land, wanted to shoulder the burden of paying for roads and bridges in his own county? Again, the act confirmed two grievances of long standing: the colonists continued to bear the whole cost of the convict establishment and they gained no share in the disposal of Crown lands and revenues.

The high property qualifications required of Council members (a minimum freehold value of £1000 or £100 in annual rentals) made it certain that candidates would be drawn from an affluent minority of the population: merchants, landholders, professional men. Less certain were the effects of the franchise, £200 in freehold property or £20 paid annually in house rental. The *Sydney Morning Herald* thought this 'next door to universal suffrage'. [21] So did Bishop Broughton and W.C. Wentworth. [22] Less conservatively, the *Australian* commended the franchise as laying the basis for popular representation while excluding those who had disqualified themselves as voters by 'not having exercised prudence and economy' [23] By this standard the improvident made up the great majority of the colony's 40 000 adult males who lived within the nineteen countries, since only 9315 were on the electoral rolls in 1843. The few surviving electoral records of that year do not show the occupation or marital status of voters. But few single men were likely to be on the rolls. Many, if country dwellers, lived in rent-free quarters provided by their employers; if city men, in the innumerable boarding-houses which graced (or, sometimes, disgraced) the streets of Sydney. Leasehold farmers, tenants of such great squires as the Macarthurs, Bowmans and Lawsons, might easily be excluded because, however much they paid in rent for their land, their dwellings only were assessed for franchise purposes. [24]

No one doubted that the influence of those whom the *Sydney Morning Herald* called 'operatives' (as distinct from the 'respectable classes') [25] would be greatest in Sydney. *Herald* correspondents complained that Only the city's worst hovels rented for less that £20 a year, [26] and they were backed by the opinion of the attorney-general, J. H. Plunkett. [27] Nearly two-thirds of Sydney's voters held a rental franchise; the corresponding figure for the Hunter Valley electorate of Northumberland was one-quarter. The power of demos had been shown by the results of the city council election, but Sydney had only two seats in the legislature, and gentlemen might look to country voters for support. Sir George Gipps planned the elections for the winter of 1843, but even before the electoral boundaries were set in January, prospective candidates were canvassing their local electors. Their speeches filled the columns of the colonial newspapers, and editors passed judgement on them with solemn sincerity and a fine disregard for libel laws. Yet such activity helped only to reveal a basic lack of certainty about the shape of colonial politics. The bitter Emancipist-Exclusive struggle of the 1830s had been buried, or at least concealed, beneath the weight of merging economic and political interests, and neither old contestants or new immigrants had yet much thought of anything beyond simply making a living in a drought- and depression-ridden land. Grievances over land, labour supply and the 'extravagance' of the executive tended, during the election campaign, to merge into a more or less amorphous opposition to 'government' on the part of most candidates and newspapers.

In trying to clarify the situation, the press fell back upon the terminology of the 1830s. The *Sydney Morning Herald,* leading newspaper of New South Wales, was controlled by Cowper's friend and staunch fellow-Anglican, Charles Kemp, in partnership with the cautious Scot, John Fairfax. Together with Statham and Forster's *Australian,* damned (wrongly) as 'the hired organ of the Macarthur family', [28] the *Herald* held to a 'moderate conservative' stance, which meant little more than approval of free trade and candidates of property, high moral standing and social eminence. The self-styled 'liberal' press, headed by J. D. Lang's *Colonial Observer* and the Catholic newspaper *Australasian Chronicle* under the fiery editorship of William Duncan, linked the conservative organs to the old Exclusive faction, accusing them of religious intolerance and of trying to deny the lower classes a share in government. [29] By implication, then, liberalism meant religious tolerance and support for a wider franchise, but the conservative journals took greater care to avoid religious controversy than did their liberal counterparts. The *Observer* 'set its face as flint against the whole Papal system', [30] and Duncan would rather have consorted with the Devil than with Lang. Proud, articulate and obstinate men, these two agreed only in their antipathy to the Church of England and approval of Bourke's Church Act. Nor were they notably more 'liberal' than the conservative press in their attitudes towards the working-class voter. The *Observer* shared the initial uneasiness of the *Herald* at the low franchise figure. [31] The *Australian* and the *Chronicle* were satisfied with it. [32] Newspapers, too, were inconsistent in the candidates they supported. The *Herald* commended avowedly liberal candidates and claimed as conservatives men whom the *Observer* considered to be liberals. [33] Not to be outdone in adding to the confusion, the fiercely liberal *Port Phillip Patriot* defended wealthy landholder Dr Charles Nicholson from the charges of rank Toryism heaped upon him by Lang. [34]

Candidates were equally uncertain of their ground: 'In the present uncertain state of all measures related to our colonial politics', M. C. O'Connell told the Sydney electors, 'professions of political opinion must necessarily be to some extent vague and undefined...I will therefore, at present limit myself to declaring, that my political opinions are guided by a profound veneration for the true principles of the British Constitution, a decided enmity to all intolerance...and an earnest wish to promote the present and future welfare of this country'. [35]

Duncan railed against such weak efforts, [36] but without effect. Uncertainty remained the keynote of the campaign. Probably Richard Windeyer, 'liberal' candidate for Durham, was as perceptive as any in remarking that British political terminology had little meaning in New South Wales and that colonial politics would turn mainly on the differences between Imperial and colonial interests. [37] An old bogey raised its head when wealthy gin distiller Robert Cooper, an emancipist, stood for the Sydney electorate. This was too much for the conservative newspapers. Reluctant to reopen old wounds, they confined themselves to berating the 'laird of Juniper' [38] for his ignorance and the evils of his gin. [39] They need not have feared for the good name of Sydney. Though Cooper claimed to be 'the working man's friend', [40] and backed himself with free samples from his distillery, he suffered annihilation at the polls, thus proving at least that a coherent emancipist cause no longer existed. It is hardly surprising that, in the words of the *Sydney Morning Herald,* most election contests 'took a personal turn' [41] The campaigns in which Charles Cowper took part were no exception.

Cowper hoped to stand for either the Camden electorate, in which his Wivenhoe estate stood, or for Cumberland, part of which lay just across the Nepean River from his property. James Macarthur was the most influential politician in the district, and Cowper confidently awaited an offer of help in this, his first, political campaign, not knowing that to secure his own position Macarthur had made other arrangements in both electorates. Macarthur saw clearly that political control had escaped the grasp of the old Exclusive interest. In order to remain a major political figure he needed to widen his electoral appeal and set out quietly to do so. By the end of 1842 he had succeeded in forging an electoral compact with his old adversary, W. C. Wentworth, still the acknowledged 'liberal' leader. This move reflected both Macarthur's readiness to move from Exclusivism and Wentworth's increasing conservatism. Neither appears to have thought his following would fully accept the alliance and they kept the arrangement secret until the last days of the election campaign. Each agreed to use his influence in the other's favour, [42] and Macarthur was to run for the two-member seat of Cumberland in coalition with William Lawson, friend and political protegé of Wentworth. For Camden, Macarthur had in view the liberal-minded Catholic lawyer Roger Therry, then commissioner of the Court of Requests and, if the absence on leave of J. H. Plunkett, acting attorney-general. In supporting Therry, Macarthur could hope to gain both the votes of Cumberland's Catholics and widespread approval of his religious tolerance.

Unaware of all this, Cowper angled cautiously for Macarthur's backing. But on 28 December 1842 William Macarthur asked him to give support to Therry [43] and Cowper must suddenly have realized that he had been squeezed out of both electorates. When Cowper, rejecting the momentary hope of aiding Therry in return for Macarthur's backing elsewhere, refused to follow the dictates of Camden Park, the Macarthurs were too deeply committed to alter course. As soon as their intentions were known, Anglican landowners of Camden County pressed Cowper to stand against Therry and on 6 January 1843 he entered the field. [44] The Macarthurs may have been appalled at Cowper's opportunism in accepting sectarian support, [45] but they had brought the problem upon themselves by their own political manoeuvring. A third candidate, Dr John Osborne rose, found little support, and sank.

The campaigns of 1843 laid the basis of electioneering tactics for many years to come. Country electorates were large and voters were few. The Camden electorate encompassed the whole of the Illawarra and Picton-Berrima districts and in 1843 only 282 electors mustered to the polls. Candidates found it vital to have the backing of voluntary committees in every area, ready to turn out pamphlets, canvass each voter and organize the political meetings and dinners which greeted the candidate as he travelled through the electorate. And travel he did, incessantly, climbing on to the boards of the hustings, in some hotel or hall or under the sky on a street corner, to listen to his friends extol his worth, to follow up with his own visions of the Land of Promise while the audience cheered or jeered as the mood took them, to meet local dignitaries at a gargantuan dinner where the day's speeches were rehashed amid toasts to the Queen, to 'Home', to the governor (if he was not in disfavour with the parties concerned) and to the Ladies, God Bless Them, though none of them were present. Next day the candidate climbed on to his horse, or into his carriage or gig, and made his way over the wheel ruts which passed for roads to the next settlement where another group waited to take part in the sport of electioneering.

Stamina and leather lungs were mandatory for aspiring politicians, and Cowper lacked neither. He was heard at Camden, Picton, Kiama, Berrima, Wollongong and in the wilds of Jamberoo, Dapto and Jer-

ringong (now Gerringong). Therry matched his travels, often shadowed
by the faithful James Macarthur. Like most candidates, they had little
to say on the future of the colony. The Therry camp based its campaign
on Cowper's alleged bigotry, smearing their opponent with the taint
of intolerance. Cowper was in a difficult position, for sectarianism
was indeed the basis for much of his support. But it could be dangerous
to admit it, since neither Catholics nor Dissenters loved the 'Established'
church, and even 'liberal' (often synonymous with 'nominal') Anglicans
might resent the raising of dormant religious tensions. So the Cowperites
played down religion and tried to exploit the general antipathy to
government by flaying Therry as the servile holder of an official post.
Therry exposed Cowper as a signatory to a petition of 1840, against
allowing emancipists to hold local office. [46] The shot rebounded when
Cowper showed that the Macarthurs had signed it too, and he implied
that he now approved of full civil rights for emancipists. [47] 'Cowper and
Constitution—The Agricultural Interests of the County of Camden—God
Save the Queen' proclaimed his placards [48] — all sound conservative
sentiments, if not very enlightening. Privately, Bishop Broughton
boasted of Cowper as his 'protege', [49] but he had the good sense to refrain
from meddling in the campaign and to Duncan's great indignation
'a whole host' of Catholics attached themselves to Cowper's cause. [50]
Duncan probably contributed to this result himself; to the horror of
Therry's men he persistently lambasted Cowper and James Macarthur
equally. Therry did not gain a consistent press ally until, on 23 February,
the Catholic vicar-general, John McEncroe, quietly removed Duncan
from the editor's chair and took his place. Lang's *Colonial Observer*
obligingly condemned Cowper as 'a starched Episcopalian Exclusive'
but did the same for James Macarthur and thought 'Sir George's
Government-man' only a little less obnoxious. [51]

Cowper's backers, it seemed, had cause to congratulate themselves
on the prospects of their candidate. [52] But he and some of his Anglican
supporters, resentful of the government aid received by Catholics under
Bourke's Church Act and uneasy at the Vatican's moves of 1842 to
establish territorial sees in Australia, [53] found it difficult to conceal their
fears of papal domination. On 20 March his Anglican supporters at
Dapto gave a dinner for him. No one ever accused Cowper of insobriety,
so it must have been the *bonhomie* of his co-religionists which overrode
his usual common sense as he rose to speak. 'Gentlemen,' he proclaimed,
'I have never desired to conceal that I was induced to stand for the
county of Camden, partly on account of Mr. Therry being a member
of the Church of Rome ... For my own part I acknowledge that I cannot
view altogether without alarm the strenuous endeavours making [sic]

by the followers of the Church of Rome to obtain a political ascendency among us ... Would that the members of our own Church were equally zealous and consistent!' [54]

This public admission of prejudice probably cost Cowper the election. the *Australasian Chronicle* gleefully seized upon it to damn him as a High Church Tory, [55] brushing aside his belated protestations of religious toleration, and, according to Cowper himself, not one Catholic voted for him on polling day. [56] He lost the election by a margin of ten votes. But James Macarthur had hardly time to express his delight at Therry's triumph before he was faced with a dire threat to his own election for Cumberland, once thought to be a foregone conclusion. [57] The Cumberland election was set for one week after the Camden poll. Because of the pervasive anti-government sentiment, it is probable that many Macarthur supporters were never happy about backing Therry, and the Anglican majority of Macarthur's main election committee shared Cowper's fear of Catholic ambitions. [58] If Therry won Camden, they resolved, Cowper must supplant Macarthur in Cumberland. Accordingly, as soon as the Camden result was known, Macarthur found himself deserted by all but two of his Sydney committee, and 'an army of eager and voluntary canvassers winged their way through the county' [59] on Cowper's behalf. At the same time, Wentworth and Lawson broke publicly with Macarthur. Alarmed at the rapid erosion of Macarthur's support, Wentworth had acquired an additional and potent motive for wishing to see him defeated. On 15 June Wentworth and his friend Dr William Bland had won the Sydney seats. He knew that, without Macarthur, he would stand alone at the head of the elected members in the new Council, and there was much he wanted from that body. Lawson's defection was planned before the Camden election. Bland, who had once signed Macarthur's requisition to stand for Cumberland, became the first to sign for Cowper, and Cowper's new electoral committee (ex-Macarthur) immediately took over the electoral headquarters of Wentworth and Bland. These two did not admit to the link with Cowper, but neither did they contradict the assertions of the *Sydney Morning Herald* and Macarthur that such a compact existed. [60] Macarthur's danger was increased by two further candidates, J. R. Brenan and G. R. Nichols, who attacked him as an Exclusive and enemy to emancipists. [61] His remaining supporters had little time to respond. Bitterly, Therry prayed that intolerance, 'like a sickly exotic', might perish in Cumberland as it had in Camden, [62] but in vain. To the astonishment even of Cowper's warmest supporters, he topped the poll with 502 votes in an electorate where, as G. W. Rusden said, 'every vote had been pledged to others before he became a candidate'. [63]

Lawson, with 380 votes, narrowly defeated Macarthur for the second seat. Feelings ran high at the declaration of the poll and the Parramatta crowd greeted Cowper with a storm of mixed cheers and hisses. Richard Sadleir, a defector from Macarthur to Cowper, could not obtain a hearing at all and the crowd took the horses from the shafts of Macarthur's carriage to draw it through the streets of the town themselves. But the sympathy of the Parramatta crowd could not restore the influence of Camden Park in the political life of New South Wales. James Macarthur had lost his chance to lead the forces of conservatism into the new era and, refusing with dignity Gipps's offer of a nominee's seat in the Council, he retired to private life.

Conversely, Cowper's gamble in opposing the Macarthurs had paid him well. He had removed himself from their political shadow, taking with him solid support from Anglican landowners, and it says much for his personal qualities that Catholics were amongst the friends who hailed his triumphant return to Wivenhoe. [64] Yet he owed his victory to city men. His merchant friend Robert Campbell and the colony's sheriff, William Hustler, managed his campaign while Charles Kemp lent him the powerful backing of the *Herald*. He gained his majority at the two metropolitan polling places, Sydney and St Leonards, [65] for Cumberland electorate included the raw new suburbs of the city, Chippendale, Camperdown, Newtown, the Glebe, Balmain and the villages of the lower North Shore. Cowper was not to forget that he owed his seat to the city and he came to look upon it as his power base for most of his long political career. Nevertheless he had come forward, as one of his supporters remarked, 'to fight the battle of conservatism' [66] and he could not then have foreseen how far he would move in later years from the political ideals of a rural landowner.

2

Principles and Popularity 1843–1848

Under the 1842 Constitution Act the first Legislative Council was to serve a five-year term. When Cowper first entered the 'Macquarie Street Club' he seemed no different from the other landholders who filled most of the elective seats: thoroughly conservative, absorbed in the problems of their class and sure that they, the social and economic elite of the colony, had a natural right to rule. Cowper soon established a reputation for fluent speech, hard work and organizing ability, but at the end of the 1843 session no one could have predicted that within five years he would be considered a major political leader and something of a popular hero. Indeed, Cowper seemed more likely to end up as quite the reverse, since the first notable cause he championed, that of church schools, was anathema to a large and increasing number of colonial citizens. In and out of the legislature he defended church schooling so fervently that the crusty Alexander Berry, 'Laird' of the Shoalhaven and nominee member of the Council, dubbed him 'Member for the Church of England'. [1] The imputation that he was, as J. D. Lang put it, 'The Bishop of Australia's Man-Friday', [2] never left Cowper in his lifetime and has clung to his reputation ever since, undeservedly. Cowper, like his father, followed his personal conscience in religious matters, but his differences with the Anglican hierarchy have not received the attention given to his support of the church's schools policy.

Still, Cowper's ultra-church image was overcome by the part he played in two issues which divided him from most of his fellow-landholders: tenure of Crown lands and the threatened renewal of transportation. His attitudes to both questions established Cowper, in a manner unexpected even to himself, as a leader of the rising urban middle class and, in time, of the lower classes, against the pretensions of the squatters. At least three-quarters of the elected members of the 1843 Council and five of the six unofficial nominees were large landowners and, like Cowper, many of them were also squatters. Few had any legislative experience, and only one man, wealthy merchant Thomas

Walker, represented the commercial interests of the colony. It was a landholders' Council, and landholders' problems were to dominate its proceedings.

In 1843, colonial graziers had little else but problems. The lands had not recovered from prolonged drought and the great commercial depression had just hit bottom. 'Persons who have nothing but Colonial property (such as Sheep, Cattle, Houses or Lands) wherewith to meet pecuniary engagements, are driven in crowds to the Insolvent Court', Gipps told the Colonial office, [3] and colonial property was all that Cowper and most of his fellow-councillors possessed. Gipps knew well that they were inclined to blame their economic ills on the Home government. They resented the discontinuance of land grants, the lack of cheap labour, the burden of paying for the upkeep of convicts, the high (£1 per acre) minimum price of Crown lands, the nominee section of the Council and the civil list which they could not touch, and the governor foresaw the first direction their resentment would take. Even before the elections, he considered ways to circumvent the severe cuts in the estimates which he expected the Council to make and he was correct in assuming that his new councillors were too preoccupied with economic problems to concern themselves with constitutional advance. Wentworth spelled out to a cheering Parramatta crowd the immediate battles to be fought, as he saw them: 'economy, retrenchment, the civil list and the territorial revenue'. [4] Most others approached the first session of the new legislature in the hope of taking action to ease their economic problems without being at all sure what form such action would take. Cowper was amongst them. Beyond a promise to place first 'all measures connected with the moral and religious improvement of the colony' and a warning that they should not be 'too sanguine' in their hopes for the Council, he told his constituents virtually nothing of his intentions. [5]

The press classed Cowper as a 'moderate conservative' [6] and the 1843 Council session confirmed this impression. Sharing the general belief of his class in the extravagance of governments, he flung himself with enthusiasm into the general scramble to cut down the estimates which Gipps placed before the Council. Whole government departments were wiped out as the councillors cut off their funds; those that survived were heavily slashed and the governor himself was threatened with a cut in salary. No item was too small for Council attention. Even the keeper of government clocks suffered a cut in his annual allowance from £32 0s 6d to £12 0s 6d. Gipps complained of debates as disorderly as they were useless, and after six weeks of this even the *Sydney Morning Herald,* which had at first approved of the economy campaign, turned in exasperation on the 'carping and cavilling...retail nibbling and wholesale demolition' of members in reducing important estimates. [7]

Cowper was prepared to put economy even before the interests of his own church. With Wentworth's help he succeeded in cutting the overall church vote by £6000. [8]

However, Cowper showed moderation and caution over the main economic issues of the session, Wentworth's lien on wool and solvent debtor's bills and Richard Windeyer's monetary confidence bill, all specifically aimed at alleviating the financial problems of the land-holders. On the first he did not speak, to the second he suggested one minor amendment, and he opposed the third which sought, in effect, to have the government bolster landowners by becoming their mortgagee and financial guarantor. Though such ideas were radical indeed in that age of laissez-faire economics, Cowper did not oppose the bill on that ground. As much as anyone, he thought government help to be vital, but he balked at usurping the governor's sole power over money bills. With a series of amendments and changes of front, Cowper tried to prevent the progress of the bill, until the exasperated Windeyer denounced him, in wildly mixed metaphor as 'fond of trumping the winning horse just before he gets in…of feeling the pulse of the House and then launching his cockboat to bear away all who will go with him'. [9]

Cowper's ability to sense and make use of the feeling of the legislature was to be a vital factor in his political fortunes. He showed, too, a capacity for painstaking research in another clash with Windeyer, again in defence of the governor. Windeyer, pointing to the lower salaries paid to Brisbane and Darling, moved to claim for the Council the right to reduce the £5000 paid annually to Gipps. Cowper countered by showing that both Darling and Brisbane had drawn army pay as well as their official salaries, and had other perquisites (which he listed in detail) not available to Gipps. Sensing defeat, Windeyer amended his motion to encompass only future holders of the governorship, and Cowper, having won his point, allowed it to pass unchallenged. [10]

The 1843 Council session saw the first rumblings of the coming battles over convictism, immigration and land policy. Paradoxically, one of the greatest concerns of the landholders in that year of depression was shortage of rural labour. There was no lack of unemployed men in Sydney but they were reluctant to face the dreary life of a back-country shepherd. When they petitioned for relief works, the resulting debates and select committee proceedings showed that every landholder in the Council, with the notable exception of the liberally minded W. H. Suttor, wanted to increase the supply and cut the cost of rural labour. In this they were representative of their class. When Gipps, reluctantly, provided local relief works for the city unemployed, he was thoroughly abused for not forcing them into the interior.

Still, united as they were in their demands for more labour, landholders fell into disarray over the means of providing it. Wentworth demanded the renewal of transportation. 'It was the cheap labour of the convict system which was the cause of the prosperity of the colony', he told the Council. 'It was the absence of that labour which was the cause of the present distress', and he eulogized transportation as 'the most humane, the most inexpensive, the most benevolent, the most efficient and the most reformatorysystem of punishment that ever was invented'. [11] Cowper immediately countered by hoping that the House would never have to consider the subject, since, he said, 'a very strong feeling existed against its revival'. Other members, whatever their private feelings, probably agreed with Cowper's assessment of public opinion on the matter. They put forward other solutions. A select committee on immigration, packed with landholders and chaired by Dr Charles Nicholson, medical man and station owner, blamed the depression upon the export of Land Fund money to pay for immigration, and the 'annihilation' of the cash reserves in the fund upon the raising, in 1842, of the minimum price for Crown lands to £1 per acre. Their answer to the labour shortage was to recommend the lowering of the land price on the assumption that sales would boom and fill the coffers of the Land Fund, which could be used as security for British loans sufficient to bring out 4000 shepherds and farm labourers annually. Others proposed different means. Monaro squatter and landowner T. A. Murray not only approved a low land price but proposed that immigrants with capital be given land grants. J.D. Lang thought this too generous; they should merely pay less than the standard price. Cowper, Windeyer and a group of others counselled caution, thinking it too early to gauge the effects of the existing land price. Outside the Council, a meeting of the lower classes demanded free grants of small allotments. Gipps, never a man to countenance unorthodoxy, ignored them all, merely noting that 'as...we sell no land, we of course have no funds applicable to Immigration'. [12]

The Council struggled to the end of the session in December 1843 without, as Gipps reported wryly, having done 'perhaps much more harm than was to be expected of it'. [13] Bold measures, forceful oratory and strong personality had established Wentworth and Windeyer as leaders of the elected members. Cowper had done well in debate, even against this formidable pair, but hardly seemed a rival for them. His talents were of a different nature. Patient, subtle, tactful, hard-working and capable in administration, he needed the opportunity to develop his leadership qualities in the furtherance of some popular cause. Instead, he championed church education.

The zenith of Anglican influence on education policy was reached in 1839 when Bishop Broughton's well-organized campaign induced Gipps to abandon plans for a secular system of schools in New South Wales. As Michael Roe has remarked, 'the recurrent Anglican theme... was that secular knowledge had no intrinsic virtue; that without the foundation of true belief it could become an instrument of evil'. [14] Cowper held this view and Broughton relied on him to continue the defence of church schools in the Council. The first attack, in September 1843, came from the impetuous Lang. He tabled a series of resolutions designed to set up a complete secular education system based upon the British and Foreign Schools system which Gipps had abandoned in 1839. Anglican opposition swiftly formed. Clergy-organized petitions with more than 7000 signatures poured into the Council. Cowper and fellow-Anglicans, Hannibal Macarthur, James Bowman and William Lawson, presented them, and Lang withdrew his motions. He must have known he could not succeed where Gipps had so recently failed. It was his way of flinging down the gauntlet to the denominationalists and within a month he returned to the attack with a bid to give the new city corporations of Sydney and Melbourne the same powers to build and maintain schools as were possessed by the district councils. Lang pointed out that, as parliament had intended education everywhere in New South Wales to be controlled by local bodies, it was necessary that the city councils should have the same powers as did rural councils. Realizing that the logic of Lang's bill was hard to refute (he was the only speaker to oppose its introduction), Cowper concentrated on delaying it. It was November, the shearing season was under way and members were impatient to end the session and return to their stations. Some had already gone when Cowper rose to argue that, before giving away any of its powers, the legislature should decide the overall guidelines for education in the colony. Cowper relied on the reluctance of a thin and impatient House to take up such a thorny problem. His judgement was sound. When he proposed a six months' postponement of the bill, the Council thankfully shelved the issue, by 11 votes to 2 [15] and the church could breathe easily for another year.

The respite was temporary. Public dissatisfaction with the poor standard of church schooling continued to grow and in 1844 Robert Lowe, barrister, nominee member of the Council, orator of power and biting wit, took up the cause of secular education. An Anglican himself, Lowe leaned towards the evangelical group within the church which hoped to reduce the temporal power of its spiritual leaders, and the education question gave him the chance to attempt it. On 21 June 1844 he moved for and gained a select committee on education. Of its ten members, Cowper was the only one completely opposed to a **general** education system. Lowe easily overrode Cowper's 'total dissent'[16] to write a report declaring that 'the very essence of a denominational system is to leave the majority uneducated in order thoroughly to imbue the minority with peculiar tenets', and recommending the immediate introduction of a secular system. [17] As before, the Anglican clergy were quick off the mark, and petitions, most presented by Cowper, flooded the Council. This time the secularists were ready. Lowe, having fallen out with his mentor Gipps, resigned from the Council as soon as his report was complete, but Wentworth, Lang and Quaker landholder J. P. Robinson took over his cause, organizing and bombarding the Council with counter-petitions, while the issue was being debated at great length and with considerable heat. It was soon apparent that members fell into three broad groups which cut across the .(by then) accepted government-opposition lines: those favouring general education only, those who wished to continue the denominational system relatively unchanged and a third, probably largest, group who wanted to try both systems together. This group decided the issue when most of them supported Wentworth's compromise proposals to set up a National Education Board and at the same time to continue government aid to denominational schools with more than fifty pupils. Stubbornly, Cowper tried to reopen the question the next day, was overruled by the Speaker and then saved by Gipps. The governor rejected Wentworth's plans, remarking that a system which did not have the co-operation of the clergy could not succeed and that, in any case, under the Constitution Act the district councils were to have control of future education needs. Wentworth, personally hostile to the governor since Gipps had thwarted his plans to acquire most of New Zealand's South Island for a pittance, was furious. He moved when the education vote came on that no money be granted for schooling except as the Council approved. In a close vote Cowper defeated him, but most members who voted with Cowper were anxious only that education of some sort should be carried on in the coming year. Thus, no vote, no education, given the governor's attitude. They shattered the church cause a few days later in passing, by 22 votes to 5, a motion by Robinson which placed £2000 for secular schools on the 1845 estimates. When Cowper's counter-motion, demanding an equivalent extra sum for church schools, was rejected out of hand, he and Broughton saw clearly that their cause in the legislature was lost. Cowper, with pragmatic acceptance of that which he could not prevent, abandoned his active opposition to the coming of secular education and tried instead to gain extra government funds and better conditions for church schools until they passed under control of a government-financed board in 1848.

Broughton and Cowper both believed that Anglicans lacked fervour in the cause of their church and its schools. To remedy this, Cowper, with the carefully hidden backing of his bishop, founded the Church of England Lay Association and became its first president. Middle-class townsmen such as Robert Campbell, T. S. Mort, Charles Kemp and James Norton, gave the association keen support, but it never gained a great following and was largely ineffective. The newspaper *Southern Queen*, begun as a prop to the association, lasted only from January to June 1845, failing, it seems, through Anglican apathy exacerbated by the deadly dulness of its pages. Cowper quietly resigned from the association presidency in 1848 and the organization petered out soon afterwards. Yet during its short life it raised passions entirely at variance with its real insignificance, because it was suspected of being a 'Puseyite' organization designed, in Lang's words, 'to promote clerical ascendency and patristical authority'. [18] 'Puseyism', a derogatory term for the Tractarian movement which emphasized the holiness and catholicity of the Anglican church, tended to enhance the status of the church hierarchy and thus was detested by dissenters and the evangelical group within the church itself. Robert Lowe and James Martin, successive editors of the *Atlas*, were particularly virulent in their attacks on Puseyism and the association. Lowe, returned to the council as an elected member in April 1845, proved to be Broughton's greatest enemy. Already triumphantly guiding the campaign for secular education, he struck again at the bishop in September 1846 by in-troducing a bill to secure the benefices of Anglican clergymen under the control of a board of trustees. This would have deprived Broughton of his powers of patronage and thus of much influence over the clergy. Cowper became the bishop's chief defender. He took the line that, since the Anglican church was not the official church in New South Wales as it was in England, the legislature was not competent to interfere in its internal affairs, and he arranged for Broughton to be heard at the bar of the House, where the bishop pressed, in much stronger terms, the same argument. The House wavered and Lowe, sensing defeat, withdrew the bill.

Cowper's defence of church education and of Broughton's powers, together with his presidency of the association gave credence to accu-sations that he was simply a spokesman for his bishop. Nor was his public image improved by such a lapse into open bigotry as occurred in 1845 when he opposed the voting of funds for support of the Jewish religion on the ground that 'it was the duty of the government to support truth and truth only'. [19] In fact, apart from the education question, his relations with Broughton were far from harmonious. He had cut the 1843 church estimates. He had told the Council, with Lowe's clergy bill before them, that they had no power to regulate the internal affairs of the church, yet he admitted that he himself had hoped to introduce a similar bill and had desisted only because the clergy could not agree on what they wanted. [20] This could hardly have pleased Broughton. In 1847 Cowper again irritated the bishop by publicly disagreeing with him over the general cemetery bill, which authorized non-denominational burial grounds controlled by government-appointed trustees. Charles Kemp expressed the deep resentment the Anglican clergy and pious laymen felt towards this measure. 'This bill is only one of a series of attempts to destroy the individual character of the church and reduce her merely to the level of a 'denomination' instead of a branch of Christ's Holy Catholic Church here on earth', he wrote, 'and also we always find that our own people, those who profess to be members of the church, and often those who like Mr. Lowe, owe their station in society to her are the foremost of the attack'. [21] Kemp might well have included his friend Cowper in his strictures. He had presented petitions on behalf of the church, he had defended Broughton from Lowe's by now almost routine attack, but he also favoured Lowe's bill and even implied that Lowe might be correct in claiming that the governor and not the bishop could be considered the head of the Church of England in the colony. In fact, the only time he showed real fervour during the debates on the cemetery bill was in contesting Wentworth's suggestion that the choice of epitaphs be left entirely to the individuals concerned. Cowper indignantly contended that 'blasphemous and indecent' epitaphs should be prevented by law, whereupon Lowe with his ever-ready wit suggested that 'it would be better to create a kind of 'Old Mortality' office, and appoint the Honourable Member for Cumberland Inspector of Tombstones'. [22] Soon afterwards, Broughton sought another spokesman in the Council. In September 1847 Cowper defended the bishop from Wentworth's charge that he had once favoured transportation, but it was a new nominee member, Henry Watson Parker, whom Broughton expressly authorized to act as his spokesman.

There were deep-seated causes, both religious and political, for the tensions that arose between Broughton and Cowper. Though Broughton had been forced to deny it in 1844, there is little doubt that he and those closest to him in the church hierarchy, particularly his right-hand man, the Reverend Robert Allwood, had strong Tractarian leanings. [23] Conversely, Charles Cowper's father and his half-brother, the Reverend (later Dean) Macquarie Cowper, were both strongly anti-Tractarian, [24] and during the controversy which reached its height in 1848 with the defection of two Tractarian ministers, R. K. Sconce and T. C. Makinson, to the Catholic church, Charles, too, showed that he stood with his family. [25] The Cowpers had too much respect for the man and his office to be publicly disloyal to Broughton, but their views on doctrine and church management were their own. However, it was in the political field that Charles most clearly showed his independence of the bishop. From 1844 he drew increasingly closer politically to Robert Lowe, arch-enemy of Broughton. Lowe and Cowper always remained firm and often bitter opponents over church matters, yet during the 1848 election campaign Lowe was to tell Cowper's constituents that 'if they did not return Mr. Cowper at the head of the poll, they would deserve to be branded with the stigma of blackest ingratitude'. [26] The curious combination of opposition and alliance which grew up between Lowe and Cowper was due to common interests in land and constitutional questions, and the recognition by both men that religion and education were, at that time, matters of secondary importance. As Lowe said in retrospect, 'In colonies, the object of government is not in the first instance so much the amelioration of law as the acquisition of power'. [27] Lowe's constant preoccupation with the constitutional side of political questions showed that he followed this axiom from the start. Initially, Cowper's interest was in the immediate future of Crown lands but gradually he came to share Lowe's wider sense of the need for constitutional change—a significant step in his political evolution.

With the well-meant intention to gain a greater revenue from the Crown lands, Gipps published new occupation and purchase regulations in April and May 1844. [28] He immediately ran into bitter opposition from the larger squatters, whose token payments to the Crown were to be steeply increased. Cowper was amongst them, joining thirteen other Council members on the committee of the Pastoral Association, formed under the chairmanship of Ben Boyd, largest squatter of them all, to fight Gipps's proposals. The legislative session of 1844 began with, seemingly, the whole colony aligned against Gipps in support of the squatters. Only one newspaper, William Duncan's *Weekly Register,* raised its voice in defence of the governor. Even the working-men of Sydney, under the auspices of the Mutual Protection Association, supported the squatters, though when they also opposed the renewal of assisted immigration and pressed for small land grants, the *Sydney Morning Herald* had the effrontery to rail against their 'narrow considerations of class interests'. [29] Two days after the session began, Cowper moved for a select committee to examine 'all grievances connected with the lands of the Territory', [30] and supported his motion

with a recital of almost every conceivable grievance of both squatters
and landowners: the financial aspects of the new squatting regulations,
the powers of the Crown lands commissioners, the low character of
the border police, the enforcement of quitrents on granted land, the
unfairness of stock assessment on squatters, and the high minimum
price of Crown land. He had no lack of fervent support, and even the
chief government spokesman, Colonial Secretary Deas Thomson,
conceded that 'it would be well that there should be a full and fair
investigation'. [31] He and Gipps were soon divested of that hope: the
election of the committee resulted in Cowper presiding over six other
members of the Pastoral Association. Clearly, this was the consequence
of collusion, and Cowper probably owed his leading role to the reputation
he had built up in 1843 as an efficient, energetic organizer and good
committee man. With Lowe's collaboration he wrote the bulk of the
committee's report, setting out fully the complaints of both landowners
and squatters much as he had listed them in moving that the committee
be formed, demanding Council control of Crown lands and their
revenues, and questioning the government's right to raise 'taxation'
from the squatters without reference to the legislature, Quite unjustifiably
the report made vicious attacks on the governor's personal integrity,
which moderate men, including the Macarthurs and even Cowper's
friends Charles Kemp and the Reverend James Hassall, rejected with
horror. Bishop Broughton, too, was bitterly offended by the report,
for he strongly supported Gipps's land policy.

Why did Cowper so completely abandon his natural caution and
moderation? The acidic Lowe probably influenced him, and Cowper's
landership ambitions were certainly involved but, most importantly,
it appears that his own financial position was desperate and Gipps's
proposals to increase the burden had acted as the last straw. 1844 was
a year of slow recovery from the depression in New South Wales, but
for wool-growers the long delay in gaining their returns meant that many
reached the nadir of their fortunes in that year. Throughout the 1840s
Cowper could not pay the £850 he owed to Archdeacon Scott and by
1849 the debt had accumlated £238 in unpaid interest. Towards the
end of the 1844 session, ill and overworked, he was desperate enough
to contemplate the virtual abandonment of his political ambitions
by making a bid for the speakership on the mere rumour that the
aged incumbent, Alexander Macleay, was about to resign. 'The temp-
tation of a seat of honour and £750 a· year has been found too strong
for Mr. Cowper's political virtue', remarked William Duncan, [32] regret-
fully. But Cowper's political virtue was saved. Macleay clung to office
for a further two years and by the time he did resign, Cowper had

recovered his nerve. He quashed rumours of his own renewed candidature by vigorously proposing the successful candidate, Charles Nicholson, and by pouring scorn on Wentworth's attempts to have the Speaker's salary doubled.

Apart from the land committee, Cowper took little part in the continued attacks of Wentworth and Windeyer upon the government, showing no interest in the constitutional questions raised by Wentworth's select committee on general grievances, and joining the majority who voted down an attempt to throw out the entire estimates for 1845. He had turned most of his vast energy into the work of the Council's select committees. There, he realized, the basic policies of the Council were formed, and his talents were well adapted to the unspectacular but exacting grind of committee work. In 1845 he led all others in the field, chairing four of the twenty-four select committees and sitting on sixteen others. The tempo of the lands question was quiet in that year, as the squatters expected much from Gipps's more conciliatory attitude and the activities of their London lobbyists. Cowper seemed preoccupied with quitrents, those recurring debts to the Crown incurred by owners of granted land. Gipps was the first—and last—governor of New South Wales to make a real effort at collecting quitrents, and Cowper, in persistently (and unsuccessfully) badgering the government to alleviate the hardships caused by their efforts, was probably taking a personal view: Wivenhoe and the granted parts of Chatsbury would certainly have been subject to these debts.

By October 1845 the initial anti-government frenzy, which had swung landowners and townsmen behind the squatters in the previous year, had faded. Landowners, having been forced to buy their lands or pay quitrents, realized that the squatters would have a competitive edge over them if they gained their objects of long-term, low-cost leases and the pre-emptive right to buy the lands they occupied. Lowe and others concerned with constitutional advance feared that the squatters in the Council might combine with government members in a bloc resistant to change. Lang feared the effects upon his dream of an immigrant yeomanry, and the lower classes saw their visions of independence on the land about to vanish. On 22 October Windeyer, a landowner with a liberal soul, voiced the suspicions of them all. 'A sort of coalition had been formed between the government and the great squatters', he told the Council, and he feared that in 'satisfying the appetites of these cormorants', the government would 'bind up the lands of the colony' for ever. [33] The cracks in the alliance were papered over for a dinner given to Wentworth on 25th January 1846. In early February the press openly acknowledged the split, and the

Atlas put its finger on the key issue for that group of councillors who, over the following two years, became a more or less coherent opposition to the squatters as the 'constitutional' party. This issue was the minimum price of Crown lands. [34] Belatedly, they realized that high prices protected the squatters. Who would dispossess them from lands worth only a fraction of £1 an acre to any buyer? In retrospect Cowper said that he and Lowe had opposed the high upset price because they wanted to see the land sold to 'the people', [35] but both had other motives, Lowe's as always constitutional, and Cowper's more complex. Under Lowe's influence Cowper became steadily more interested in the constitutional issue, but even in 1848 he did not advocate full responsible government for New South Wales. Believing, as did most landholders, that his class was the backbone of the country, his main concerns were a market for his surplus stock and the procurement of a sufficient rural labour supply at a cheap price. With immigration lagging, the problem became steadily worse during the mid-1840s and Cowper, after 1845, seemed to be almost obsessed with it. Hostile as he was to renewed transportation and to Ben Boyd's attempts to introduce coloured labour from the Pacific Islands, he could look solely to Britain for immigrants. The British government had made it clear that only the Land Fund could be used to finance a stream of new settlers. Cowper reasoned that, if the price could be lowered sufficiently, sales of Crown land would boom as they had before 1840, funds for immigration would be assured and immigrants with capital would rush to buy surplus stock to put on their newly bought lands. Hence Cowper's course in the major controversies (apart from education) which shook the colony between 1845 and 1848.

The growing divergence between squatters and constitutionalists did the unfortunate Gipps, probably the most honest man of them all, little good. Finding in early 1846 that current British proposals for settling the land question did not give them the security they sought, the squatting representatives again turned on Gipps by combining with Lowe, Windeyer and Cowper to reject the renewal of the Squatting Act, thus depriving the government of much of its control over them. Wentworth went on to prevent the passing of the estimates by moving successfully that the Council adjourn until after Gipps's impending departure from the colony, whereupon Gipps prorogued the Council and brought the whole bitter farce to an end. When he left New South Wales a few days later, he carried with him a testimonial signed by only one elected member of the Council, W. H. Sutter. For the last time in the life of the first Council, the elected members had turned their full wrath on the executive government. Under the casual and conciliatory rule of the new governor, Sir Charles Fitzroy, the representatives of the people turned to rending one another.

In September 1846 the squatting representatives, led by Wentworth and Robinson, clashed head on with constitutionalist leaders Lowe and Windeyer, when Lowe moved that the Council declare its support for a lower minimum Crown lands price. For the first time, a squatting representative ceased to be evasive on the issue when Robinson declared that a lower price would mean 'utter ruin for every squatter in the colony' as speculators would scramble to buy up existing runs.[36] Windeyer, Murray, and even Deas Thomson spoke in Lowe's support. They were men who believed, with W. H. Sutter and wealthy merchant John Lamb, that the pastoral base of New South Wales society must eventually be superseded by a more intensive land use. Thus they voted with Lowe to beat the squatters by 10 votes to 8 and prevent the lands from becoming, as Lowe said, 'a sheep walk for ever'.[37] Cowper, as usual, spoke for a lower land price, but to the amazement of all, he backed Robinson's attempts to divert the issue into a maze of generalities and he voted with the squatters.

Less than three weeks later Cowper surprised another group which looked to him for leadership—those opposed to transportation. In spite of some agitation, principally from squatters, for renewed transportation to New South Wales, few colonists had ever believed it could be resumed, until W. E. Gladstone succeeded Lord Stanley at the Colonial Office. Impressed with the urgency of solving Britain's ever-pressing convict problem, Gladstone wrote in April 1846 to Fitzroy, asking him to sound out colonial opinion on the renewal of transportation. Two weeks after the passing of Lowe's lands resolutions, Deas Thomson laid Gladstone's despatch before the Legislative Council. The prospect of cheap labour delighted the squatters. Hastily, Wentworth moved for a select committee on the subject, sweeping aside Gladstone's clearly expressed intention to abide by colonial opinion with the claim that 'whether it met with the approval of the colonists or not the system would in some shape be forced upon them', 'They must take the labour that was offered to them or have none', declared Wentworth and he bluntly defined the purpose of the committee as being 'to settle the terms on which they might accept it'.[38] Predictably such great squatters as Henry Dangar and J. P. Robinson supported him. More surprisingly, not one speaker unequivocally opposed the renewal of transportation. Lowe and Windeyer did not speak. Self-styled 'liberal' M. C. O'Connell first pointed out, correctly, that Gladstone had agreed to abide by colonial opinion, then pondered at length on the best ways to employ the convicts. William Bowman, a declared anti-transportationist, was carefully non-committal and so, unexpectedly after his strong stand against Wentworth in 1843, was Cowper. He complained that Britain had always been niggardly in paying for the convict establishment; he was sure that free institutions could not exist with the assignment system; he even spared a thought for the mechanics who might be 'deprived of the reward of their industry' by the introduction of convicts; but nowhere did he say that he would directly oppose their coming. Wentworth got his committee, packed with pro-transportationists.

Cowper's friends must have wondered at the weakening of his stand over land price and labour supply. Certainly the lure of labour, any labour, was strong, but they did not know that Cowper had made a most embarrassing blunder. Not foreseeing either the squatter-constitutionalist split or (as he admitted in later years) the possibility that transportation could ever be resumed, he had eased his labour problems in 1845 by allowing J. P. Robinson to import for him seven ex-convicts from Van Diemen's Land to work at Chatsbury. Unlucky man! If he failed to oppose the squatters, his friends would turn on him. If he did oppose them, Robinson might denounce him, with the same result. So he temporized, and he might have dithered for months if matters had not suddenly escalated beyond his control.

Obsessed with their labour problems, landholding councillors had failed to anticipate the strength of public reaction against renewed convictism. In 1841, as transportation ended, New South Wales contained 130 000 people. Nearly half of them had come as free men and women into the colony since 1832. By 1846, despite depression and shortage of funds for assisted immigration, 15 000 more had followed. As the landholders lamented, the new settlers filled the urban areas rather than the countryside, and they were bitterly opposed to both the moral influence and job competition offered by convicts. The *Sydney Morning Herald*, so recently the champion of the squatters, now turned on them, to become the leading organ of the anti-transportationists. 'The very men whom our suffrage had placed in the Senate to represent our wishes, to assert our rights, to protect our interests have been the foremost to aid and abet a policy by which those wishes would be mocked, those rights trampled upon, those interests deeply and irremediably injured', declared the *Sydney Morning Herald* [39] and flung its weight behind the organizers of Sydney's first protest meeting, held in the city theatre on 22 October. At the last minute, the mayor could not honour his promise to chair the meeting. Who better as a substitute than the man thought to be the legislature's leading anti-transportationist? Cowper, pressed by the men who had helped him into the Council in 1843, could only agree. The theatre was crammed, the proceedings swept along on a swelling wave of anti-felon fervour, and Cowper was carried along with it. The meeting demanded an anti-convict petition and speedily elected a committee to organize it. The crowd cheered as Cowper was placed at the committee's head and delegated to present the petition to the Council, and when Charles Kemp praised him as one who, against the interests of his class, had 'all along' been opposed to transportation, the theatre shook with roars of assent. [40]

Overnight, it seemed, Cowper had become the city's hero, and the leader of a cause through which he might go far. Inevitably, Ben Boyd and other squatters used the story of his seven convicts in a prolonged and vicious campaign to discredit him. Cowper made matters worse by trying to evade the issue and throw the blame on Robinson, which caused Lowe, with his usual acid wit, to dub him 'Little Ingenuity'. [41] Yet in the end, Cowper escaped largely unscathed, probably because the anti-transportationists needed their most articulate and influential leader badly enough to overlook his minor transgressions.

Alarmed by the rash of anti-transportation meetings which spread over the country and the flood of petitions which reached the Council, Wentworth dodged Cowper's repeated demand that he table the report of his select committee on transportation. Only in the last minutes of the session, when the House was thin in members and crowded with visitors for the closing ceremony, did Wentworth produce the report. Backed by his well-drilled supporters, he moved successfully that it be printed, thus ensuring that it would be forwarded to the Colonial Office as an official document of the Council. Cowper's counter-motion for the printing of the anti-transportation petitions lapsed for lack of a quorum when most members hastily lost themselves in the crowd. Temporarily outgeneralled, Cowper was not beaten. He quickly called a meeting of the Sydney anti-transportation committee and had them request Fitzroy to send the petitions to England, and he did so.

As expected, the committee's report favoured Gladstone's proposals and throughout the early months of 1847 the opposition of the colonial lower classes—artisans, shopkeepers, labourers, free men everywhere in New South Wales—continued to mount under the guidance of their middle-class leaders. But before the new Council session opened on 4 May, much of the heat was taken from the issue by the news that Peel's conservative government had fallen in June 1846 to Lord John Russell and the Whigs, who were thought to be against transportation. In that belief, the legislature shelved the subject and turned urgently to the question of free labour. On 18 May Cowper, trying to transfer the matter to his preferred medium, moved for a select committee on immigration, Robinson told the Council that the squatters' need to 'buy on the cheapest market and sell on the dearest' required that Asian and South Sea Islands labour be considered, [42] but the majority shared Cowper's distaste for 'cannibals', and coloured races were excluded from the committee's terms of reference. Still, the squatting representatives were not disposed to be too contentious. They had heard from their London representatives that the British government was about to grant them the long leases and pre-emptive rights which were their chief goals. Lowe had heard rumours of this, too, and he used the immigration debate to launch a passionate attack on the prospective locking up of the lands. In June, a despatch from Earl Grey at the Colonial Office confirmed Lowe's fears and he again carried the battle to the squatters by moving that the legislature reaffirm his resolutions of 1846 on the need for a lower land price. Wentworth, secure in his gains, sneered at those who had once belonged to the 1844 land grievance committee and had now turned against the squatters. Both Cowper and Lowe answered that thrust by declaring that in 1844 the squatters had been threatened with oppressive taxation and thus merited support, but now the squatters were the oppressors because the price of land had not been lowered when they gained their leases.

The vote on Lowe's motion clearly separated the squatters from the constitutionalists. Unluckily for the latter, the official members, offended by Lowe's attacks on the government's land policy, joined the squatters to defeat the motion by 14 votes to 10. The combination of squatters and government members which Lowe had feared seemed to be forming and this drove the constitutionalists into their first really concerted action. When squatting representatives Foster and Robinson decided to extend a rather limp olive branch to the constitutionalists by proposing a select committee on Crown land price, the election of members resulted in the two squatters being joined by Cowper, Suttor and six other opponents, who elected Lowe chairman instead of giving the post, as convention prescribed, to the mover of the motion, Foster. A stream of squatter witnesses received a rough handling from Suttor's blunt questioning, Lowe's ironic wit and Cowper's barrage of subtle thrusts. No one was surprised when the committee's report turned out to be a complete statement of the views of the landowners and of Lowe who wrote it.

Blustering Ben Boyd, who detested Cowper for his leadership of the anti-transportation cause, was next to be attacked. He had brought in New Hebridean islanders to man the 1 million acres of Crown lands he controlled—a move disapproved by most of the constitutionalists and official members. When the Masters and Servants Act came up for renewal, Deas Thomson, to the surprise of the elected members, moved that 'savages' be excluded from its provisions. Backed by the constitutionalists and government members, his move succeeded, thus depriving Boyd of legal control over his New Hebrideans. Furiously, Boyd denounced his opponents in the pages of the *Australian,* which he then controlled, reserving his greatest malevolence for Cowper, but his case was not helped by the islanders, who walked off his stations in droves, or by incidents like that gleefully recorded by the *Sydney Morning Herald* on 1 November 1847. 'About noon, on Saturday' reported the newspaper, 'a party of a dozen or more of these creatures [islanders] marched through the city, along its principal thoroughfare, to their proprietor's place of business. The sight was the more refreshing from the circumstances of only three of their number being encumbered with the article of clothing generally considered to be the most indispensable of male attire'. Boyd's experiment was doomed.

Boyd and his London connections vigorously pressed the British government to resume transportation. Cowper knew of this and decided that, as a counter to Boyd, the Council must decisively reject Wentworth's transportation report. Since Wentworth refused to table the report for discussion, Cowper moved that its principles and recommendations be rejected. He knew that the strength of public feeling was behind him. So did the members of the transportation committee and when Cowper rose to speak to his motion, three of them, Lowe, Windeyer and Foster, were discreetly absent. This was Cowper's finest moment in the life of the first Council. With his usual smooth delivery heightened by a touch of passion he attacked the report and the motives of the men who made it. The transportationists sat stonily as Cowper condemned the social evils of the system and claimed that crime in New South Wales had steeply declined since its suspension. He waxed eloquent on the wrongs done to free immigrants by bringing in convicts. 'He contended the humblest man, woman or child had a right to be heard on this question—aye! they had a right to a double voice, for these were the classes that would come into contact with the immigration and suffer by their presence here'.[43] It was a well-prepared, effective attack and it was solidly endorsed by Bowman, Lamb, Murray and the liberally minded attorney-general, J. H. Plunkett. The transportationists had no effective reply. Barrister J. B. Darvall blustered of 'yielding to clamour' from outside, Robinson mouthed pious humbug, Dr Bland made an incredible blunder, remembered for years, in declaring that it was not the convicts but the immigrants who had ruined the colony, and only Wentworth was impressive, more for his bold disregard of unpopularity than for the effectiveness of his arguments. Official members swung their votes behind Cowper to pass his resolutions by 11 votes to 7 and it seemed that Earl Grey was to be left in no doubt as to the distaste felt by New South Welshmen for transportation.

More than ever, landholders were now obsessed with the need for an influx of rural labour. Cowper's immigration committee urged it in their report. On 21 September 1847 Cowper moved resolutions pressing for renewed efforts, 'an increase of 30,000 in...labouring population', he suggested, and he was prepared to finance this human flood, if the Land Fund would not suffice, by means of loans, debentures or even a direct tax. Cowper's fellow-members balked at the idea of a tax (though 800 country landholders whose petitions for labour Cowper presented did not), but all were impressed with the need for workers. With only minor amendments, the resolutions passed and Cowper saw them off to England. He felt with justice that the session had gone well for him and he spoke of retiring from politics on that note—not that he had the least intention of so doing. The Council elections, it was generally expected, would take place before the next session was due, and Cowper no doubt anticipated that talk of retirement would stir into early action those who might support him to stand again.

Unfortunately for Cowper's anti-convict record, the Council did meet again before the elections. In March 1848 Fitzroy called the members together to consider proposals from Earl Grey for a new kind of transportation. Grey suggested that men be sent out as holders of tickets-of-leave or conditional pardons after a reformatory term in one of Britain's new penitentiaries. Good conduct would enable them to have their families sent out, equal numbers of free immigrants were to be sent and the whole expense was to be paid by Britain. 'At present', admitted the *Sydney Morning Herald* of Grey's offer, 'we cannot deny that under the exigencies of our labour market, it wears a very attractive aspect', [44] and it did so for nearly every man in the Council. There were good reasons for this. Cowper's immigration report, like its predecessors, seemed to have vanished into some British limbo; the price of wool was falling, increasing the flock-owners' desire to force down wages, and without new settlers they could not sell their surplus stock; the lack of cost to the colony in implementing Grey's scheme appealed to all; in direct contrast to the reception given to Gladstone's proposals, Grey's despatch brought very little public reaction. Most importantly for those like Cowper who had based their objections to transportation on moral grounds, it was possible to draw a valid distinction between previous proposals for receiving newly sentenced convicts and the coming of 'exiles'[45] who had first been 'reformed' by the new methods of treatment in Pentonville or another British penitentiary. In this manner the *Sydney Morning Herald* justified its change of front, and so did Cowper in telling the Council that Grey's proposals 'ought to have a trial'. [46] Of all the councillors present during the debate on Grey's plan, Plunkett and nominee member George Allen were the only ones to oppose transportation unequivocally, and Grey's terms were approved without a division. No doubt Lowe was right when he remarked ironically of the anti-transportationists who supported the coming of 'exiles'; 'having been placed on the rack, another turn of the handle had caused a different feeling'. [47] Cowper felt genuinely the moral distinction between convicts and exiles, yet he had allowed his personal interests to affect his moral judgement and he was uneasily aware of it.

Probably the main reason for the quiet public reception of Grey's exile scheme was that colonial attention was then focused on another British idea which presented a more immediate threat—the constitutional proposals which reached Fitzroy in December 1847. Britain wished to separate Port Phillip from New South Wales and give both colonies and Van Diemen's Land identical constitutions. Elected regional councils were to govern locally and the members of these bodies were to elect a central assembly which was to form the lower house of a bicameral legislature. The central legislature in turn was to elect delegates to a federal congress which was to regulate intercolonial matters. The colonists were not happy with any of this, but opposition focused immediately on the proposal for local councils with elective powers to the central body. This implied that the hated district councils, created by Gipps under the 1842 Constitution Act (and which the Council had been doing its best to destroy ever since), were not only to be resurrected but were, as the colonists saw it, to have the voting powers they now enjoyed as individuals. A storm of protest swept the country. Wentworth, badly needing to regain ground lost in his Sydney electorate through his pro-squatter tactics, immediately leapt into the fray. So did Lowe and Cowper, both hoping to weaken the squatting group and Wentworth's standing as a leader. All three found themselves on the platform together at a crammed public meeting in Sydney on 19 January 1848, where speaker after speaker condemned the proposed constitution to the cheers of a crowd amongst which, according to the *Sydney Morning Herald* 'were fairly represented the landowners, the magistracy, the learned professions, the farmers and graziers, the merchants, shopkeepers, mechanics, labourers, and the men of every degree'. [48]

Unity vanished when the issue moved to the Council chamber in May. By this time both Wentworth and his opponents knew that Grey was on the point of withdrawing the whole scheme, but they were all willing to flog a dead horse to serve their own political ends. Lowe and Cowper, drawn closer together by the lands question in 1847, had yet differed over .transportation, but when Cowper accepted the exile scheme, the way of alliance was clear except for church matters which were, in any case, dormant in 1848. Windeyer, the third of the constitutionalist leaders, had died in December 1847. He had been the only real friend Lowe possessed in the Council; Lowe's acid tongue had struck too often. Still, Cowper, who had felt its edge as often as any, seldom let passion colour his political judgement and he readily combined with Lowe on the constitutional and lands issues.

Wentworth seized the initiative in the Council by moving resolutions condemning the British constitutional proposals. Cowper and Lowe, realizing that the government members and even the squatters were unhappy at the contemptuous tone of Wentworth's submission, managed to substitute more softly worded resolutions of their own, which passed easily, with one exception; a demand for a bicameral legislature scraped through by only one vote. Lowe then made a slip. He reopened the question by trying to have a clause reconsidered and Wentworth abruptly moved that the whole matter be postponed for six months. To the dismay of Cowper and Lowe, this move succeeded by 10 votes to 5. As Fitzroy told Earl Grey, 'the result of this last step was clearly to prevent the Council from placing on record any opinion whatsoever'. [49] Cowper and Lowe had underestimated the strength of the elected members' belief that the existing single-chamber house worked to their advantage and also, probably, the reluctance of the government members to give the appearance of censuring the British government. The result was stalemate. A similar fate met Lowe's attempt to revive the matter of land price at a time when few of his supporters were in the House. It was voted down by the squatting representatives. Cowper had better luck in moving an address to the Queen aimed at easing the quitrent regulations since the squatters, indifferent to imposts they did not pay, allowed it to pass unchallenged. In the end, however, Cowper's appeal gained nothing. The British government rejected it.

On 20 June 1848 the Legislative Council sat for the last day of its five-year term. If the councillors were sometimes inclined to take more credit than was due to them, they had still been an energetic group, sitting for over 400 days, passing more than 150 bills, and influencing major changes in education, transportation and lands policies. The very core of their work was in the select committees, and here Cowper was without peer. Of the 107 select committees, created by the Council between 1843 and 1848, he chaired 18 and was an active member of 55 others. No one else approached these totals, and his name became a byword for 'peculiar zeal and untiring energy in the accomplishment of any objective in which he is interested', as the *Sydney Morning Herald* put it. [50] The press judged him to be amongst the best speakers in the House. [51] He lacked the rough power of Wentworth, the polished phrases and ironic wit of Lowe or the wilting blasts of Windeyer; at his worst he could be infuriatingly specious, but his speeches were usually well researched and prepared and with his smooth unflurried delivery and persuasive manner — 'the lavender of Mr. Cowper' [52] — he thrust home his points firmly. He was one of the very few members who tried to improve the efficiency of the Council's proceedings, pressing for the appointment of a legal draftsman and extra secretarial staff. Also he was developing a shrewd political judgement, except for church matters where, as as *Atlas* remarked, 'the usual good sense of Mr. Cowper forsakes him entirely'. [53] Still, in 1848 his religious principles were not wholly a political handicap. His consistent stand for denominational education added nearly as much to his reputation as a man of principle as was detracted from that reputation by his bigotry. His work on immigration and the lands question enhanced his popularity with landowners and, while his major concerns certainly lay in fields where he had a personal interest, he had not forgotten the Sydney mercantile men who backed him so successfully in 1843. At their request he pushed through the reluctant Council bills for the licensing of auctioneers and publicans, and much of his select committee work was related to city affairs.

Resentment of government expenditure was strong amongst the Sydney entrepreneurs as it was amongst the landed gentry. Cowper, the most consistent estimate-trimmer in the Council, won the approval of these groups by his efforts, though they sometimes had unexpected results, as in 1844, when J. P. Robinson complained of the 'almost impassable' bogs of the Parramatta Road. For once, the urbane Deas Thomson had the perfect answer. He explained that maintenance was difficult because the Council had abolished the department that carried it out. [54] The only estimates which Cowper would not cut were those for humanitarian purposes. He strongly supported the votes for orphan schools and headed an inquiry into conditions at Tarban Creek Lunatic Asylum which led to great (and expensive) improvements in the organization of that Australian Bedlam. The compassion he showed for these neglected sections of the population earned him considerable credit in the colony.

Under Lowe's tutelage, Cowper's views on the future government of New South Wales had broadened greatly. By 1848 he believed, with Lowe, that the existing Council formed only a step in a continuous process of evolution towards self-government. Yet his was still a conservative view. Like most of his landowning and mercantile friends, he assumed that power would be transferred, not to the people as a whole, but to the 'natural' leaders of the colony—the class of propertied men who made up the existing Council. Unlike Lowe, he had not yet sensed the growing political power of Sydney's shopkeepers, artisans and labourers. His popularity stood high with them because of his leadership of the anti-transportation cause and his association with Lowe in fighting the squatting cormorants who had swallowed the land. But he politely evaded their efforts to have him appear at their anti-convict meetings, and his speeches on the subject revealed concern for morality rather than political advantage. It took the general elections of 1848 to press upon him a first consciousness of far-reaching changes which stirred in the land.

3

The Evolution of a Liberal 1848–1856

By 1848 Sydney had far outgrown its early years as an untidy village hugging the shores of Sydney Cove and even the image of a 'large busy town' which in 1839 had reminded Mrs Louisa Meredith of Liverpool or Bristol.[1] Sydney had become a city in its own right, the bustling commercial centre of New South Wales. Some forty-two thousand people inhabited the city proper and there were seven or eight thousand more in the suburbs, Woolloomooloo, Paddington, Surry Hills, Redfern, Chippendale, Camperdown, Newton, the Glebe and St Leonards, which crept outwards into the surrounding scrub, swamp and sandstone ridges. Nearly one-third of the total population of New South Wales lived within 5 miles of Sydney harbour. Fine stone buildings of two and three storeys, banks, auction rooms, shops and 'fashionable emporiums' lined the main streets of the city, and the residents could take their ease in coffee-houses, theatres and the many hotels or improve their minds at the School of Arts and the Australian Library. There was another side to the city. Even in the major thoroughfares the rotting carcasses of dogs and cats mingled with raw sewage and the uncollected droppings of a thousand horses in the dust of summer and the mud of winter. While the city council bickered and did nothing, the pestilent slaughter-houses of Sussex Street, cheek by jowl with warehouses and homes, continued to kill in conditions of indescribable filth, to toss the offal to the pigs standing belly-deep in rotting mud as they awaited their turn to go under the knife, and to create a stench that spread downwind for miles. Still, this Australian metropolis teemed with vigorous life. Into it were crammed not only the bulk of the colony's professional men and greater merchants, but a fast-growing, migrant-augmented swarm of small shopkeepers, tradesmen, artisans and some whose only assets were a ready tongue and a quick wit. Many were men who had taken part in or clearly recalled the recent movements for lower-class political rights in Britain, and they meant to assert such rights in New South Wales. By virtue of Sydney's high rents, many of them possessed a vote — for the Sydney electorate if they lived in the city or for Cumberland if they lived in the suburbs. Robert Lowe allowed them, under the leadership of toy-shop owner Henry Parkes, auctioneer J. K. Heydon and manufacturer J. R. Wilshire, to draft him into the fight for the Sydney electorate, where they won him a notable victory on the strength of his opposition to the squatters.

Cowper, too, had fought the squatters, and his leadership of the anti-convict cause gave him an advantage over Lowe who had condoned Wentworth's transportation report. Yet when he decided to stand again for Cumberland, he ignored the lower classes, probably because he thought, with most of his middle-class supporters, that class interests could not and should not form a basis for the election of parliamentary representatives. The lower orders, used to attempts by their masters to cut wages at every opportunity, were more realistic, though their leaders were too shrewd to admit it openly. Lowe's campaign committee, after waging what amounted to a class-based campaign to elect him, blandly hailed their victory as that of 'justice and the people's right over class-interests and the intrigues of faction'. [2] Confident that his record of sevice in the Council would be enough to secure his re-election, Cowper retired to Wivenhoe and left•the running of his campaign to the same group of supporters—middle class, urban and protestant—which had helped him to office in 1843. His confidence seemed to be justified. The entire Sydney press commended him, except for Ben Boyd's ramshackle *Australian,* then staggering to its end. Even the Catholic-run *Chronicle* supported him, a thing unthinkable five years earlier. After Therry's appointment to the Bench in 1845, the only Catholic in the first Council had been J. H. Plunkett, who made no secret of his support for government-run schools and became the chairman of the National Schools Board. Thus the Catholic hierarchy, fighting like the Church of England to retain government aid to their schools, had found Cowper a useful, though unwitting, ally.

Sir Charles Fitzroy, scion of the ducal house of Grafton, feared that the 'Mob of Sydney' might become sufficiently infected with the revolutionary spirit then sweeping Europe to descend upon the £700 000 which lay in Sydney's banks. [3] So he shortened the election campaign to six weeks in order to keep down a revolutionary fervour which did not exist in Australia. Cowper's committee put up another candidate, wealthy retired merchant and landowner H. G. Smith, for the second Cumberland seat. Old William Lawson did not stand again. But two weeks before the election date (2 August) Lawson's son Nelson, a flamboyant character noted for his wealth, huge landholdings and some heavy sowing of wild oats in younger days, suddenly decided to stand and, in a furious campaign which was said to have cost him £1500, swept through the county appealing to latent rural resentment of the city. Scenting danger, Cowper hastily disassociated himself from Smith and entered the fray personally, supported by Lowe, while Ben Boyd, unable to resist the chance to have a personal crack at his enemy, weighed in to help his fellow-squatter, but his aid did Lawson more harm than good. Furious at Cowper's insulting response to his attacks, Boyd challenged him to a duel. Cowper prudently declined and Boyd's cause was lost in the laughter of the colonists.

Nomination day, 26 July, at Parramatta saw scenes of wild enthusiasm for both Lawson and Cowper, particularly sweet to the latter, for Parramatta had gone heavily against him in 1843. Had he done his duty? he asked the crowd. 'Yes,' they roared, 'better than any man in the Council and we'll put you in at the head of the poll'. Did they want to hear his principles? persisted Cowper, to great cheering and cries of 'No, no—we know you', and the only sour note was struck by a sepulchral voice asking, 'Why did you vote against the Menangle bridge?'[4]

The electors were as good as their word. Cowper topped the poll with 632 votes to Lawson's 556 and Smith's 489. He exulted in his victory, yet it was apparent that he was even more dependent on the city voters than he had been in 1843. In that year, 52 per cent of his total vote came from the two city polling places. In 1848, this had risen to 67 per cent. The trend towards separation of city and country interests was clearest in the cases of Lawson and Smith. Smith received 82 per cent of his vote from the city, Lawson only 44 per cent. 'They had fought the battle with the merchants and people of Sydney manfully', declaimed Lawson to the uproarious cheering of the Parramatta crowd. 'As the tables of the money-changers in the temple were overturned, so they had driven the money-changers out of the County of Cumberland'.[5] But what they had really done was to illustrate the power of local prejudice.

Cowper's increased dependence on the city vote did not escape his notice and he could not fail to see that Lowe's victory was due to lower class organization and support. Background, training and social status made Cowper a conservative, in the sense of one who believes in a clearly defined hierarchical society, but he was above all a pragmatist in politics. Realizing that his future lay with the voters of the metropolis, he turned increasingly to strengthening his ties with Sydney's mercantile-professional class, a move congenial to him since he had long enjoyed the friendship of Robert Campbell and Charles Kemp and had a wide acquaintanceship with the Anglican middle class through his church connections. He saw the rapid growth of this class in numbers, wealth and prestige[6] and he came to share their 'liberal' view of the kind of government the colony needed: a popularly based and therefore stable ministry which would promote the economic development of New South Wales.

Alliance with lower-class political activists, those who became known as 'radicals', did not come so easily to Cowper. He could never forget social distinctions, but after the 1848 election he clearly saw the growing political influence of the radicals and took care not to offend them. When the unemployed of Sydney held a meeting on 20 December 1848 to petition Fitzroy for relief works, they invited Lowe, Wentworth, James Martin and Cowper to speak. All declined, Lowe sharply rejecting this 'attempt to prevent labour finding its level',[7] Wentworth and Martin sending evasive answers, and Cowper pleading a previous engagement, 1851 he could forbear to protest the *Empire*'s inclusion of his name as 'the letter of a gentleman' in contrast to Lowe's 'insulting document'.[8] Cowper was similarly circumspect a month later when the new radically based Constitutional Association asked him to speak in favour of a lower franchise. In 1844 he had opposed the lowering of the municipal franchise to £10 rental value because he felt that 'persons not desirable as voters' might obtain that right.[9] In 1849 he told the Constitutional Association that he was not prepared to give an opinion on the subject. He would neither oppose the radicals nor join them. But he was soon to be forced into collaboration with them through the sudden revival of the transportation issue.

On 26 February 1849 the *Sydney Morning Herald* printed a despatch in which Earl Grey announced his intention to send 'exiles' to New South Wales without the promised free settlers. Public opposition, centred in Sydney, rose immediately, and Cowper, backed by the same urban mercantile-professional group as in 1847, sprang to the head of it. He justified his renewed anti-convict fervour by charging Grey with a breach of faith in proposing to send convicts without free settlers, a suggestion which dismayed even the most fervent Anglophiles. 'A very nice mess your great statesman Lord Grey has put us in', wrote squatter E. W. F. Hamilton to his partner in London. 'How I who would sooner cut out my tongue than join a colonial outcry against the Home Government shall be able to say a word in his favour I know not'.[10] Yet Cowper had also realized tardily that the great majority of free settlers would never again countenance the entry of convicts on any terms. Lowe and many others who had earlier condoned some form of renewed convictism saw it too and hastened to change sides.

The renewed agitation was at first dominated by the middle-class liberals.[11] Only one prominent radical, Dr Isaac Aaron, gained election to the new anti-transportation committee formed under Cowper's chairmanship, and even he was not so democratically inclined that in 1851 he could forbear to protest the *Empire's* inclusion of his name 'among simple *Messrs.* while *Tradesmen* were distinguished by the title of Esq.' [12] Without strong radical support, the first of the committee's public meetings lacked a large audience. The liberals sought closer co-operation with their lower-class counterparts when, Nelson Lawson having died, they decided to run barrister Archibald Michie in the resultant by-election against Wentworth's protegé, Robert Fitzgerald. Leading radical Richard ('Dirty Dick') Driver, licensee of the Three Tuns Tavern, and several of his political friends joined Cowper, Lowe, Campbell, Kemp, lawyers James Norton, G. K. Holden and Gilbert Wright and other members of the anti-transportation committee in supporting Michie. Fitzgerald, a prominent Cumberland landowner, shrewdly added to his natural advantage over the unknown Michie by declaring himself, at the last minute, to be against transportation and he won handsomely, but the pattern of radical-liberal co-operation had been set and it weakened thereafter only when the radicals tried to take control of the anti-convict movement from those who considered themselves the natural leaders. This happened when Fitzroy promised the citizens of Melbourne that he would divert Earl Grey's exiles away from Port Phillip and into New South Wales proper. With the new Legislative Council in session, Cowper and Lowe prepared to attack Fitzroy's promise. Their first anti-convict motions were blocked by Wentworth but, as he openly acknowledged, they had the upper hand and in return for some minor watering-down of the resolutions, the squatters allowed them to pass unopposed. However, in early June 1849 the ship *Hashemy* with a cargo of exiles arrived in Sydney harbour and promptly triggered off two mass meetings of protest. Though some liberals, including Lowe, Campbell, Michie and John Lamb, took part, Parkes, Lang, Wilshire and other radicals were the organizers. With most other leading liberals Cowper held aloof, mainly, it seems, because they were reluctant to follow a lower-class lead. Grey took the heat out of the anti-convict movement by calling a halt to the shipment of exiles, but he did not rule out the possibility of resumption.

Pressed by financial stringency and his deep involvement in the affairs of the Sydney Railway Company, Cowper resigned his Council seat in March 1850 and did not return to the legislature until September 1851. In his absence Wentworth and the squatters managed, on 30 August 1850, to postpone John Lamb's attempt at petitioning the Queen to remove New South Wales from the list of places to which convicts could be sent. Immediately, the anti-transportationists were in full cry. The liberals made certain that they dominated the revived movement. No other of their leaders matched Cowper's ability and prestige and he easily gained the chair of the newly formed New South Wales Association for Preventing the Revival of Transportation. The twenty-eight men on the managing committee included five members of the Legislative Council, a majority of Sydney business and professional men and not more than half a dozen who could be classed as radicals, Still, these men, particularly bookseller W. R. Piddington, merchant E. C. Weekes, Wilshire, Parkes and the 'Reverend agitator' J. D. Lang were to be of vital importance to Cowper, not only for the vigorous part they took against convictism but also for their significance in the growing liberal-radical political movement of the 1850s.

By now the colony's transportationists were in full retreat and, as Cowper warned, the main danger lay in 'indirect transportation', [13] the movement of convicts from Van Diemen's Land, which continued to receive British felons, and the threat of a new penal colony at Moreton Bay. The association turned to petitioning against transportation to all of the Australian colonies, to active canvassing for British support with the help of Robert Lowe, who had returned to England in 1850, and to cooperation with sympathetic groups in Van Diemen's Land, South Australia, New Zealand and the new colony of Victoria.

In February 1851 the Victorians set up an intercolonial anti-convict organization. Cowper and his fellow committee members, ever conscious of the superior age, population and dignity of the parent colony, refused to join this upstart organization, the Australian Anti-Transportation League, until the smaller colonies, suitably chastened, sent delegates to Sydney to dangle the bait of leadership in the league before their eyes. Within ten days of the delegates' arrival, the association was converted to a branch of the league. Cowper became president of the whole body and the New South Wales committee was elected executive board of the league for the current year. Thus Cowper and New South Wales led the first great intercolonial political movement. A few weeks later Cowper noted ironically that Wentworth, James Macarthur and others of the transportationists in the Council were scrambling to modify their views before the 1851 elections fell due. [14] The league turned to hammering away at their Imperial masters with increasing bitterness as the flow of felons continued. Even Cowper, the man of 'mild, affable and benignant character', as Henry Parkes put it, [15] and a loyalist to the core, hinted at rebellion. Parkes and Campbell backed him up and the *Sydney Morning Herald* smugly pointed out that Earl Grey was driving them to it. [16] They were saved the need for blood and fire or the embarrassment of swallowing their seditious words when, in April

1853, news reached Australia that all transportation was at an end. Lowe in London and Parkes in Sydney had hopes of retaining the league organization to fight for common political rights for the colonies. Cowper, more realistically, saw that there was too much diversity of political opinion within the league and between the colonies to allow this idea a chance of success, and advised against it. Its task ended, the league was dissolved in May 1854.

Cowper's leadership of the anti-transportation cause made him one of the best-known men in Australia, gave him valuable contacts with the rising leaders of the radical movement and, above all, brought him into ever closer co-operation with the middle-class city liberals. This trend was accelerated by another interest which he shared with them, the building of railways in New South Wales. Only a network of lines radiating from Sydney, they believed, could ensure the economic development of the lands and the continued primacy of the city. They were the main force behind a series of public meetings, committees and route surveys which took place between 1846 and early 1848. Cowper took part in this activity from the beginning, and when, in mid-1848, the railways movement bogged down in a welter of local jealousies and bitter squabbles over routes, surveys and the economics of various projects, he helped to divert the whole inquiry into the hands of the legislature. There he quickly took charge of it, chairing the investigating select committee, nominating its personnel and writing its report himself. He recommended that private companies build and run the railways and that government help be given in the form of free land grants and a guaranteed 6 per cent interest rate on the first £100 000 of capital subscribed — terms favourable to colonial investors, but not particularly attractive to British capitalists who could obtain a better return on their money elsewhere. Cowper was determined that the railways would remain in local hands. The whole Council, it seemed, suffered from railways fever and they approved the report with enthusiasm.

Teetering as he was on the brink of genteel poverty, Cowper hoped to turn the railways movement to his own advantage. His work on the select committee won him the chairmanship of the provisional committee when the Sydney Tramroad and Railway Company (a title later shortened to Sydney Railway Company) was set up in October 1848. Energetically he sold the company's shares and quietly collected the proxy votes of country shareholders for use when a permanent directorate should be elected. Backed by the major city shareholders, Kemp and Fairfax of the *Sydney Morning Herald,* Robert Lowe, businessmen T. S. Mort and Daniel Cooper and fellow-councillors

Charles Nicholson and John Lamb, Cowper won the chairmanshop on 2 November 1849 'with the vote of every shareholder', according to Lowe. [17] Kemp, Lamb, Cooper, Nicholson and ex-councillor William Bradley joined him on the board. The full extent of Cowper's influence became apparent later in the day when the new directors met. He was not only elected unopposed as president of the company but was also appointed manager at a salary of £600 a year. Was it entirely coincidental that Cowper soon appointed John Lamb's son to a clerkship in the company's office? Lamb had moved that Cowper be given his dual post.

The company planned to build a single-track line from Sydney to Parramatta as the first stage of the route to Goulburn. Cowper looked forward to a safe career at a salary sufficient to end his immediate financial problem, but his position proved to be neither safe nor permanent. Almost immediately, the pressure of his managerial duties forced him to resign his seat in the council. His dual appointment raised bitter opposition from a section of the shareholders, and a prolonged power struggle resulted. The dissidents forced Cowper to relinquish the presidency to John Lamb in order to keep his salaried post. In a complex series of moves Cowper rallied his supporters, spilled Lamb and nearly all the directors and forced his way back onto the board, though he cautiously allowed Charles Kemp to take the presidency. By this time the company was in dire financial trouble. High costs and shortage of labour followed the gold rushes of 1851, the company's engineer and other staff quit when their salaries were cut, Cowper clashed with the new engineer, Mais, over the latter's slack administrative work, landowners on the Parramatta route demanded wildly inflated prices for their land, and by the middle of 1852 the company's share sales were virtually at a standstill. By this time Cowper had realized that only under government control could the project have any real chance of completion and he believed that, sooner or later, the state must take it over. But he had no intention of relinquishing his own interest in the enterprise. In July 1852 he persuaded the directors to return him to the position of power he had enjoyed in the first days of the company. They abolished the post of manager, Charles Kemp stood down from the presidency in favour of Cowper and the board voted him an annual allowance of £600 as its chief executive officer. Thus were his enemies disarmed, but thus, too, did Cowper come to bear much of the responsibility for the blunders which followed.

As a critic said, Cowper 'was never on, or saw a railroad in his life.' [18] He and his fellow-directors stood in awe of their new engineer, James Wallace, specially imported from England. They meekly accepted his recommendation that the earthworks on the Parramatta line be extended to double-track size, worsening greatly the company's already perilous financial position; they stood by and even defended Wallace when he coolly allowed his protegé William Randle to monopolize the company's contracts, sometimes without bothering to call tenders or even to inform the board; worst of all, they permitted him to change the gauge of 5 ft 3 in previously agreed upon and confirmed by a bill which Cowper had piloted through the Council. Victoria and South Australia had followed suit for the sake of standardization, but no sooner had Wallace arrived than he persuaded the directors to change to the British gauge of 4 ft 8½ in. From this decision stemmed the problems and costs of differing gauges that Australia has borne ever since and, considering Cowper's hegemony over the board, he bears a good deal of the blame.

Late in 1852 the government, faced with the ever-increasing burden of shoring up the company financially, demanded a share in its management. Three government-appointed directors joined Cowper and two other shareholders' representatives on the board. Cowper hoped to retain the presidency, but deadlock ensued when the three official directors voted for one of their number, F. L. S. Merewether, and the others voted for Cowper. By virtue of a provision inserted by Wentworth in the enabling bill, the governor had the power to resolve this situation and he promptly appointed Merewether. Furious, Cowper resigned his directorship, charging the government and Wentworth with a 'vindictive and tyrannical spirit' in getting rid of him because he was a political opponent. [19] As Deas Thomson pointed out, the government had a sound claim to make the appointment because they had by then contributed three-fifths of the company's capital. Yet all three government directors were chosen from the minority of seven who had voted against Cowper's re-election to the board at the last shareholder's meeting, and Merewether had warned the executive council that he could not spare the time to attend properly to railway affairs. Cowper was then a leading opponent of the conservative constitutional proposals put up by Wentworth and supported by Fitzroy and the principal government officers; he was probably correct in assuming official animus against him. Perhaps Fitzroy bore a guilty conscience. Soon afterwards he offered Cowper the post of chief commissioner for the City of Sydney with a salary of £1000 a year. Indignantly Cowper refused, which suggests, at least, that concern for his personal solvency was not the only reason for his interest in railways. To the Council he proclaimed his vision: twin threads of steel linking Sydney to the farthest parts of New South Wales and to Melbourne and Adelaide. [20] Tirelessly he hammered away at his constant theme: the government must build and run the whole rail system. In England railways linked already populous areas to one another, and private companies could reap immediate profit from their operation. In New South Wales, conversely, settlement must necessarily follow the building of railways and only the government could bear the initial costs and long wait for profitability. Acceptance of this argument was no great step for the officers of government to take when they already controlled the board of the Sydney Railway Company. In 1855, they took the full burden, beginning the hegemony of government over public transport which exists in Australia to the present day.

Under the Australian Colonies Government Act of 1850 the Port Phillip district won from the Imperial Parliament the separation from New South Wales which they had long sought. With the withdrawal of their six representatives from the legislature of the parent colony, a recasting of electorates and new elections for that body became necessary. With true conservative distaste for representation according to numbers rather than interests, the government saw to it that Sydney gained only one of the six redistributed seats. Still, the very size of the electorate and the fast-growing commercial power of the city gave the Sydney seats prestige above all others and it was natural that Cowper, rescued from looming penury by his railway company salary and impatient to re-enter politics, should try for a metropolitan seat at the 1851 elections. Once again, men of the urban mercantile-professional group took charge of his campaign. Many were shareholders of the railway company, members of the anti-transportation movement and, as in the case of T. S. Mort, T. W. Smart, Thomas Holt, Gilbert Wright and James Norton, also associates of Cowper in the management of two newly formed companies: the Australian Mutual Provident Society and the Australian Gas Light Company. Cowper stood on his record in the anti-convict movement and his furtherance of colonial railways, but clearly he saw, too, the need to make concessions to the radicals. E. J. Hawksley, editor of the *People's Advocate*, laid down the tenets of a 'true liberal' as manhood suffrage, vote by ballot, and representation by population. [21] Only one of the five candidates for the Sydney seats, J. D. Lang, met these requirements, and Cowper's position fell far short of them. He promised an unspecified extension of the franchise, a greater share of representation for Sydney, and declined to commit himself on the question of a secret ballot, but even this was a significant change from his attitude in 1848, and Hawksley, Driver, Wilshire, Piddington and other leading radicals gave him support, as they did also to the other 'liberal' candidates, John Lamb and Lang. Wentworth and a Catholic candidate, A. Longmore, made up the field, and the radicals soon realized that a concerted campaign for their three candidates gave the best chance of success. It was not to be. Lamb, furious at being dumped by Cowper from the presidency of the railway company a few months earlier, refused to have anything to do with him, and Cowper's middle-class supporters shied away in horror from the arch-radical Lang. Cowper was unconcerned. He felt that, as in 1848, the electors would return him on his record. Instead, Lang, Lamb and Wentworth took the Sydney seats and he fell to the bottom of the poll. Outwardly he accepted his defeat with grace and good humour. Inwardly he was deeply shocked and his easy win in the country seat of Durham a few days later did little to ease his resentment. Even three years later his bitterness remained at having been 'dragged in the dirt most ignominiously'.[22] It was fuelled by Deas Thomson and other political opponents who, knowing Cowper's pride in his dignity and standing in the House, gleefully made play with his status as the 'second' or 'junior' member for Durham. 'All this has its *meaning*—and though I now have worked all through it, and it is gone by it forms part of one's *political experience* and *training*', Cowper told Henry Parkes.[23]

As Lang said, the subject of transportation was 'as dead as the feudal system' at the 1851 elections.[24] By then it was apparent to all that the advocates of transportation, both in Britain and in the colonies, were in full retreat and the flood of immigrants begun by the gold rushes would soon disperse them completely. Cowper had failed to see the change in public interest or that railways had not yet captured the people's imagination as they were later to do. Lang and Lamb went into the electorate and won votes personally; Wentworth edged his way into third place through the lingering popularity of former days; Longmore's loss proved, not for the first time, that Catholics did not necessarily vote for their co-religionists; and Cowper failed because he tried to rest on his laurels instead of pursuing, in J. M. Ward's apt phrase, 'the art of winning votes'.[25]

In 1849 Cowper had shown such zest for the work of the legislature that he sat on seventeen of the twenty-two select committees. During the 1851 session the level of his activity dropped so sharply that it drew the notice of the sporting newspaper *Bell's Life in Sydney*, which dismissed him as a 'lamentable failure' because Lowe was no longer there to instruct him.[26] It was well for *Bell's Life* that it could assess horses with greater accuracy than men. Lowe had worked, as Cowper said, in 'singular unanimity' with him in 1849,[27] for each man's talents were a complement to the other's, and Cowper's equable temperament enabled him to work with the irascible and unpredictable Lowe where others could not. With one or two exceptions, Cowper was as close a friend as Lowe possessed in New South Wales, and the two spent much time in discussing politics as they meandered on horseback over the sand dunes near Lowe's Coogee home. If Lowe was the leading spirit in lands and constitutional questions, Cowper was equally so in transportation and railway matters, and until Lowe departed from the colony for ever in January 1850, they continued to differ strongly, even bitterly, over moral and religious issues. Thus, when the Myall Creek massacre of 1838 brought about a scarifying debate in the legislature during the following year, Lowe cynically advised that settlers and blacks be left alone to 'fight it out amongst themselves' so that the 'universally inferior' blacks should gain a wholesome fear of the white man. Cowper took the opposite view and condemned the 'atrocious crime' of the white murderers[28] and shortly before Lowe's departure for England, Cowper rose 'with feelings of exquisite pain and deep disgust' to castigate him for his last attack on Bishop Broughton.[29] Allies, even friends, they were; leader and follower they were not.

Cowper had reasons other than hurt pride for his diminished political role in 1851. The railway company absorbed much time, and Wentworth had seized the initiative in the legislature. Transportation, education, religion were all dormant issues; land problems were fast merging with the great unresolved question of constitutional change and in this field Wentworth, profiting from the absence of Lowe, re-established his undisputed ascendancy. 'He is Master of the House, whenever he chooses', wryly acknowledged Parkes's *Empire* after the 1851 session.[30] He instigated and chaired the general grievance committee of that session which produced a report attacking the new constitution of 1850 and demanding local control of colonial revenues, taxation and patronage. Neither Cowper, a member of the committee, nor any other elected member could quarrel with Wentworth's report and they fell in behind him in support. Without the opportunity to shine in the legislature, Cowper quietly worked at strengthening his ties with the Sydney merchants. In the euphoric atmosphere of the early gold-rush years, wild hope or sober assessment of increased trade caused city commercial men to create a spate of new companies. From 1851 to the peak year of 1853 it was Cowper, and not the holders of the city seats, who patiently shepherded most of the company incorporation bills through the legislature. During the same period he steadily extended his social contracts with the urban middle class as, increasingly, they took the place of landholders on the boards of social, charitable and church organizations. In 1852 Cowper was an active member of eleven organizations of this type, ranging from the New South Wales Vineyard Society

and the Australian Subscription Library to the Sydney Female Refuge
Society and the Church of England Clergy and Widows Fund — a
happy linking, it seems, of charitable instincts with political advantage. Yet, apart from his special interest in railways, he made no
serious attempt to enter the commercial world himself. He remained
a countryman at heart. Only the love of politics drew him to Sydney.

The early gold-rush years were critical in the evolution of Cowper's
political views. His election defeat of 1851 had shown him the importance
of the lower-class vote in the prime city and it was apparent that the
power and prestige of Sydney were growing fast. It was almost to
double in a decade its 54 000 people of 1851, and the population which
it served in outlying areas grew even faster. Cowper saw, more clearly
than did most of the landholders and the wealthy urban middle
class, that they could hope to remain the political leaders of the colony
only if they came to terms with the democratic ideas of the radicals.
After 1851, Cowper moved increasingly towards a political stance more
radical than that taken by most of the greater merchants and professional
men who had backed him since he first entered the Council. By
1853, radicals ·were hailing him as their champion. 'He stands alone',
proclaimed the *People's Advocate,* 'to do the battle of democracy, against
the government on the one hand and Mr. Wentworth and the
oligarchical party on the other'. [31] Still, Cowper took care that he did
not alienate his middle-class support. He would not join such purely
radical movements as the Political Association of 1851 or the Democratic
League of 1853. He gave covert encouragement to Parkes when he stood
as the 'popular' candidate at Sydney by-elections in 1853 and 1854,
but would not side openly with him, since his opponents, Thomas
Holt and Charles Kemp respectively, were both influential members
of the commercial community.

Such fence-sitting tactics occasionally tried Cowper's political dexterity
to the limit. Such a situation occurred in September 1853 when Cowper
succeeded in abolishing Australia's first democratically elected local body,
the Sydney City Corporation. By 1849 that body had become notorious
for the slovenliness of its proceedings and the blatant self-interest
displayed by its members. In that year a select committee of the Council,
chaired by Lowe and with Cowper as a member, condemned it for
gross corruption and demanded its replacement by three government-
appointed commissioners. No action was taken and in 1852 Cowper,
disgusted at the continued sorry record of the city fathers, obtained
and chaired another select committee on the subject. A rate-payers'
meeting, called to petition for the abolition of the city corporation,
broke up in uproarious disagreement, but, in general, merchants

and the *Sydney Morning Herald* were for abolition, while radicals and the *Empire* demanded the preservation of an elective body. Cowper's committee was equally divided and eventually produced the novel proposal that six aldermen be elected by voters who were to hold from one to four votes each according to the value of city property they held. Cowper, presiding over a public meeting on these proposals, was carefully non-committal, but even a ringing defence of him by Parkes did not prevent radical speakers from savagely assailing the unfortunate chairman over the sliding scale of franchise. On the other hand, the *Sydney Morning Herald* condemned the committee's proposal as tantamount to continuing the existing rotten system. A majority of the Legislative Council members thought similarly. They rejected Cowper's report in favour of a proposal by J. B. Darvall that the corporation be replaced by three paid commissioners. Again an indifferent government took no action and Cowper faced an embarrassing dilemma. Given the Council's attitude, he had either to press for city commissioners, thus incurring the wrath of the radicals, or give up his reforming mission. Reluctantly he moved that the corporation be suspended and commissioners appointed, won easily the resultant division, and so consigned the corporation to oblivion. 'After the stand he has made against nomineeism in the legislature', lamented the *People's Advocate*, 'it appears to us most incongruous and illogical on his part to have proposed this resolution'. [32]

Luckily for Cowper, his 'stand against nomineeism', in the controversy over the form which representative government should take, far outweighed his preference for efficiency over democracy in city affairs. Both liberals and radicals demanded an elective upper house while Wentworth, the squatters and most of the government members of the Council favoured a nominee body. 'Our doom is now sealed' complained the *Empire*, [33] with good reason, when Cowper and William Thurlow became the only liberals elected to Wentworth's select committee on the constitution. Consistently, Cowper voted for liberal tenets; with equal consistency, he lost to the conservative majority, and their report proposed a nominee upper house and a property franchise for all voters. Cowper, with Robert Campbell and Darvall, fought the resultant bill through every stage until December 1853. A hastily convened body, the constitution committee, met in August to produce a liberal alternative to Wentworth's bill and to whip up public fervour in their cause. They failed in both objects. Only Wentworth's proposals for a hereditary upper class, the 'bunyip aristocracy', aroused the people and they swamped the idea with irony and laughter. By December, Cowper and Darvall, both enthusiastic early members of the constitution committee, had realized that internal disunity would prevent that body from producing a worthwhile alternative to Wentworth's plan. [34] Disgusted at liberal discord and the apathy of a population which could raise no more opposition to Wentworth than six or seven public meetings throughout the whole colony, [35] Cowper told the solid phalanx of squatters and government members which faced him across the Council chamber that he, Darvall and Campbell would no longer carry on a futile resistance. [36] For months he had pinned his main hopes of killing Wentworth's constitution bill upon the Imperial parliament. He believed that the known views of Gladstone and Newcastle (then secretary of state for the colonies) against colonial nominee houses could cause delay or even rejection of the bill. Above all, he counted upon Robert Lowe, from his seat in the House of Commons, to oppose the bill and to lobby for its rejection. Throughout 1854 the liberals were buoyed up by such hopes and equally their hopes were the fears of the conservatives. Wentworth followed his bill to England to see it through parliament and as late as December 1854 George Macleay of Brownlow Hill wrote to William Macarthur (then in England), 'Remember me kindly to Wentworth...[Impress upon him] the necessity of his returning here immediately if the New Constn. Bill is sent back to us as I grievously expect it will.' [37]

By this time, Cowper was clearly identified with a small but reasonably coherent group of liberals in the legislature. The term 'liberal' carried more democratic overtones than it had five or six years earlier. These men were placed near the centre of a line joining the extremes of earlier radical and liberal thought. From the radical side came Parkes, Lang and William Thurlow, the latter replaced by J. R. Wilshire in 1855. From the liberal end came Cowper, Edward Flood, George Oakes and J. W. Bligh, while Robert Campbell had long planted a foot in both camps. Of these, Campbell, possessor of that rare combination, great wealth and a generous heart, a man renowned for his honesty and a wild incoherent speech when excited, was Cowper's oldest friend and also his closest political ally.

But Cowper drew increasingly close to Parkes as the latter gradually shed his more extreme radical views. In his early middle age at that time, Parkes lacked the striking appearance and oratorical flourishes of his later years. His looks, said a writer for *Freeman's Journal*, were 'cold, heavy and dull' and his speech resembled the dark, stagnant waters of an Irish bog, [38] but Cowper, like the writer of that assessment, saw the shrewd political sense and organizational ability of the man. He saw, too, that Parkes's control of the *Empire*, the colony's second daily newspaper, would become increasingly important to him as he moved to gain radical approval and, in doing so, risked the loss of the *Sydney Morning Herald*'s long-standing support. Campbell formed a bridge between the two men. Once landlord to Parkes in his Hunter Street toy shop, Campbell scorned Cowper's cautious tactics and from 1849 joined wholeheartedly in radical activities—so wholeheartedly that he found himself barred from Government House for his part in the anti-'exile' protests of that year. The *Empire* backed him strongly in his successful bid for the Sydney seat vacated by the near-bankrupt Lang in 1851 and Campbell reciprocated by helping Parkes to another Sydney seat in 1854. He even organized the payment of Parkes's election expenses through a subscription fund, which should have earned the gratitude of that ever-impecunious politician. Campbell seems at first to have played a mediating role as Cowper set out from 1851 onwards to seek the political help of Parkes. Cowper's letters to Parkes, preserved in the Parkes Correspondence of the Mitchell Library,[39] show a gradually developing political intimacy until, by 1855, the two men worked in close harmony, with Cowper pouring out advice and comment on the *Empire*'s policies and expressing his personal feelings with candour and even, as in the expression of the humiliation he continued to feel at his 1851 defeat in Sydney, with deep passion. By 1854 Parkes had become Cowper's most effective and, next to Campbell, his closest political ally. Yet they were no more than 'political friends',[40] as Cowper put it. Colonial society had sharp divisions, the frontiers of which, noted that perceptive observer G. C. Mundy, 'are not the less arbitrary because they are not very apparent'.[41] Parkes, the self-made working-man and keen social climber, would probably have welcomed a closer friendship, but Cowper, being a member of the colonial social elite, would probably have not. Cowper's elder son, Charles, married in 1855, at a time when Cowper regularly expressed to Parkes a biting criticism of conservatives such as wealthy merchant Stuart Donaldson, James Macarthur and the Macleay family. Yet at the wedding reception, Macarthur and Donaldson made the major speeches and Parkes appears not to have been invited.[42]

Perhaps the strangest feature of Cowper's relations with the radical wing of the new liberal group was the mutual regard which grew up between him and the arch-radical J. D. Lang, who had once condemned Cowper as a starched Episcopalian Exclusive. Lang had been won over by Cowper's stand against transportation. His efforts to help Lang settle his debts in 1851 confirmed the friendship. Thereafter each showed a warm respect towards the other which lasted till the end of Cowper's life.

By 1854 these men were consistently demanding electoral reform and the breaking of the squatters' hold upon Crown lands. Yet they

Charles Cowper, aged 25 years, painting by
Richard Read jun., 1832
(In possession of Sir Norman Cowper)

R. Campbell

E. C. Weekes
J. F. Hargrave
(By courtesy of the Council of
the State Library of N.S.W.)

knew that major reforms must now await the coming of representative government. There was truth in H. C. Douglass's charge that they continued to harass the conservative majority in the legislature mainly because they were striving to impress 'the multitude out of doors'. [43] Therein lay the main reason for their growing hostility to Governor Sir Charles Fitzroy. They needed to impress their own position upon the electorate by increasing their opposition to the governing structure which he headed. Thus when the able and efficient Deas Thomson left for England in December 1853 the *People's Advocate* libelled him as 'The Great Sham' who was 'about to quit for a time the country he has well-nigh ruined by years of misgovernment'. [44] The city merchants did not share this view. They packed his testimonial committee, and Cowper, with typical caution, neither criticized Deas Thomson nor contributed to his testimonial. Until that time Cowper had been reluctant to criticize the vice-regal representative, but Fitzroy's action in deposing him from the presidency of the railway company and his open support for Wentworth's constitution bill helped to propel Cowper into the vanguard of the liberal attack. Furthermore, when Wentworth departed for England early in 1854, the last shred of unity amongst the elected members vanished, for, as Cowper acknowledged, [45] the old lion of colonial politics was the only man in the Council who could hope to be leader to them all.

The small group of liberals drew closer together and Cowper began to lend a ready ear to the accusations of immorality which Lang had been hurling against Fitzroy since 1852, in particular the story of the 'Berrima incident', in which Fitzroy or one of his two sporting sons (sporting in more ways than one, said the colony's gossips) was said to have fathered a child upon an innkeeper's daughter during the vice-regal travels around New South Wales. Parkes, too, believed this story but he was too prudent to adopt Cowper's suggestion that he publish the child's certificate of baptism in the *Empire*. [46] In the privileged sanctuary of the Council chamber the liberals used such allegations as the basis for attacks on Fitzroy's fitness to govern. With a considerable degree of co-ordination they also attacked the government throughout 1854 over inefficiency in public works and Crown lands administration, opposed an increase in Fitzroy's salary, tried to reopen the constitutional question and had a field day with the estimates. Finding holes in the government's armour was made easier by the replacement of Deas Thomson as colonial secretary by C. D. Riddell, a plodder, though he probably did not deserve the judgement placed upon him by the *People's Advocate* of being 'one of the most ignorant men in Her Britannic Majesty's dominions'. [47] Cowper launched the high point of the liberal attack on 13 September 1854, bringing up a motion of no confidence in the government and demanding a complete stoppage of supply until responsible government was granted. Most of his opponents were baffled by these moves, for all knew the liberals were certain to be soundly defeated and, as the *Sydney Morning Herald* pointed out, a new viceroy and a new constitution were already on the way. [48] But, as liberal actions and Cowper's letters to Parkes make clear, these moves were all part of a plan to establish the liberals as a valid political opposition to the conservatives and, on Cowper's part, as James Martin suspected, to further his own leadership ambitions. [49]

The liberals tried new tactics when Sir William Denison, forsaking his long-held governorship of Tasmania, replaced Fitzroy in 1855. They knew that Denison favoured elective upper houses and hoped that he would, if suitably petitioned, dissolve the Council and hold new elections which might result in a liberal majority and give them another bite at the constitutional cherry. Cowper's response to this proposal gave a clear indication of both his native caution and the great value he placed upon his personal dignity. He first agreed to join the prime movers of the petition, Parkes; Lang and Darvall, but soon withdrew, fearing that hasty action might turn Denison against them and that his standing in the Council would be damaged if he became 'a decided partizan and not a deliberative senator'. Besides, he added, 'at a Public Meeting such as will assemble some very *wild* notions will be broached. [50]

Cowper kept his dignity, and Denison nonplussed the liberals by firmly rejecting their petition. They did not know their man. 'I look upon change as an evil of great magnitude, not to be encountered unless for the removal of some greater evils, or the introduction of some special goods', wrote Denison in explanation of his attitude. [51] The liberals got no constitutional help from him. By August 1855 they had conceded that Wentworth's constitution would pass relatively unchanged and had even begun to realize that its form was not necessarily inimical to their interests.

Early in June 1855 the Legislative Council convened for the last time. Denison, energetic and autocratic, sent a heavy programme of government legislation to them, only to find that it ran into a solid wall of opposition which he attributed, with some degree of truth, to members being 'loth to commit themselves on any subject which they think will involve them in difficulties at the next election'. [52] More importantly, elected members thought that all but the most urgent legislation should be left for consideration under the responsible government which was to begin a few months later. Foremost amongst those who felt this way were the liberals, for they were sure that they would be the leaders in the new era.

Their opposition to government bills was more effective than ever before, because they were joined by others, G. R. Nichols, James Martin, Ă. T. Holroyd, and more, men castigated by Cowper, just before the session began, as 'this miserable faction...slippery members who join the Government Ranks on all important questions'. [53] But these were astute men who looked to their own political futures and had no desire to see the existing officials returned to power under responsible government. Increasingly during the 1855 session Martin, Nichols, Holroyd and other 'independent' members such as Stuart Donaldson and J. B. Darvall, joined the liberals in opposition to the government, forging their own image of independence before they had to face the electors of a fully responsible government. Where strong differences of opinion were coupled with this attitude, as in the opposition of liberals and independents to Denison's plans for the fortification of Sydney harbour, feelings were bitter indeed. The government members had to endure a sixteen-hour sitting and thirty-two motions of amendment before they could force through the defence vote. By August, Denison was conceding privately that much of his legislation would fail. He was right. On 19 December 1855 the Council ended thirteen stormy years of existence. Cowper delivered a eulogy on the retiring Speaker, Charles Nicholson, still a personal friend in spite of the ever-widening political gap which had separated them for ten years. Few turned out to watch—a sad end to a body which had been so useful to New South Wales. The thoughts of all were on the future.

Cowper seemed well placed to enter the new and independent parliament soon to be elected. Thanks to his blend of principle and pragmatism he enjoyed wide support across the whole urban radical-liberal spectrum, without having committed himself to the extreme views of either group. He had consistently maintained his record as an enemy to the extravagance which the public was ever ready to believe existed in government spending. At the same time he earned the approval of public servants by instigating an inquiry which led to pay rises to compensate them for gold-caused inflation. He had continued to strive hard for the poor, the lunatic and the prisoners of Darlinghurst Gaol where, during an inquiry of 1849, he uncovered administrative corruption that scandalized the colony and embarrassed the government. But if these actions were those which a man of principle might support, it was still clear that others were dictated by expediency. Such was the case when he refused to support Parkes openly in his 1854 election campaign but did so warmly in secret, and when, in 1853, he backed T. A. Murray's complaint that the government's action in cutting up Crown grazing lands for sale as small farms had forced adjacent landowners to buy these blocks at high prices where previously they had grazed them free.

this attitude contrasted strangely with his demands for the breaking of the squatters' land monopoly. As J. H. Plunkett said, 'his hon. friends opposite admitted that the principle was good, but they did not like these small proprietors to tread upon their toes'. [54]

In other issues Cowper displayed a blend of realism and principle which was often misunderstood. Thus, when he came out against state aid to churches at the 1851 elections, some observers believed, erroneously, that he had modified his religious views. 'He is clearly getting the better of his former high church notions', wrote William Kerr to J. D. Lang. [55] But Cowper had merely come to the conclusion that, since his beloved Church of England had now no practical hope of becoming the 'established' church, it was better to end state aid than to continue the financing of error as well as truth. [56] For different reasons the other leading liberals also favoured the abolition of state aid; Campbell partly agreed with Cowper, but was mindful that under a voluntary system the numerically superior Anglican church could expect to be comparatively better off than its smaller rivals; this viewpoint was shared by many, laymen and clergy alike; Parkes thought state aid unjust and inequitable. Cowper's belief explains his changing attitude to the recurring question of state aid for the Jewish religion. He opposed it in 1845 and 1849, avoided any commitment in 1853, and a year later conceded that the Jews had as much claim as others (with the implication that he meant other perpetrators of error). He even contributed five guineas to a fund for the distressed Jews of Palestine.

Cowper applied similarly pragmatic reasoning to the education question. He actively supported the proposal for an Anglican college at Sydney University and in 1853 he told the legislature that children who attended government schools were 'trained up to sedition in this world, and to peridition in the next'. [57] Yet in 1854 he joined Parkes in gaining Council approval and funds to set up the non-denominational Sydney Grammar School and he told the Council that he 'never was opposed to the national school system'. [58] At that point a just God might well have struck him with a thunderbolt. Instead, lovers of truth had to make do with one indignant schoolmaster who wrote to the *Empire* in condemnation of Cowper's 'barefaced effrontery'. [59] By Cowper's own admission, he had realized that the public wanted the national schools [60] and he adapted his actions accordingly. A similar sensitivity to the demands of the non-religious seems to have moved him a few weeks later when he joined Martin and Nichols in insisting that heads of denominational colleges at the university need not be clergymen, and again in 1855 when he added to Plunkett's marriage bill a clause allowing secular ceremonies by a registrar.

As New South Wales advanced to the edge of responsible government it was apparent that few could hope to challenge Cowper for the leadership of the embryonic liberal party. His social standing was high, a point important even to the radicals. His long political service, his organizing ability, his pleasant and conciliatory personality and his tremendous capacity for work were widely acknowledged. Able men such as Nichols, Martin and Darvall had not yet established a liberal image. Of those who had, John Lamb had left the colony in 1853, Campbell was Cowper's loyal follower, Lang's republicanism had isolated him except from the extreme radicals, and Parkes, perhaps the ablest of them all, was yet a relatively untried new man. The only man whose rivalry Cowper feared was the enigmatic Stuart Donaldson, who had shown himself to be an able politician and one highly skilled in the art of compromise, but Cowper's jealousy of him, revealed in his letters to Parkes, [61] was more a symptom of his own desire for the leadership than a reflection of any real threat from Donaldson, who had too much inclination towards conservatism to be a serious danger.

A greater problem was the lack of unity amongst the liberals themselves. Partly, this stemmed from their failure to develop a coherent liberal ideology. As Loveday and Martin have noted, liberal aims were then too ill-defined to offer a basis for party action. [62] Cowper acknowledged the need 'to bring down good principles of government, [63] but he was not the man to define them. He was a practical politican sensitive to the demands of the electorate, not a party theorist. It is unlikely that anyone could have imposed an orderly party structure and unified aims upon the liberals at that time, since the ideals they held in common amounted to little more than a belief in the inevitability of progress towards a world of more equal opportunity. They shared with their conservative opponents the view, long out of date in British politics, that the duties of a parliamentarian included that of speaking and voting as individual conscience dictated. This led to a degree of disunity even on issues where liberal members were basically in agreement. Thus, disagreement over tactics led Campbell to vote for second reading of Wentworth's constitution bill where Cowper and the other liberals voted against it, and in 1854, while Cowper was striving to retain the support of Sydney commercial men, Campbell publicly accused two of their leading members, Charles Kemp and T. S. Mort, of treachery to Cowper over the railway company's affairs and proclaimed that Mort had 'turned renegade' by leaving the constitution committee. [64] Again, while Cowper persuaded Parkes not to support Donaldson for a Sydney seat in 1855, both Parkes and Campbell flung their weight behind him when he stood instead for a surburban seat. As the *Sydney Morning Herald* said when Donaldson won, he had been returned 'by active persons dissenting from his opinions, and under the patronage of journalists who lateiy denounced them'. [65]

In these instances and in others, it seems that Cowper might well have given a stronger lead than he did towards securing liberal unity and emphasizing his leadership. But with the current of ambition in his mind ran a strain of disillusionment, deepened greatly by overwork and recurrent illness. 'The field of Politics is a stormy one and I sometimes, especially when I am as at present suffering from sickness, sigh for shelter from its exposure', he wrote to Parkes. [66] The peaceful country life of Wivenhoe drew him as often as he could get away from the turmoil of politics. 'It is astonishing how...continued residence away from Sydney affects ones [sic] concern about politics and State affairs', he reflected, [67] and he penned to Parkes his ever-recurring doubts as to the value of his work. 'For years I have been incessantly engaged in hard uphill work', he wrote, 'and during that period I have often asked myself *what good* have I been in any respect the means of accomplishing'. [68] He yearned nostalgically for what he saw in retrospect as the unity of the elected members during the early years of the Council and, at least until the end of 1854, nursed the improbable hope that a strong leader (presumably himself) might restore it. The only effect of this dream was to weaken still further his chance of exerting strong leadership over the liberals. The nature of colonial politics made it extremely difficult for Cowper to impose real unity; his own nature made it doubly so. As the year of independence, 1856, approached, he was indeed the leading liberal politician of New South Wales, but not yet, in any real sense, the liberal leader.

4

The Quest for Power 1856–1857

In 1856 Sydney held over 20 000 people more than it had possessed five years earlier, but it was still recognizable as the city of pre-gold-rush days. The treeless sandstone of Pyrmont supported more closely packed houses, and the spacious homes of the Glebe were more deeply sunk in exotic greenery. Rows of surburban cottages lined the Parramatta Road for six or seven miles out of the city, and the villas of the North Shore and eastern bays clustered more thickly along the shoreline, but in the main this growth was consolidation of earlier expansion. The greatest changes since 1851 had taken place in ways not so readily seen, in the commercial life of the city. The gold rushes had greatly accelerated the previous steady growth of the metropolitan commercial community, in numbers, wealth and power, for Sydney had retained and extended its prime role in New South Wales. The railway, opened in 1855, ran only to Parramatta, but all roads led to Sydney, and the traffic in men and freight upon them helpéd to pour wealth into the new banks, insurance companies, warehouses, wholesale and retail businesses, which had sprung up initially to cater for the gold seekers and survived after the boom years by supplying the same people as they turned from gold to seek a living in the towns. For those with capital, for professional men, for anyone with energy and a desire for business, Sydney held the greatest promise, and while its population remained proportionately much the same in relation to the whole colony as it had been in 1851, the concentration of wealth, enterprise and political awareness within the city had greatly increased.

The liberals were well aware of these changes. The trend of city elections since 1848 had been clearly and strongly in their favour. They saw the four Legislative Assembly seats which had been allocated to the city as the basis of their political strength in the new House. since each elector could cast as many votes as there were seats to fill in his electorate, it would obviously be of help to the liberals if they could put up four candidates in some sort of coalition for Sydney, to minimize the risk of 'plumpers' or misplaced votes by liberal electors.

Realizing this, Hawksley and another veteran radical, William McCurtayne, promoted a public meeting on 25 October 1855 in the hope of forming an Electoral Association to select and back suitable candidates. Their move was premature. The liberal leaders stayed away and without them the meeting reached no conclusions. But Parkes, loftily proclaiming his intention not to stand while waiting for someone to ask him to, had been turning the matter over in his mind and in mid-December he suggested to Cowper that the two of them plus Campbell and Wilshire might support one another for the Sydney seats. The elections were due in March, but Cowper was in no hurry to consider the matter. He went home to Wivenhoe for Christmas and moved on to Chatsbury without making any decision on his candidature.

While Cowper was away, the liberals were forced into action by the news that J. H. Plunkett was to stand for Sydney. He was the colony's most prominent Catholic, and non-Catholic liberals still feared that chimera, the Papist bloc vote. Additionally, his enlightened attitude to social questions, to law reform and to secular education could be expected to draw support from uncommitted voters. Liberal activists met at Piddington's bookshop, approved J. D. Lang's suggestion that they set up an electoral organization to promote a coalition against Plunkett, and recommended Cowper, Campbell and Parkes as candidates: Wilshire's reputation for laziness nearly cost him the fourth place but, no more suitable person being found, his name was added to the list. The choice of candidates, all men of some standing, showed clearly the ascendancy of the middle-class liberals over their radical allies. Even the arch-radical Daniel Deniehy insisted that liberal candidates must have 'some claim to social respectability'.[1] A public meeting approved the four candidates, but Cowper hesitated. He still remembered the city's rejection of him in 1851. He also seemed unwilling to oppose Plunkett, whom he respected for his ability as a law officer and for his role as Cowper's sole defender on the Executive Council in 1853 when that body urged Fitzroy to depose him from the chairmanship of the railway company. He told Parkes, 'I suppose I must go for Sydney',[2] Yet he left his ally to bear the brunt of the campaign for weeks thereafter while he remained in the country.

The liberals, repeating the tactics they had been perfecting since 1848, organized a series of local area committees and public meetings to push their candidates. Plunkett acknowledged the efficiency of their methods by copying them and battle was joined. The liberal 'Bunch', without a clear-cut policy to offer and harassed by differences of opinion within their own ranks, ran a rather negative campaign, condemning the provisions of the 1851 Electoral Act and the new constitution without suggesting any positive remedies, and trying to label Plunkett as a conservative of the deepest dye. Plunkett declined to accept the role and stood on his record of public service. His meetings, well attended by the Catholic Irish of the city, were orderly affairs. The same Irish made sure that the meetings of the Bunch were disorderly. Playing upon the public dislike of 'faction', of combination for personal gain, Plunketts supporters forced each Bunchman in turn to deny what everyone knew was true, that he was part of a coalition. Plunkett himself, for all his earlier amiable relations with Cowper, dug so far into his past that he dredged up the matter of the seven Vandemonian convicts and hammered his chief opponent for religious exclusivism. As always when any colonial candidate tried to rally the Catholic vote behind him, Plunkett found defectors everywhere. Self-proclaimed 'Tipperary boys' campaigned for the Bunch,³ and Cowper held on high a letter promising to vote for him from that most senior and respected churchman Archdeacon John McEncroe. McEncroe had worked amicably for years with Cowper in the anti-transportation campaign. Like many another Catholic who came to know Cowper well, McEncroe seems to have felt that the personal charm and liberal tendencies of the man outweighed his occasional bigotry. 'His only weakness is Anglicanism', the editor of the *Sydney Chronicle* had once remarked,⁴ 'but we fear not his influence in this subject', for the era of Anglican supremacy had long passed the point of no return.

The 1856 campaign in Sydney and its suburbs showed clearly that the split which had long been forming between the greater mercantile men and the small fry of the early liberal movement had become an unbridgeable gap. Such eminent commercial men as T. S. Mort, Gilbert Wright, David Jones, Charles Kemp, John Fairfax, M. E. Murnin and Thomas Holt, all of whom had taken part in the early liberal and anti-transportation movements, now rallied to back Plunkett against their old ally Cowper, while the main supporters of the Bunch were men who had been called radicals a few years earlier: Hawksley, Piddington, Driver, McCurtayne, Edward James, B. Mountcastle, Martin Guest; shopkeepers, publicans, tradesmen; with only a sprinkling of such greater traders and merchants as Thomas Walker and J. L. Montefiore. Plunkett's mercantile supporters were well on the way to becoming a new breed of conservatives, not so opposed to democratic ideals as the old officials and landholders, but wary of 'mob rule' and counselling a gradual constitutional evolution rather than the bold leap into majority rule demanded by followers of the Bunch.

Still, the line of demarcation was blurred, for the boundaries of conservatism and liberalism in New South Wales had not been set.

Thus Cowper chaired a meeting for W. M. Manning—once solicitor-general under Deas Thomson and now a candidate for the South Riding of Cumberland—only to withdraw his support quietly when Manning attacked a leading tenet of the liberals, electoral redistribution on a population basis. Parkes gave consistent support for a North Cumberland seat to J. B. Darvall, who, in the old Council, had been liberal in his opposition to the constitution bill and conservative in nearly everything else. Another strange bedfellow for the Bunch was James Martin, once Wentworth's protegé, who, barely eight months earlier, had attacked the 'levellers' of the liberal party 'who appeared to delight in cavilling at everything that was really good and proper. [5] When he turned out to speak at a Bunch political meeting, Parkes hailed the event as a step in building 'the first great powerful party that ever existed in this country'. [6] This happy prospect was stillborn. Martin made it clear that his personal enmity towards Plunkett was the sole cause of his appearance and said not a word in praise of the Bunch. At least one man, Daniel Cooper, candidate for the suburban seat of Sydney Hamlets, received support from both Plunkett's backers and the Bunch. Neither group had any great influence outside the immediate environs of Sydney, though Parkes actively intervened on behalf of liberal candidates in at least three near-city electorates and Cowper canvassed the Cobbitty-Narellan district for liberal Elias Weekes.

The Bunch swept the board on polling day and in topping the poll, Cowper expunged the lingering bitterness of 1851. Yet Plunkett ran the fourth man, Wilshire, very close and had a double, if indirect, revenge in winning the Bathurst seat from Cowper's old colleague J. W. Bligh, and the Argyle seat from James Chisholm, who was supported by Cowper's son Charles. Though Plunkett chose to sit for Argyle, the humiliated Bligh would not stand again for Bathurst, and Cowper lost a valuable ally.

While the election campaign progressed, Denison reviewed the situation, decided that the conservatives would gain a majority and approached Deas Thomson to form a ministry. Thomson declined and Denison turned to James Macarthur for advice. The upshot was that Stuart Donaldson received the commission to form a ministry. He hoped to head off political strife by forming a middle-of-the-road government. Well aware that he could not succeed without Cowper's support, Donaldson offered him first the Treasury, then the key post of colonial secretary with the highest government salary, £2000 a year. The new premier said later that Cowper refused him with the sharp comment, 'Well, Donaldson, all I can say is—had the Governor-General sent for me to form an administration you would have been the first person I should have sought to assist me.'[7] No doubt Cowper would have resented the commissioning of Deas Thomson or of anyone other than himself to head the first responsible ministry, but he was specially antagonized by the appointment of the one man whom he felt could threaten his position as the liberal leader. Denison's own conservatism seems to have been the chief factor in his rejection of Cowper, but the latter may not have been entirely wrong when he blamed Macarthur. 'I distrust him [Cowper] as being a needy man, and associated with needy men, and in being a man who from what I know, and from what I have heard has never gone straight towards any object, but has always worked a tortuous course in utter disregard of honesty being the best policy', Denison told a friend in London,[8] and who other than his conservative advisers would have painted that picture for the governor?

In the words of the *Empire,* Donaldson 'was forced to throw himself into the arms of the pastoral party'[9] to form his ministry. His ministers, Holt, Manning, Darvall and Nichols, were all city men but only the support of pastoral representatives could keep them in power. Denison, reviewing the election results, decided that a conservative majority of ten or twelve would exist in the Assembly and renewed Donaldson's commission. Since no one could be certain where the boundary lay between liberalism and conservatism, Cowper arrived at a different conclusion. He calculated that liberal and conservative numbers would be roughly equal, refused Donaldson's renewed offer of the Treasury and tried unsuccessfully to 'pot' the new premier by offering him liberal support for the speakership. Donaldson's selection of ministers with identifiable conservative tendencies helped to define political attitudes more clearly, to Cowper's advantage. The liberals, as Denison said, were 'out',[10] and their desire to be 'in' led them to more coherent support of their leaders, Cowper in the Assembly and Parkes in the electorates.[11] Even Martin, who had little time for democracy or for Cowper, collaborated with the liberals. Still, Cowper found it necessary to be cautious in defining the common interests of the liberal group, those members, he said in August 1856, 'who are supposed to entertain similar views in reference to the Crown Lands, the Electoral Districts, and the financial policy of the Government'.[12] On 7 May 1856 those men met at the mansion of one of their number, wealthy merchant and investor Daniel Cooper and agreed on concerted action against the ministry. As soon as the Assembly's first session opened in May, they put up Cooper for the speakership against conservative candidate H. W. Parker and won the resultant division by one vote. Seeing government within his grasp, Cowper threw caution to the winds and tried to topple the ministry on a vote of no confidence. The Assembly rejected his move and he was forced to recognize that uncommitted members, and even such an out-and-out liberal as the ebullient Hunter Valley landowner John Robertson, would not overturn the government on what they saw as trivial grounds.

Cowper's pangs of thwarted ambition were suddenly submerged by personal grief. His second and favourite son, William Harrington Cowper, died in London where he had been sent to complete his education. Cowper left the Assembly and rode home to Wivenhoe, where for weeks he brooded in anguish. On 5 July he wrote gloomily to Parkes, 'I am not yet of heart for politics. The unexpected loss of my son has depressed me sadly', [13] but the lure of politics was not to be denied and a week later he commented to Lang on the proceedings of the Assembly and the blunders of the government. [14] Shortly afterwards he returned to the House. Yet his depression and inaction lingered until the *Sydney Morning Herald* remarked that Martin, with his articulate and aggressive opposition to almost everything the ministry attempted, seemed to be the new leader of the opposition. [15] Martin was too isolated to be a serious threat, but thereafter Cowper joined wholeheartedly in a liberal campaign of indiscriminate obstructionism which led Donaldson to complain that the opposition had spent the session in trying 'to exhaust the ministers and render them incapable of doing anything'.[16] Even John Robertson opposed his own colleagues when Cowper led them into dogged obstruction of an innocuous government motion for a select committee to inquire into the necessity for appointing a new minister. The ministry narrowly won the divisions, only to resign the next day, 'chattered to death', as the *Sydney Morning Herald* put it. [17] Darvall nicely expressed the ministry's feelings in saying that the opposition had made it impossible that the government could be carried on by gentlemen. Men of all shades of political opinion, the conservatives believed, should join in the promotion of sound measures, and governments should only be overturned on matters of great moral principle. Liberals felt the force of this view. Because factions were thought to lack real principles, they denied that they were a faction, and perhaps, in 1856, they were justified in so doing, for it seemed that the trend of politics was towards two well-defined parties. They could not then foresee the coming extinction of the conservatives as a political force. But their leading men had already grasped the pragmatic concepts which were to form the basis of faction politics; the purpose of politics was to gain and keep power, for without it nothing could be done, and to this end the means, within the limits of conscience, were subordinate.

The *Empire* expressed the astonishment which liberals felt at Donaldson's resignation for so 'frivolous' a reason as having won a few divisions by small margins.[18] A group of uncommitted ('cross-bench') members led by W. H. Sutter, Cowper's old ally of anti-transportation days, thought similarly and decided to move a motion of confidence in the Donaldson ministry in the hope of persuading them to resume office. They showed how little they understood the liberal attitude to power by approaching Cowper for support. With Denison's commission to form a government already in his pocket, Cowper refused and, forewarned, forced immediate adjournment upon the Assembly by withdrawing his followers *en masse* from the House. The *Sydney Morning Herald,* mouthpiece of the evolving core of urban conservatives, conceded Cowper's skill as a tactician but shuddered at his naked ambition and ruthless tactics. The mercantile supporters of this viewpoint turned out to oppose the ministerial re-elections of Cowper and his treasurer Robert Campbell. Cowper's supporters, they claimed, were no longer 'citizens of influence', [19] but they could not field a candidate who was reckoned to have a chance against him, and the new ministers went to the poll opposed only by a certain Dr Duigan, who stood for Sydney seats for years without ever rising above the bottom of the poll, and this occasion was no exception. Nevertheless, Cowper realized that liberal tactics could lose them electoral support and he justified his moves by developing a new argument: that the constitution required Deas Thomson and the old officials to remain in power until defeated on a vote of no confidence. Thus, he argued, Donaldson's ministry had been appointed illegally and the liberals were justified in using extreme means to oust them.

Cowper's negotiations to fill his ministry revealed an incipient division in the liberal ranks. On 23 August the *Empire* understood that 'the more decided section of the liberals have determined not to take office'. This attitude probably resulted from the knowledge that they would not be asked. The composition of a future ministry under Cowper's leadership had been discussed at opposition meetings before Donaldson's fall and it seems that the 'more decided' members had agreed that the practical need for wide electoral support outweighed ideological purity in the selection of ministers. The most urgent need was to find an attorney-general and solicitor-general, posts held conventionally by members of that solid bastion of conservatism, the Bar of New South Wales. One Martin's advice Cowper decided to offer the senior law post to Plunkett. The cool effrontery of such an offer must have staggered their allies, but Martin and Cowper judged that Plunkett might take the post, if only to save the bar from the ignominy of seeing Martin, about to be admitted as the most junior member, given the dignity and precedence of the attorney-general's office in default of any other candidate. They prepared their moves with care. Cowper first secured T. A. Murray for the lands and works portfolio. Murray, who had once battled the squatters with Cowper and Lowe over Crown lands policy and transportation, had gone on to support Wentworth's constitution bill and to side with Plunkett against the Bunch, but when he came to the Assembly, he favoured Cowper as first premier and joined liberal attacks on the government. A veteran in politics and widely popular in the Argyle and Monaro districts where he held his lands, he seemed well suited to the ministry. Moreover, Plunkett respected him. Murray and Cowper tried hard to secure Plunkett. They tried harder still when Richard Jones, editor and publisher until 1855 of the colony's leading country newspaper, the *Maitland Mercury,* and a man esteemed by conservatives and liberals alike for his courtesy, erudition and dignified behaviour in the House, agreed to take the Treasury if Plunkett filled a law post. In the end Plunkett refused to join the ministry, Jones withdrew in consequence and Cowper gave the Treasury to Campbell. Left with the problem of the attorney-generalship, Cowper hawked the office around to at least four other members of the bar. When all refused, his dignity had suffered enough. Was it proper for him to give the post to Martin? he asked Chief Justice Alfred Stephen, and when Stephen, a personal friend, saw no objection, [20] Martin filled the breach, reluctantly, since he foresaw the howls of indignation which his learned colleagues would raise. A.J.P. Lutwyche, one of those who had refused the senior law post, eventually took the solicitor-generalship, and the ministry was complete.

The abortive move of the cross-bench members to prop up Donaldson's expiring ministry had warned Cowper that he would find it hard to command a majority in the Assembly, and his failure to secure Plunkett and Jones, together with Martin's appointment, further worsened his position. Still, he hoped to attract cross-bench support with a vigorous programme of legislation, in contrast to the Donaldson ministry's slow progress. The conservatives moved to forestall him. On 10 September, twenty-two of them held a meeting (the 'Kellet House conspiracy') at Donaldson's home to perfect their tactics against Cowper's government. Cowper rallied his supporters just before the Assembly resumed but, two days later, Riverina squatters John Hay moved a direct motion of censure against the new ministry and, after a marathon five-day debate, won the resultant division by 26 votes to 23. The liberals showed they were of sterner mettle than Donaldson. They met, decided to defy Hay's motion and advised Cowper to seek a dissolution of the Assembly rather than resign. Cowper did so, telling Denison that no strong government was possible, given the existing composition of the Assembly. The governor disagreed and the ministry reluctantly abandoned office. Approached by the new conservative leader, H. W. Parker, to join an all-party government, Cowper told him bluntly that the idea was impossible and retired with his fellow-liberals to the opposition benches.

Cowper had tried too soon for power and paid the penalty. Yet his leadership of the liberals was strengthened rather than weakened by the rapid fall of his ministry. Liberals everywhere were indignant that 'their' government, far from being tried and found wanting, had not been tried at all. In Sydney they turned out in force to demonstrate their support for Cowper and when a conservative group hired the Victoria Theatre for a meeting aimed at censuring him for taking office, not one of the speakers could be heard above the roars of abuse, the stamping of feet and the sounds of strife from the pit. The voters of the suburbs gave the clearest indication of the swing to the liberals when Donaldson, Parker's treasurer, stood for ministeral re-election for the Sydney Hamlets. Four months earlier he had easily defeated his liberal opponent, John Campbell, in similar circumstances. This time Campbell, brother of Cowper's old friend, took the seat comfortably. Liberal influence was much weaker in the rural and semi-rural areas surrounding the city. Though Parkes organized the campaign of James Byrnes against Parker at Parramatta, even his skilled management could not defeat the premier, and Donaldson gained a South Cumberland seat three weeks later. Sydney, once again, proved its key position in liberal politics.

The composition of Parker's ministry showed that the urban middle-class opponents of the Bunch had now completed their alliance with the representatives of the squatters and the old officials. Parker, Donaldson, Manning and Darvall were survivors of the Donaldson ministry. The new men were squatter John Hay and the doyen of colonial officials Edward Deas Thomson. With his confidence bolstered by John Campbell's victory, Cowper tried to tip out the ministry on a censure motion when the Assembly reconvened. The motion was lost, by 27 votes to 11, with only the hard core of liberals voting for it. The next day Martin seized a trifling excuse to censure Parker again, but only Cowper and John Campbell supported him. Eight liberals left the House before the division and five voted with the government. These devastating defeats at last showed Cowper and Martin that they had little chance of returning to power until the Parker government had been tried and found wanting by liberals and cross-bench members alike. In the meantime, Cowper had somehow to hold the liberals together in the face of strong internal dissensions. Luckily Parkes, Robertson and Martin saw as clearly as he did the need for unity. With patience and skill they set about the recovery of power.

With the year well advanced and little accomplished, Parker confined the government programme for the session to the urgent matter of passing the estimates and to other routine business. No doubt he was mindful, too, that this approach would minimize the liberals' chance to use against him the tactics of harassment and attrition which had brought down Donaldson. But the generalship of Cowper, Martin, Robertson, Jones and W. M. Arnold again permitted the opposition to drive the ministers to frustration and fury. The walked out of the House to deprive it of a quorum; they filibustered far into the night, for there was no time limit on members' speeches; they disputed every minor point; and the session dragged on and on. In February 1857 Denison wrote in exasperation to Donaldson, 'For Heaven's sake get your Loan Bills and all other bills over as fast as you can or we shall have the Legislature constitute itself a permanent Body.'[21] Not until 18 March could the suffering ministers end the sitting, and the late date ensured that they would enjoy only a brief respite before having to call the Houise together again.

In concrete terms, the opposition's tactics had given them little. Their one significant gain resulted, strangely, from their continued lack of unity. Without consulting Cowper or the other leading liberals, Jones and William Forster brought up an electoral bill which aimed to increase urban representation. Electoral reform and particularly an increase in seats allocated to Sydney, which had only four out of fifty-four in the Assembly, had long been a liberal policy, but Cowper, annoyed at this unilateral move and unwilling to allow such a popular issue to pass out of his own hands, went home to Wivenhoe before the bill came on for debate. Of the city members, only Robert Campbell was present and the government rejected the measure with ease. Liberal supporters outside the House protested the loss of the bill at a well-attended meeting chaired by Hawksley. John Robertson alone appeared to represent the liberal parliamentarians, but they soon realized that public demand for electoral reform was strong enough to be forged into a useful weapon against the conservatives. They turned up in force at the next meeting, held to organize an Electoral Reform League, and gained control of the league's executive. Robert Campbell took the presidency, Cowper, absent through illness, was appointed a vice-president together with Lutwyche, Forster and Robertson, while other parliamentary liberals joined the committee

Sir Charles Cowper, K.C.M.G.
(By courtesy of Sir Norman Cowper)

Lady Cowper
(By courtesy of the Council of
the State Library of N.S.W.)

29th August 1858

Wivenhoe, pencil sketch by Conrad Martens, 1858
(By courtesy of the Council of
the State Library of N.S.W.)

of the league. They knew that Parker planned to bring on, at the next session in August, an electoral bill which could be expected to favour pastoral electorates. Cowper, anxious to return the electoral issue to the parliamentary arena, was overruled by Parkes and Jones who persuaded him that the Electoral Reform League should first whip up public support. Awaiting the right moment, they held the league in reserve. Cowper and the liberal press turned to sapping the position of Deas Thomson, the government's representative in the Legislative Council, with allegations that he was the real master of the ministry and that he hoped to form a ruling oligarchy of friends and relatives: as Cowper put it, 'Not only a Social government but a Family Compact'. [22]

Cowper knew that some liberals believed, with the *Maitland Mercury*, that his part in the events of the session amounted to little more than 'petty and paltry obstructionism' which served only to lower his reputation as a leader, [23] but he felt that liberal unity was yet too delicate a structure to withstand the launching of bold initiatives. '[Some] think I should have assumed more as the leader of the opposition', he told Parkes. 'But, however I might have voted if my Colleagues had been at my side, and there had been more agreement among us I still think I acted prudently in not adding to the length of the Debates or being instrumental in making apparent what perhaps to me seemed correct... What we want now is *Political intercourse during the recess*'. [24] Patiently, tactfully, Cowper set about consolidating the liberal members behind him during the five months of the parliamentary recess. He wrote again and again to every liberal member he could reach, commenting sympathetically on their personal affairs, canvassing their support for liberal candidates at by-elections, discreetly airing his own views on current issues, urging them to attend liberal meetings, prophesying great benefits from liberal co-operation and inviting them to meet him socially at the Sydney Club. [25] This organization, founded late in 1856, claimed to have 'no party or clique connections', [26] but with Daniel Cooper as its first president and Robert Campbell as a vice-president, it was no matter for surprise that it became for a time the unofficial headquarters of the liberal parliamentary group. 'Our Sydney Club is proving a great convenience', confided Cowper to Parkes. 'There I generally fall in with Piddington, Weekes, Flood...I think there are now more than twenty M.P.'s Members of it,' [27] and there Cowper—no drinker but no prude either—entertained his often hard-drinking colleagues in the interests of liberal unity.

Above all others, he seems to have sought the friendship and co-operation of Parkes. Beset by the growing financial problems of the

Empire, Parkes had abruptly resigned from the Assembly in December
1856. Cowper's letter of regret to him carried a hint that the liberal
leader was not altogether sorry to find that his very able colleague
was to confine himself to publishing his newspaper, [28] though he knew
Parkes too well to imagine that his parting from politics would be
permanent. Ever conscious of the value of the *Empire* to the liberal
cause, Cowper took a leading part in getting up a testimonial to Parkes
(which Parkes, probably feeling that such a gesture smacked too much
of political extinction, refused to accept), claiming his personal friendship
and commending his 'vitally important work' with the *Empire*. [29]
Daniel Cooper was the principal creditor of the *Empire* but, declining
to mix business with unprofitable sentiment, he threatened to sell the
printing plant to recover the debt owed to him. Cowper and Robertson
tried unsuccessfully to change his mind and both played prominent
parts in the subsequent public movement which raised enough financial
guarantees to allow the newspaper to carry on. Always ready to
suggest political matters for Parkes to publish, Cowper now increased
his pressure for *Empire* support. Parkes responded, rather selectively,
in assertion of his continued independence, and the *Empire* continued
to be the most valuable bridge between the liberal parliamentarians and
their constituents. Publicity given by the liberal newspaper helped
to turn out 2500 citizens of Sydney to cheer Cowper as he attacked
the Parker government and vindicated his own. Weekes and Robertson
followed his example in their electorates and Cowper remarked with
satisfaction that these meetings had 'evidently done *good*. They have
cleared up several points in the public mind which required explaining.' [30]

Nevertheless, Cowper realized that he and the city liberals were
hardly known beyond the boundaries of the County of Cumberland.
He welcomed the chance to widen his sphere of influence when his
son, Charles (then manager of Chatsbury) and Daniel Deniehy organized
a dinner at Goulburn for T. A. Murray and invited him to be the
principal speaker. Since an occasional mail coach was the only available
public transport and the roads, deluged by late autumn rains, in such
a state that wheeled vehicles could hardly traverse them, Cowper
saddled up his own horse and rode out from Wivenhoe, only to turn
back on the road. 'I rode 40 miles on horseback towards Goulburn',
he explained to Parkes, 'but the...Rain—Thunder, Lightning and
Hail—and the positive refusal of the only Mail to take my clothes or
myself—compelled me to return...Two poles were broken by the Mail
as it came down a day after time...I was sadly disappointed...The
credit will now attach exclusively to Mr. Murray and his supporters.' [31]

This episode, unimportant in itself, nevertheless illustrates one of the greatest problems of political organization in the early years of Australian independence, before a network of railways covered the land. Great distance and bad roads simply did not permit politicians to make themselves known in every corner of the country in the way that later generations took for granted. The post was a very poor substitute indeed for personal appearance. Although Cowper was unable to leave the vicinity of Sydney again before the parliamentary session opened in August, he was greatly encouraged by clear signs of a swing to the liberals in country seats. In February 1857, when Plunkett resigned his Argyle seat to preside over the Legislative Council, Deniehy took it unopposed. Three months later Manning left his South Cumberland seat through ill-health and James Byrnes, backed by the Sydney committee of the Bunch, won it with a big margin over his conservative opponent J. R. Brenan. In the previous December, Sydney elections had demonstrated clearly that the city seats were irretrievably lost to the conservatives. A Cowper protegé, young barrister W. B. Dalley, easily beat *Sydney Morning Herald* proprietor John Fairfax for the place left vacant by Parkes, in the face of formidable opposition from city merchants, members of the government, squatters and J. H. Plunkett. A few days before the opening of parliament, Cowper wrote hopefully, 'Upon the whole the Liberal side will meet in the Assembly considerably strengthened, not only numerically, but by improved feeling and a more united desire for co-operation.'[32] He knew that policy differences still existed but, he told Parkes, he had swung Jones, Piddington and Flood behind his proposal that the liberals should probe cautiously for government weaknesses and turn them out at the first clear opportunity.[33] Cowper hoped to gain 'a thorough understanding' with the other liberal members at a series of meeting where, he said, 'Robertson's earnestness, Martin's impulsiveness—Jones [sic] coldness and my diplomacy—may all be of use—and each may act as a check on the others.'[34]

He never did reach a thorough understanding with some of his colleagues. They were willing enough to guard against leaving openings for government and press to accuse them of greed for power at all costs, as had happened in 1856. Yet some were still ready to assert their independence at inconvenient times. On 14 August, when Cowper brought up a resolution condemning some ministerial appointments to public office, Jones and Weekes declared themselves sick of party strife and wanted only to get on with the business of the legislature, while Forster went off at a tangent by announcing that he would have voted for a general no-confidence motion but would not vote for such a selective one. All three abstained from the division, which the government won. The *Empire* reflected the exasperation of the liberal leaders in an outburst against 'independent' members. [35]

The conservatives were less united still than their liberal opponents. Their reliance on what Donaldson called 'the free and unbought support of the independent representatives' [36] was their greatest weakness. Parker failed to consult the squatting representatives in the Assembly before he announced his lands policy, which the squatters considered to carry the threat of higher Crown land rents and less security of tenure. They withheld their support from two of the government's minor bills, allowing the liberals to reject them, and Parker adjourned the House for a week while he considered resigning. The very thought of a liberal government whose followers had been thirsting for ten years to break their hold on Crown lands was enough to turn back the squatters to the lesser evil. They hastily mended their fences with Parker and he told the reconvened Assembly that he would continue to govern. No one could be sure that he had the numbers to continue; head-counting was a thankless task for party men when a few unpredictable independents could upset the most careful planning. Cowper, angry at Parker's resumption of power, wanted to turn him out immediately. But he would not risk failure in a direct confrontation; instead of moving no confidence in the ministry, he challenged Parker to ask the House for a vote of confidence in his government, and moved a twenty-four hour adjournment to allow the premier time to do so. Darvall turned the adjournment motion into a direct test of government support and they won the division by one vote. Frustrated again, Cowper finally triumphed the next day when Parker brought on his electoral bill. The liberals had long been preparing for this measure. Through the Electoral Reform League they whipped up public interest and put pressure on members of the Assembly in the last weeks before parliament reconvened. Cowper and Robert Campbell followed up by presenting to parliament a series of league-inspired petitions for equitable electoral distribution. These moves may have tipped the balance to the liberals. Darvall tried to adjourn the debate on the bill, Cowper beat him on the casting vote of the Speaker, moved the bill's rejection and won by three votes. Defeated in their main policy measure, the government resigned and Cowper returned to power at the head of his former ministry, with one exception. Robert Campbell surrendered the Treasury to Jones, amid general approval. Cowper once more led the country, and in one form or another he continued to lead it for most of the next six years.

5

'Slippery Charlie'

In days before their friendship grew, J. D. Lang dubbed Cowper 'Slippery Charlie'. The term was taken up by Cowper's friends with a tinge of admiration, by his enemies as censure, and it passed into legend through the writings of Parkes.[1] As W. J. V. Windeyer has said, the nickname 'was an allusion to his adroitness and astuteness as a politician, not a reflection on his personal character'.[2] Not even Cowper's most rabid opponents suggested that his years of power brought him any financial gain beyond his salary as colonial secretary or that his personal life was other than irreproachably moral. Yet he had to endure constant charges of political corruption and lack of principle. Conservatives were slow to recognize that minority governments must use tactical flexibility and widespread patronage in order to maintain power and pass legislation. Cowper, the first of the faction leaders and the head of government for most of the six years from 1857 to 1863, was the main target for their critical broadsides and interminable sniping. For several years the *Sydney Morning Herald* led the attack. In 1858 it fumed, 'Government by artifice; by tact; by playing off one against the other; by selling twice over; these are the schemes Mr. Cowper would naturally have recourse to,'[3] and sixteen months later the editor thundered, 'No one sees more rapidly how a supporter may be fixed or by what means an opponent may be caught. Men who have a profound distrust of human integrity, who believe all have their price, have often an immense advantage over blundering patriots who think there is something in professions and promises'.[4]

Light dawned, reluctantly, on the 'Old Lady' of colonial newspapers[5] when the Forster ministry of 1859—60 trusted itself to the 'free and un-bought' support of members and crashed after four months of frustration. Opposition assaults upon Cowper's corruption were 'much like Satan correcting sin', remarked the *Sydney Morning Herald* in September 1861, glumly conceding that it was useless to complain or to try reformation: 'Mr. Forster tried it, and where is he!'[6] Less realism was shown by such 'Old Guard' conservatives as Therry, Nicholson and the Macarthurs. They continued to condemn Cowper's methods, but they also cherished a lingering hope that he was driven by his democratic allies and would some day reject them to lead a conservative revival.

Alas for their hopes! Cowper himself brought the garrison of their stronghold, the Legislative Council, to heel, and by the time the Martin ministry replaced him in 1863, the conservative cause was past revival. Better for Cowper had it survived, for he faced instead a more formidable opposition from men who shortly before had been his friends and allies. When he came to power in 1857 he could claim some degree of support from every liberal in the Assembly, and the concept of him as the legitimate channel for liberal ideals, 'the great chief of the liberal party', as David Buchanan put it in 1863, [7] lingered with increasing tenuity as a prop to his leadership throughout his subsequent career. But the conservative decline removed the main basis for liberal unity, and the group gradually fragmented under the pressure of differences of political opinion, of local interests, jealousies and unsatisfied ambitions. A new opposition began to develop, men who showed when their turn came that they had learnt well the methods of faction government. Since no clear ideological differences separated these anti-Cowper liberals from their former brethren, the cry of government corruption and inefficiency became their most useful weapon. Even such usually consistent supporters of Cowper as the *Empire* (reconstituted in 1859 under Hanson and Bennett) resorted to accusations of this kind whenever they disliked some aspect of government policy. Cowper's successful bid to draw the influential Edward Flood into his 1859 ministry, condemned by the *Sydney Morning Herald* as corruption, was hailed by the *Empire* as 'a triumph worthy of the genius of Mr. Cowper'. [8] But when Hanson and Bennett disagreed with Cowper in 1863 over the financial policy which caused his fall from power, the *Empire* drew the moral that 'it should teach that no man, however able, however subtle, however praiseworthy for former services, can safely make tools of the people who have elevated him to power, and use that power for the suppression of the authority from which he derived it'. [9] There was point to J. D. Lang's wry comment that he and Cowper were 'the best-abused men in New south Wales'. [10]

However, there were few mèn who were prepared to deny Cowper's astuteness and administrative ability, or who would rather have him against, than for, them. Donaldson and Parker in 1856, Jones in 1859, Robertson in 1860 and one of Martin's ministers in 1863, all approached Cowper to join them in government. Even Forster, still bitter at the defeat of his ministry by the Cowper—Robertson forces in 1860, admitted privately that he 'by no means wish[ed] to see Cowper excluded from

Govt.'. [11] Three years later, as he took office in the Martin ministry, Forster told his electors that the man Martin was displacing had shown high ability and given great service to the country. [12] His accolade was one of many given, however grudgingly, by independent observers and opponents of Cowper.

Until 1859 there were some, amongst conservatives and liberals alike, who believed Cowper could not long hold his leading role in liberal politics. He must fall, thought conservatives, because he lacked real principles and cared only for power. Thus the defeat of his 1856 ministry led the *Sydney Morning Herald* to comment, 'That he might be Caesar, Mr. Cowper abandoned the policy of a statesman, and contented himself with being the secretary of a political club. They accepted him not because he was the man of their trust—not that they had confidence in his inward sympathy with them, but because he was the smartest and most nimble tactician. If he be still permitted to move at the head of their band it is as a courier—not as a chief.' [13] Eighteen months after Cowper had regained the premiership, the *Sydney Morning Herald* capped its repeated predictions of his fall by claiming that Parkes, 'a genuine democrat', would succeed him. [14] But the conservative collapse, the failure of the only alternative ministry (Forster's) which the Assembly could muster and Cowper's return to the premiership after a spell in the Legislative Council forced the Old Lady to concede that 'Mr. Cowper is certainly the most able man of his party and its natural leader. [15] Cowper's adroit survival of a torrid session in 1861 and the great parliamentary strength of his ministry in 1862 and early 1863 led the *Sydney Morning Herald* to comment ironically that 'Mr. Cowper has made himself indispensable—he has cleared off by his electoral laws, or his administration, all effective opposition and he may be considered rather as the founder of a dynasty than a minister'. [16] The budding dynasty fell six weeks later.

For similar reasons to those of the *Sydney Morning Herald*, a section of liberal opinion saw Cowper as merely a stopgap leader in the early days of independence. Gavan Duffy, observing from Melbourne, thought the first Cowper ministry to be 'only a jury-mast to float the vessel of the state into deep waters' [17] and advised Parkes to join Plunkett and be ready to form a succeeding government. This unlikely duo never eventuated, though rumours of its coming bid for power arose when the Cowper ministry was forced to a dissolution after the disastrous failure of their 1857 land bill, but the odium which Cowper had incurred over this bill did lead some liberals to believe, with the *Empire,* that he and Martin should make way for new men. [18] Three years later, most of the New South Wales liberal press was ready to believe, with a querulous correspondent of the *Sydney Morning Herald,* that 'the eternal Charles Cowper' was the only man who could 'keep the State Coach moving. [19] His parliamentary opponents seethed with frustration. 'Honesty is at a discount', complained Piddington in 1862 as the ministry ruled supreme. 'This last Legislative Assembly... is certainly by far the worst House we have ever had — the most corrupt — the most lazy and useless'. [20] A verse attributed to Parkes expressed their feelings succinctly:

> What more of Parliament is ever wanted? —
> Cowper's in office, and supplies are granted! [21]

As time passed, opposition cries of government corruption found a diminishing echo in the press. Newspapers remained ready to attack individual cases of blatant manipulation or patronage, but increasingly they justified Cowper's methods by his success in providing stable government and passing legislation that the people wanted. They had accepted the necessary conditions for faction government, and Cowper's ascendancy over a perennially disunited opposition led them to believe that there was no alternative to him. They could not then foresee that Martin and Parkes were to prove them wrong.

Perhaps the greatest handicap to Cowper's political standing was his reputation for being willing to sacrifice his own beliefs for political advantage. Cowper's use of compromise clashed with existing political attitudes: on the one hand the belief that sound government could only be carried on by parties based on clear-cut principles, and on the other, paradoxically, the old concept of a member's right to an independence based on his personal principles, which, as Loveday and Martin have shown, survived and flourished in the era of faction government. [22] Because Cowper was seen to sacrifice some principles for political advantage, it was widely believed that he would sacrifice them all. David Buchanan's eulogy of Cowper, written in 1863, unintentionally added to this impression. 'There is no character so much misunderstood by the general public as that of...Mr. Cowper. Many people...suppose. him to have no opinions of his own, and to be ready to act in any way a majority directs him. The people who think thus were never more deceived in their lives', claimed Buchanan, [23] but further on he said, 'There is no man more free of indecision than Mr. Cowper. Even suppose ,at first, that he does not acquiesce in certain principles, if he sees that vast body of the people resolutely bent on their adoption...he, without hesitation, 'bouts ship and runs before it.' [24] Few friends were bold enough to say, with William Spiers, J. D. Lang and Dr William Bland, that Cowper's political flexibility was the quality for which they prized him most. It is certain that both friends and enemies helped to perpetuate his reputation as 'Slippery Charlie'. So far as this reputation implied a lack of moral principle, it was less than just. His attitudes to issues involving religion were remarkably consistent, but they have been overshadowed ever since by remembrance of the subtle, supple strategy he used in handling three major issues faced by his governments: electoral reconstruction, reorganization of the Legislative Council and the settlement of the lands question. His tactical skill in the day-to-day management of parliament merely added to his slippery image.

In May 1857 Cowper told his cheering constituents that the basis of liberalism was a desire to reform the electoral and Crown lands laws, to have an elected upper house and a unified education system. A fifth question dear to Cowper was that of state aid to religion. In broad terms the Cowper and Cowper—Robertson ministries of 1857 to 1863 stuck to a consistent strategy, bringing up one of these questions for legislation each year. The land problem dominated the sessions of 1857, 1860 and 1861 and electoral reconstruction that of 1858. In the eyes of Cowper's contemporaries, the resultant legislation provided the great triumphs of his ministries. Reform of the Council never became more than an important secondary issue, education problems were eventually left for Parkes to solve in later years, and while the abolition of state aid to religion in 1862 raised great passions, it lacked the broad impact imposed by the Lands and Electoral Acts on the whole of New South Wales society.

When the Cowper ministry took office on 7 September 1857, it seemed certain that they would press on immediately with electoral reform. This issue had won them power; it was best fitted to rally liberal support to the new, still shaky, government, since press and public saw a reformed Assembly, based on a wider suffrage and more equal electoral districts, as a necessary base for other liberal reforms. Parkes and Forster demanded that it be the first consideration, but Cowper announced that he would postpone the question and begin with a lands bill. A new Electoral Act, he explained, was not possible until the royal assent was received to the act repealing the constitutional provision for change by two-thirds majorities. This was mere sophistry. He knew, unofficially, that the despatch giving assent was already on its way to New South Wales. In truth, the ministers could not agree on suffrage and ballot clauses for an electoral bill, and the lands question was the only great issue on which they could reach a reasonable compromise. Murray and Jones thought it the more important; the latter even hinted that pre-eminence for the lands bill was the price of his joining the ministry, [25] and he was the prime mover in the construction of the measure.

Cowper brought the lands bill to the Assembly on 22 October. It was by no means a radical measure of reform. Squatters in the unsettled

districts were to have their existing leases and rental levels protected
and their pre-emptive right to buy land preserved. A stock levy was to
be imposed, of £7 10s for each 1000 sheep or 160 cattle which the
run could carry, new leases were to be limited to a maximum of five
years, and auctioned land was to be classified as town, suburban,
agricultural or country lots, to be sold at minimum prices of £8, £2, £1
and 5s respectively. These provisions reflected an uneasy compromise
between varied ministerial views and recognition of the need for greater
public revenues and parliamentary support. Murray alone favoured
selection of blocks before survey (a provision omitted from the bill)
but, with Cowper and Jones, he placed first in importance the lowering
of country lands prices. Martin's main concern and a point of agreement
between all ministers was the urgent need for revenue. In later years
Cowper claimed that the Parker government had left the Treasury
so bare that only Daniel Cooper's private offer of a £50 000 loan had
enabled the liberal ministry to withstand bank demands for permission
to sell government debentures at a huge discount. [26] The provisions for
stock assessment, a structured minimum price, and cash sale by auction
all reflected the need for money.

The *Sydney Morning Herald* was quick to point out that Cowper's
figure for stock assessment was lower than that proposed in Parker's
abortive bill. [27] This provision, plus the protection of leases and buying
rights, seemed calculated to draw support from the squatters. Short-
sightedly, many of them opposed the bill because the minimum price
for their runs was to be lowered. They did not want to buy at any price;
they wanted to stop others from buying. But in opposing Cowper's
bill they risked what finally did occur, a measure worse for their interests
from a later ministry.

Bedazzled by the lower country lands price, the liberal press at first
greeted the bill with cautious approval and the public was silent.
Ironically, the *Sydney Morning Herald* was first to point out that the
measure gave no help to poor men, who must still purchase agricultural
land for a minimum of £1 per acre. [28] Public opposition sprang to
life as the liberal press turned against the bill. As usual, Sydney was
the centre of ferment, with Parkes stirring the brew. He chaired three
public meetings where men who had been, or still were, Cowper's friends
and allies flayed the measure he was pushing through parliament.
Some, shrewd enough to see that the only alternative to Cowper was
the return of the conservatives, joined Parkes and .Lang in saying they
opposed only the bill and not the ministry, but their voices were lost
in the growing public storm. On the night of 7 December, three thousand
people packed Wynyard Square by torchlight to hear speaker after

speaker condemn the ministers and their bill as fit only to please the squatters and fill the Treasury. Out of that meeting came the New South Wales Land League to lay down demands that Cowper could not and would not meet: selection before survey of blocks up to 320 acres, £1 per acre maximum price, freedom from buying competition and deferred payments.

While the citizens savaged them out of doors, the ministry battled for the bill and its own survival in the Assembly. The great danger lay not in the conservatives, but in an incipient split between those Robertson saw as 'tending to liberalism', led by Cowper, and those 'consistently liberal' members led by himself. [29] When Robertson demanded selection before survey and deferred payments, Cowper offered him a compromise. The ministry, he stressed, 'would not give way one iota' on what he termed the bill's main features: cash payment, sale by auction and the 5s minimum price. But to gain these he offered to sell all lands at the low price. [30] Robertson refused to compromise, pressed his amendment and was thoroughly beaten when the squatters combined with the ministry against free selection. Fearing that the ultra-liberals might now combine with the conservatives to reject the whole bill, the ministry threatened resignation or dissolution if the measure failed, and Cowper formed a secret compact with the five Moreton Bay members, all squatters. They were not to oppose the bill and in return were promised legislation they wanted for their local area. [31] These men walked out of the House when the 5s clause came to a vote and it passed. But their abstentions were not enough. On 9 December, two days after the formation of the Land League, Cowper made a desperate attempt to complete the bill in the lower house. With passion rare to him, he told the House that the ministry 'would not withdraw the measure, no matter what its fate might be', that he would never submit to 'the cry out of doors' or to time payment and the abolition of the auction clause [32] This extreme commitment to a rigid position, so uncharacteristic of him, shows the depth of his convictions on the lands question, but even the votes of the Moreton Bay members and a few other squatters wise enough to support the bill for fear of a worse one enabled no better than a tied vote against the forces of Robertson and the remaining conservatives. The Speaker gave his casting vote for the bill but clearly it could go no further. Cowper, bitterly feeling the loss to his personal standing at the hands of men who were his friends, told them the ministry would resign at once. Appalled, for all knew that the only alternative to Cowper was the conservatives, they called on him in a body that evening and urged him to seek a dissolution instead of resigning. Perhaps Cowper felt they deserved to suffer; he kept them pleading until 3.30 a.m. before he agreed. Yet he knew that he needed them as they did him and that he must now come to terms with their views.

Dissolution was only a respite. The danger of decimation at the polls led the liberal politicians to sink their differences and fight the elections on the promise of electoral reform. A new Bunch, Cowper, Campbell, Wilshire and Dalley, stood for Sydney and the Land League, divided over the question of opposing them, put up only one candidate, George Thornton. But some angry Land Leaguers turned out in force to show their displeasure. Amid catcalls and jeers, Bunch candidates tried hard to steer away from the lands question and into electoral reform. Listeners heard Cowper with impatience; repeatedly they drowned out the others at meetings said by the *Sydney Morning Herald* to rank with the most uproarious ever held in Sydney. Thornton topped the poll, brewer Robert Tooth, a last-minute entry after being defeated in the suburbs, followed, Campbell came next, Cowper crept into a humiliating fourth place, while Dalley and Wilshire lost their seats. The 'hideous Bunch' had been finally demolished, gloated the *Sydney Morning Herald* [33] and the *Empire* forecast 'a general breaking up and disintegration of parties', [34] In reality the political situation had hardly changed. The Land League had little influence outside the city. John Campbell and Daniel Cooper, both supporters of the lands bill were returned ahead of Robert Tooth for the Sydney Hamlets, Dalley easily won the Cumberland Boroughs seat, all the ministers were returned, and by the time the elections ended it was obvious that the political composition of the new Assembly would be very similar to that of the old.

For personal reasons both Jones and Murray had resigned from the ministry. Robert Campbell returned to the Treasury and, given Cowper's need for ultra-liberal support, Robertson was the obvious man for the lands and works portfolio. Yet Cowper first offered it to Edward Flood, perhaps in a last bid to avoid the abandonment of his long-cherished views on the lands question, perhaps because he could not forgive Robertson's defection. Only when Flood declined did Cowper turn to Robertson, to form, eventually, one of the warmest and most enduring of political friendships.

The agreed and logical policy of the ministry for the 1858 session was to regain some much-needed popularity by promoting an electoral bill. The problems were many. No less than equal electoral districts, manhood suffrage and a secret ballot would meet the demands of the city liberals. Yet moves to decrease the proportion of pastoral electorates might still be defeated in the Assembly, where the balance of power lay with twenty-three members of uncertain allegiance, [35] and the Legislative Council was filled with conservatives nominated by Donaldson and Parker. Before even the bill could be drafted Cowper had to reconcile the divergent opinions within the ministry. Martin abhorred both manhood suffrage and the ballot. Robertson and possibly Lutwyche took the extreme liberal view. Campbell shared it except that he opposed the ballot. Cowper, too, disliked the ballot and had hinted to the electors that he thought it impossible to devise equal electoral districts. [36] Predictably, the electoral bill, drafted by Cowper and Robertson, was a compromise. Martin gave way over manhood suffrage, but plural voting was permitted to those who held property in electoral districts away from their home constituency. The metropolitan area had its representation increased from 6 to 14 members, while the total membership of the Assembly rose to 68. Pastoral districts, allowed 18 seats out of a total of 104 in the defeated Parker ministry bill, were to have 12 seats under the Cowper measure, only a small proportional decrease. For the conservatives, the sting in Cowper's bill came mainly from his intention to base most country electorates on police districts, without separation of town and rural areas as Parker had planned. Urban voters tended to liberalism and in many districts they might be strong enough to swamp the more conservative vote of rural areas.

Cowper told the Assembly that the ratio of members to population would still favour such pastoral electorates as Lower Murray, with a member for 1718 inhabitants as against Sydney's figure of one member for each 5928 people, but Donaldson was quick to point out that there would be, on average, more voters in pastoral than in closely settled electorates, a clear illustration of the continuing dearth of women and children in remote areas. The ministers could not agree on the ballot. Cowper solved the problem by inserting a ballot clause and allowing a free vote on it.

Cowper's patience, tact and political skill were tried severely during the stormy passage of the bill. Diplomacy and persuasion superseded the forceful tactics which had failed him with the lands bill. He tabled the bill and waited five weeks for public and parliamentary reaction to it. The Land League supported it, Parkes threw the weight of the *Empire* behind it, the liberal country press followed suit and even the *Sydney Morning Herald* hoped that the bill could be modified into 'a useful measure'. [37] Delighted at public response, Cowper pressed on with the measure, only to come within a single vote of defeat on a postponement motion by James Macarthur. Cowper quickly divined the cause: members unhappy at alterations to their own electorates voted with Macarthur and the conservatives. Word spread that Cowper would bargain over boundary changes, and the second reading of the bill passed easily. But the committee stages proved to be little more than a prolonged squabble over electoral boundaries, with Cowper behind the scenes busily soothing frayed tempers and arranging compromises. At the same time, friend and foe alike afflicted him with torments on lesser issues. Forced to dismiss Plunkett in February from his post as chairman of the National Schools Board, Cowper suffered broadsides of conservative abuse for months. William Forster proclaimed to all who would listen that Cowper had wrecked the Jones-Forster electoral bill of 1857 so that he might hog the glory himself. Parkes, very inopportunely, brought up resolutions impinging on the composition of the Legislative Council, which achieved little but did produce the spectacle of Robertson taking sides against his chief in arguing that the Council should be abolished. Cowper's own friends defeated him to pass the second reading of a tax removal bill, and when he changed sides in the vote for the third reading, in the opposite direction, so did Martin and others who had helped to pass the bill earlier. It was thrown out. On the same day Denison, at Cowper's instigation, asked the Assembly to sanction the transfer of Royal Artillerymen from Sydney to India as an aid in suppressing the Indian Mutiny. Jones, Parkes, Piddington, Weekes and Forster opposed the ministers, and the request was rejected. Three days later, the ministers suffered another defeat in supporting Martin on a disputed point of law. When this reverse was followed by a second caning of the ministers over the Indian troops proposal, Parkes realized with alarm that liberal squabbling might drive the ministry to resign in sheer frustration. With all speed he moved a motion of confidence in them, telling the Assembly there was no chance of an alternative government which could, or would, carry the electoral bill. The liberals saw the point and carried the motion, but the harassment went on. Forster persisted in embarrassing the ministry by attacking Martin over his silence on the electoral bill and his frequent absences from the House. Even Robert Campbell added to the woes of his old friend by storming out of the House in a huff when Cowper refused to extend the franchise to the Imperial troops stationed in the colony. The pressures on Cowper must have become well-nigh intolerable when his father died on 6 July.

Two years later Cowper recalled the 1858 session as 'torture', [38] yet he never lost his political sense or slackened his efforts to pass the electoral bill. He 'bowed to the wishes of the country and House' in renouncing his personal opposition to the ballot, [39] and his patience in marshalling his followers and settling the conflicting demands of members was repaid

by the Assembly's approval of the measure, intact in its essential
features, on 26 August. The greatest test was yet to come, in the
Legislative Council. In February 1858 all but four of the members
were appointees of the Donaldson and Parker ministries. In that month
Denison refused Cowper's bid to add fifteen new members as an aid
to passing the electoral bill. But by August the ministry had succeeded
in adding thirteen new nominees, mainly by filling vacancies.
Ministerial supporters were still a minority in the upper house, and
Cowper's hopes of passing the bill depended upon the reluctance of
some conservatives to reject so popular a measure. The 'Lords' dawdled
over the matter, and Cowper's patience dwindled as he struggled to
keep the Assembly in session and his followers together. 'I shall be
very much obliged if you will kindly attend punctually and regularly',
he snapped at R. T. Jamison, [40] and no doubt others felt the edge
of his exasperation. Compensation came on 12 November; the manhood
suffrage clause, most contentious of all to the upper house conservatives,
finally passed the Council in the absence of several members who had
opposed it. Few had the grace to acknowledge with Deas Thomson
that they yielded to the popularity of the bill but, as he pointed out, their
absence was not likely to have been accidental. [41] Cowper still had to
survive a budget session made torrid by the angry conservatives. 'This
is really dreadful work', he wrote on 6 January 1859, 'All our friends
leaving us to the tender mercies of Donaldson and Co.'. [42] But the
ministry survived and the elections of June 1859, held under the new
franchise, ended the power of the conservatives in the lower house.
The Electoral Act lifted Cowper to unprecedented popularity. 'In
liberality [the bill] exceeded anything in the known world', proclaimed
a speaker at the final meeting of the Electoral Reform League. [43] Others,
more sceptical, still thought it as good as they were likely to get. The
whole of the liberal press acclaimed Cowper's leadership and Cowper
gloried in the favour of the East Sydney electors who placed him far
ahead of his prospective rivals, Martin and Parkes, in the 1859 elections.
Diplomacy had gained him what force could not, and conservative
bleats at his 'unprincipled' bargaining tactics [44] fell, for the time being,
on deaf ears.

Cowper presumed too much on the basis of his own and his ministry's
popularity. Instead of returning to the lands problem in 1859, he turned
to the even thornier question of the education system. Robertson
proclaimed far and wide his intention to bring up lands bills and he
did table two such measures in the Assembly on 28 September 1859.
They were virtually simplified versions of Cowper's 1857 bill, with
additional clauses permitting selection before survey and deferred

payments. They were never passed, because, it seems, they were meant only as an assurance that the matter had not been forgotten while Cowper pushed on with his education bill. On 19 October the bill brought down his government, whereupon Cowper resigned the seat so triumphantly won less than five months earlier and retired to the country.

In March 1860 the weak Forster ministry collapsed and Robertson, the new premier, lured back his old chief with the offer of the colonial secretaryship and a seat in the upper house. Forster had been forced by opposition pressure to bring on a lands bill which lapsed when he fell, and with Robertson at the helm, it was certain that the future of Crown lands would form the main business during the 1860 parliamentary session. The new lands bills, brought up to the Assembly on 27 September, still bore the imprint of Cowper's measure in the continued provision for sales by auction at government discretion and the five-year renewal of squatting leases in unsettled areas, but Robertson had removed a squatter's right to buy his land without competition. From the quiet of the Council, Cowper watched as Robertson directed the growing battle in the lower house. Though the squatting representatives were few, they had allies: urban conservatives like Mort, Saul Samuel, Darvall, Plunkett and Charles Kemp, and such dissident liberals as Henry Rotton, John Campbell and William Forster, men who disliked free selection. Robertson blundered badly. A convivial session at the new liberal meeting place, the Victoria Club, led him to strike a bargain with a group headed by Rotton, who promised support for the bill in return for Robertson's agreement to confine free selection to the settled districts and specially designated agricultural reserves. Robertson, alas, had failed to consult his parliamentary followers first. The common sense of the proposal escaped them entirely; men must be free to select their little blocks everywhere, no matter how useless the land for agriculture. No pandering to the squatters! They forced Robertson to speak and vote against his own compromise. In return, Rotton's group backed the conservatives and gave John Hay the numbers to reject the entire provision for free selection.

This fiasco ended Robertson's brief sway and returned the leadership to Cowper who, implied the *Sydney Morning Herald,* was thoroughly disgusted at Robertson's lack of tactical skill. [45] Twenty-eight liberal members of the Assembly met in Cowper's office and joined him in demanding a dissolution of the House. Denison granted it, Cowper topped the East Sydney poll at the resultant general election and Robertson amiably returned him the premiership. The voters, stirred to fury by the failure of Robertson's bill, filled the House with supporters of free selection, a triumph for Robertson rather than Cowper, for the new premier knew that hatred of the squatters could cause the new men to throw out his cherished 5s minimum price for grazing land. [46] On 7 March 1861 the new Assembly overruled government opinion and set the price of all country lands at £1 per acre. Cowper's last personal stake in the lands bills had gone, yet he pushed them on through parliament with power and vigour, until they passed into law. At first he tried, half-heartedly, to justify his complete change of front on the lands question by claiming that his 1857 bill had been meant as an interim measure only. Eventually he admitted openly that he had changed his stand to suit the people's wishes, [47] thus laying himself open to opposition charges of unprincipled opportunism. '£500 reward will be paid to any person who can discover either perpetual motion...or any of Mr. Cowper's views or principles upon any subject', proclaimed an anonymous advertisement in the *Sydney Morning Herald* during the 1859 election campaign, [48] and that newspaper, with Martin and Plunkett, attacked him savagely a year later for his opportunism over the lands bills. Cowper would have called it realism and certainly it was sound political strategy. The passing of the lands bills gave the ministry such popularity that in November 1861 Cowper wrote gleefully, 'Our enemies are puzzled what to conjecture next', [49] and the government effortlessly dominated the next year's parliamentary session.

For more than a century, John Robertson's name has been inseparably linked with the lands legislation of 1861, and rightly so, if its final form is the criterion. Yet the generalship which passed the bills belonged above all to Cowper. This can be seen most clearly in the superb skill with which he overcame the greatest obstacle which stood in the way of the lands bills, their passage of the upper house — a skill which enabled him not only to pass the bills but to use the issue as a basis for shattering the hostile conservative bloc within the Council and rebuilding it to suit himself with little regard for the opinions of others. Several modern historians have suggested that Governor Sir John Young and W. C. Wentworth were principally responsible for the composition of the 1861 Legislative Council. [50] It seems, rather, that Cowper manoeuvred Young, Wentworth, and the old Council into such a position that he gained exactly what he wanted — a Council 'respectable' enough to attract conservative support to him and to check the extreme liberals in the Assembly, yet amenable to the passing of popular legislation which his government needed to stay in power.

During the constitutional debates of 1853 Cowper had been a leading advocate for an elective upper house. He never did publicly change his attitude, and so long as the conservatives were in government or seemed likely to regain it, there is little doubt that he believed, with most liberals, that an elective body best suited their needs. Repeatedly he promised to try for it, but legislation for electoral reform, lands and education took precedence when he came to power. It seemed that 1861 would be the most favourable time to attempt reform of the Council, since the Imperial parliament, in passing the constitution bill, had enacted that the first appointed upper house should sit for five years only and was to be followed by a permanent body with members appointed for life, unless the colonial government could master enough support in both houses to change its form. While Martin remained in the ministry, Cowper dared not raise the question of reform, for he was unalterably opposed to it. That obstacle was removed when Martin resigned his office in November 1858, but ministerial opinions continued to differ. Publicly Cowper, with Robert Campbell, continued to reiterate the opinion that he had expressed in 1853, that the Council should be 'conservative [but] popular'[51]—that is, though members should have a property qualification, they should be elected by a manhood suffrage vote. Robertson and W. M. Arnold, who joined the ministry in March 1860, openly favoured the abolition of the upper house,[52] but Robertson knew that he had little public or parliamentary support for a single-chamber government and in 1859 he let it slip that he favoured a nominee upper house because it could be more easily controlled by the Assembly than could an elected body.[53] Though Cowper remained silent where his ebullient colleague could not, he had probably reached this conclusion even earlier. In August 1856 he had remarked that reform of the Council could afford to wait because that body was amenable to lower house control by means of 'swamping' it with new members.[54] During the next four years he had ample cause to see that an appointed Council (provided, of course, that he nominated its members) suited him best.

As early as August 1858 Forster and Cowper's confidant, Dalley, had suggested that the nominee Council of New South Wales was preferable to Victoria's elected one.[55] The New South Wales Council had shown itself amenable to public pressure in passing Cowper's electoral bill. The Victorian body, entrenched behind a property franchise for both electors and elected, rejected a popular lands bill in 1857, entirely reshaped another in 1860 and seemed to be impervious to public pressure. The awful example of Victoria was enough for the liberals of the parent colony. No such body could be permitted in New South Wales. By 1860 Cowper was fully convinced that a Council elected under manhood suffrage was equally undesirable. It could, all too readily follow the pattern of opposition in the Assembly where, from 1859, a section of the more 'democratic' liberals replaced the vanquished conservatives as the leading opponents of the Cowper-Robertson ministries. Their leaders were able men and formidable enemies. Martin's conservative attitudes to electoral and lands reform kept him in isolation for years, but other friends turned enemy proved to be more troublesome. Daniel Deniehy, a Cowper supporter until 1859, attacked the government bitterly in that year, over their appointments to the Crown Law Offices, a sad misuse of his considerable critical powers, for few disputed Robertson's tart remark that Deniehy had gone into opposition because the ministry had not made him solicitor-general. [56] Parkes, breaking away from his old allies under the drive of ambition, was far more dangerous, and scarcely less so was goldfields member Dr John Bowie Wilson, a man notable for his sharp tongue, grim tenacity and abiding dislike of the Cowper ministry. These men, backed mainly by members who came into the House after the electoral reconstruction of 1858, harried Cowper and Robertson constantly. In September 1859 Parkes managed, briefly, to drive the ministry from power when new members helped him to reject government duties on tea and sugar. Six weeks later these men brought down the ministry again when they helped to throw out Cowper's education bill, a measure to which he was deeply and personally committed. The Robertson ministry of 1860 continued to suffer from the attacks of those whom their leader had condemned as 'recreant so-called liberals [who] sought to drive the government from power after it had borne the heat and burden of the day'. [57] On 3 May 1860 the *Sydney Morning Herald,* hardly a government supporter, complained that policy was being taken out of the ministers' hands, pointing to successful motions by Wilson to abolish the duty on gold, by John Lucas to bring in a Chinese immigration bill which forestalled the ministry's intentions, and by Parkes for an inquiry into railway construction and management. In vain, Cowper and his ministers condemned Parkes as an obstructionist, and the liberal opposition as having no common interests except greed for office: [58] the 1861 session gave the government no respite. Wilson moved to have the church and school lands (the remnants of those Cowper had administered thirty years earlier for the Clergy and School Lands Corporation) defined as ordinary Crown lands, thus opening them to selectors should the lands bills pass. Believing that these areas should be preserved for the benefit of the churches, Cowper bitterly opposed the motion. He found himself defeated by liberals, as he had been over his education bill eighteen months earlier. In these two matters, which Cowper

meant to settle once the lands bills had been passed, his main hopes
rested on the upper house conservatives, particularly on the members
of his own sect who formed a majority of the existing Council and of
the materials available for the reconstruction, on conservatively
appointed lines, of any new Council. When Wilson's bill passed its
final reading in the Assembly, Cowper declared bitterly that 'he looked
upon it as a matter for gratification that there was not the slightest chance
of the bill being passed by the other House'. [59] He was right. The
Council threw it out without a second reading.

Gratifying as this aid was to Cowper, he still knew well that the
existing Council was dangerous to any liberal government. His own
sojourn in the upper house of 1860 gave him first-hand knowledge of
the utter intransigence of conservative members where their own powers
and privileges were concerned. Led by Deas Thomson, R. J. Want,
R. M. Isaacs and Robert Johnson, the upper house brought the
Robertson ministry almost to its knees over conservative demands that
the Council's right to alter money bills be recognized. They refused
to equate their position with that of the House of Lords, as Cowper
insisted they should, [60] and the government was saved from a financial
debacle only when Denison persuaded the influential Deas Thomson to
relax his opposition to their indemnity bill. [61] Moreover, by 1861 Cowper
was sure they would not pass the lands bills.

It was apparent, then, that Cowper must rid the Council of the
old-guard conservatives. By April 1861 he knew that the new governor,
Sir John Young, stood squarely in his way. The Duke of Newcastle,
secretary of state for the colonies, had advised him to reappoint the
existing councillors when their five-year term expired. In turn Young
had made it clear to Cowper that he would reject attempts to 'pack'
the House in the interests of party and that he expected to reappoint
at least 27 of the 35 members. [62] As Loveday points out, [63] Cowper
himself had tacitly acknowledged the governor's right to reject ministerial
recommendations to seats in the Council by accepting Denison's refusal
of his request for 15 new members in 1858. How was Cowper to
overcome that obstacle? Equally importantly, how was he to prevent the
lower house from attempting to replace the Council with an elected
body, a move demanded by almost every liberal in New South Wales?
He dared not even breathe the thought aloud; in fact he must convince
the Assembly and the country that he was bent on exactly the
opposite course to that intended.

At least Cowper had the support of his ministers. They saw how
the wind blew and fell in behind him. The public got its first hint of
Cowper's intentions early in 1860. The Forster ministry, just before

its fall, had tried to pass an elective upper house bill, and with public and parliamentary interest focused on this topic, the incoming ministers of Robertson's cabinet deemed it politic to stress that they intended to follow up the issue. Elias Weekes, Robertson's treasurer, told his electors that Cowper had entered the Council mainly to push through the coming bill for an elective Council, [64] but when he revealed that it was going to the upper house first, a few perceptive persons began to doubt the honesty of the government's intentions. Parkes hit on the truth in accusing the ministry of procrastinating so that they would be in a position to make the life nominations when they fell due in the following year. Weekes blandly replied that the bill, being democratically based, would fail in the existing Council whether it was sent there first or last, [65] and Cowper made little attempt to press it. Nevertheless, he could not afford to drop the matter. Public demands for a democratic body became louder as the expiry date of the old Council, 13 May 1861, drew nearer. So Cowper introduced the bill to the lower house in January 1861. All knew that there was not time to pass it through both houses before May, but Cowper disarmed suspicion by promising that appointments would be made only from those who agreed to give way to an elective body. The bill passed the lower house; the councillors sank it three weeks before their final sitting day, 11 May. At the same time they sent Robertson's lands bills back to the Assembly with additions designed to protect the squatters' tenure. Young condemned these actions as 'impolitic and ill-judged'. [66] From his point of view, and theirs, he was right. They had done exactly as Cowper had expected and their actions handed him the initiative. Forcefully he pushed through the Assembly the rejection of the Council's main amendments to the lands bills, telling the House, 'If these bills are rejected eventually, upon the head of those who reject them be the responsibility'. [67] The next morning, 10 May, the ministry call on Young, presented him with a list of twenty one men, and demanded that he 'swamp' the Council by appointing them members immediately, so that the lands bills could be passed on the next and last sitting day. Young summed up his position accurately when he wrote, 'The choice, if choice it can be called, placed before me on the morning of Friday, May 10, was either to accept the advice of the ministers or break with them backed as they are by six-sevenths of the Assembly and by the people in a cry which was all powerful on the hustings'. [68] To him, as N. I. Graham remarks, 'It was better temporarily to swamp a house due to expire in three days time than to tempt the ministry to pack a new and permanent council'. [69] But Young was far from having the full measure of Cowper's subtlety. He freely promised the governor that the new appointees, a strongly liberal group, would not be guaranteed seats in the new Council, for he had no intention of reconstructing that body on such a liberal basis. He used the swamping issue only to demonstrate to a public 'driven wild'[70] by the lands question that the ministry had made every possible effort to pass the bills and to place Young in a position where he could not prevent the government from 'packing' the new Council. In fact, he had no intention that the swamping members should sit at all. If the old Council had passed the lands bills, he would have failed to discredit it sufficiently to give him the leverage he wanted with Young in making permanent appointments and he would have lost the chance to vindicate his choice of a new body by having them pass the bills instead.

The first intimation of their intentions that the ministry gave to stiff-necked William Burton, president of the Council, was Robertson's brusque verbal notification of the imminent swamping on the morning of 11 May. Burton resigned immediately and left the House in high dudgeon, followed by most of Cowper's enemies. Graham has noted that Burton had a suitable excuse for thus bringing the Council to an abrupt end because Young was ignorant of the local convention that the governor informed the Council president in writing of all new nominations,[71] but Cowper and Robertson knew it well and they knew the irascible Burton too. Their failure to enlighten Young suggests that they hoped for precisely the result that did occur. Cowper's opponents in the Council had blackened themselves beyond redemption in the eyes of the great majority of voters and Assembly members who demanded the lands bills above all else, and Young had been neatly deprived of his chance to renominate most of the old Council as he had hoped to do only a month earlier.

Old W. C. Wentworth arrived home from a seven years' absence just in time to chair a committee set up by Young to recommend men for life membership of the new Council, but the surviving correspondence on the subject between these two and Cowper suggests what the outcome made clear, that Cowper had much the greatest voice.[72] He rejected at least four of Young's nominees, only thirteen of the retiring councillors were offered reappointment and a mere five of these were men who had walked out with Burton on 11 May. Six of the others had been consistent supporters of the Cowper ministry. Cowper made the most of his chance to select men who would safeguard the ministry, telling Young, 'Much of my difficulty as regards "names" would be removed, if when attacked, as attacked I shall be, most unmercifully when the list is made public, I can show *clearly* that

I had taken reasonable precautions for securing a majority for the government and that those appointed...would pass the Land Bills and were prepared to reconstruct the Council upon an Elective Basis', [73] Young had little choice but to acquiesce. The official correspondence with six of the new appointees survives. It shows that all consented to Cowper's conditions. [74] Wentworth, president of the new Council, agreed only on condition that in future that body should not be swamped 'until after the rejection by it of some vital question upon which the opinion of the country has been previously taken, after a dissolution of the Assembly for that express purpose. [75] Cowper, not wishing his hand-picked house to be vulnerable to attack by his liberal enemies, agreed with alacrity. Furthermore, he himself was almost certainly responsible for Wentworth's appointment to the presidency.

Cowper had realized that Wentworth, the father of the constitution and the most widely respected of colonial conservatives, was the very man for the presidency if he could be secured on the ministry's terms. His ship reached Sydney on 18 April 1861 — a 'very opportune' return, wrote Cowper smugly. [76] With cool effrontery he and Robertson set aside their long-standing enmity to the old lion, joined his welcoming committee, and Cowper was amongst the first aboard the ship to welcome him. 'It was rich to see CC [Cowper] in...[Wentworth's] train', wrote William Macarthur. [77] to his brother James. But three weeks later he was forced to admit that Cowper had paid very effective court to Wentworth. [78] On 22 June Cowper himself told James Macarthur, with sly humour, that Wentworth had arrived with 'strong prejudices which are gradually being dispelled'. [79] Two days later the great man became president of the Council.

Most of Cowper's new appointees were, as James Macarthur said, 'men of experience and respectability', [80] if not known conservatives. Young commented that the ministry had 'evinced moderation' in reconstructing the Council, [81] and colonial conservatives were pleased and surprised. Cowper basked in the rare commendation of the Sydney Morning Herald, and even the Duke of Newcastle, horrified as he was by 'so violent a measure' as trying to swamp the Council, approved the presence of many 'gentlemen of eminence and tried ability' in the new upper house. [82]

Liberal reactions to the new Council varied greatly. To Cowper's astonishment, William Forster praised the 'impartial spirit' of his nominations. [83] The promise to pass the lands and elective upper house bills which Cowper had exacted from members dampened public protest, as the wily premier had calculated. The liberal press was wary, but prepared to wait and see how the Council turned out before

condemning it, and the *Empire* showed it had clearly absorbed the
lesson of the swamping affair, that the threat of such ultimate coercion
could make a nominee house more acceptable than an elected one to
liberal governments. [84] As the ministers had expected, the real opposition
came from the parliamentary liberals. Parkes had been temporarily
neutralized by being sent to England as an immigration commissioner,
but just before the Assembly resumed in September twenty-three
liberal members met under Wilson's chairmanship and issued an
ultimatum to the government: they would refuse supply until the
ministry carried the lands bills, an elective upper house bill and a
measure to settle the problem of Chinese immigration. Furiously
assailed in the House by old enemies, Wilson, Holroyd, Lucas,
Piddington, Forster and W. B. Allen, the ministry also came under
fire from former supporters led by David Buchanan and goldfields
member James Hoskins. The government seemed to be tottering,
but Piddington proved to be correct when he told Parkes that '[though]
the nominations have given great offence to some of the Cowper
mob...there [sic] wrath will expend itself in words'. [85]

Wentworth fully justified Cowper's confidence in him by ramming
the lands bills through the Council by mid-October, cutting off the
threat of alteration to the free selection clauses by ruling that the
proposed change was a monetary clause and thus outside the Council's
jurisdiction. Three months later he brazenly told the councillors that
his first ruling was an error, [86] but the lands bills had already passed
into law. The Council also passed the ministry's measure to restrict
Chinese immigration, and Cowper promised an elective Council
bill. These moves were enough to split the opposition and keep the
ministry in power. Buchanan and others returned their allegiance to
Cowper, and the ministry was able to vote down most opposition
attacks with ease. The only issue which endangered them was one
which cut across normal political lines. On 12 November 1861 they were
saved, it must have seemed almost symbolically to Cowper, from
Wilson's censure motion over the control of church and school lands
funds by the single vote of squatter John Hay. From this time, Cowper
felt his government was safe. 'Holroyd, Lucas, Hoskins, Wilson...&
such like are everlastingly at work concocting...attacks—& always
getting well beaten:...I believe I stand stronger in the confidence
of the House than ever,' he told Parkes on 23 November, [87] and his
pleasure at the turn in political events—increased when the Council
rejected three measures which were carried against his personal
opposition in the lower house—a motion excluding Chinese from gold-
digging, Wilson's renewed bill to bring the church and school lands
under Assembly control and Hoskins's bill to lower the salaries of future

governors. 'Mr. Wentworth has behaved admirably as President of the
Council; and so indeed have all the Members: the construction of
that House has been a great success', he exulted at the end of 1861. [88] All
he needed now was to make that body permanent.

Public demand for an elective Council, stirred by Cowper's political
opponents, was still too great for Cowper to ignore. He needed time to
bring about a greater change in favour of the existing body. His elective
Council bill was not reintroduced until 14 November and it went to
the upper house first. Understandably, that body showed little enthusiasm at the prospect of helping to end its own existence. Members
toyed with the bill while the ministry looked the other way, and almost
a year went by before the measure came to the Assembly, heavily
amended to provide for a property franchise, proportional representation
of parties and the addition of ten nominee members. With shrewd
forethought Cowper expunged the latter two provisions but kept the
property franchise in the version he presented to the Assembly on
12 November 1862. Twelve months' delay had wrought the change he
sought in public sentiment and, as the *Sydney Morning Herald* was
quick to point out, the principal feature of the debate on the bill was
the number of members who had changed their opinions in favour of
the existing Council. [89] When the bill barely passed its second reading,
Cowper judged the time right to drop it. The government, he told
the Assembly, would proceed with the bill only if the £50 voting
franchise was preserved. This move split his opponents. Given the
strength of Cowper's following, they could not hope to remove this
provision against his wishes; they had either to accept it or vote against
the whole bill. Some took the latter course and supported Forster's
move to have the bill withdrawn. The whole ministry voted with them
and the bill was thrown out by 34 votes to 15. Only the *Empire* bothered
to protest and Cowper never again made any move to alter the constitution of the Legislative Council.

It was a remarkable victory. Cowper had succeeded in breaking down
the belief, held strongly by most of his own followers, his political
enemies in the lower house, and the voters of New South Wales, in
an elective Council, to the point where he was able to establish a
permanent Council of conservative nominees without seriously
endangering his ministry. At the same time he had manoeuvred the
governor into a position where he could not prevent the purging
from the upper house of the men most obstructive to the government.
He even earned Young's gratitude for the moderation of his appointments
which protected the governor's own standing with his British masters.

The effects of Cowper's victory were mixed. In his long-term aim,
that of establishing the ascendancy of the lower house over the upper,

he had considerable success. Legislative Councils of New South Wales continued to be fractious at times but, as Loveday remarks, they 'could no longer claim power to the point where it could threaten the existence of a ministry'. [90] In the short term, he succeeded in passing the lands bills and·giving his ministry a further two years' tenure of office. For a time, it seemed that his hopes of attracting conservative support to balance that lost to his 'ultra-liberal' opponents, would be realized.

In 1862, one of his Council nominees, E. W. Ward, reflected the rising hopes of the conservatives for him. 'Cowper firm in his Saddle insofar as I can see, possessing both great ability and with every desire to do right', wrote Ward to James Macarthur. 'His moral view has improved as also his policy, according as his political position has gained strength. The way to get most out of him is to keep him in power'. [91] Macarthur and other conservatives, even Cowper's old opponent Roger Therry (then in England) wrote of their hopes that Cowper would lead a conservative revival, but William Macarthur was nearer the mark when he told his brother, 'I have had hopes that he [Cowper] might have been induced to join the conservative party...but there is now no conservative party'. [92] After 1861, landholding conservatives such as John Hay and William Macleay were rare in the Assembly and the trend of politics did not continue as Cowper had anticipated. The Martin ministry which replaced his in 1863 contained elements from the extreme wing of the liberals, but on balance it was more conservative than his own.

In seeking his goals, Cowper had no hesitation in misleading the public, the opposition, his own followers and the governor, in fact everyone except his ministerial colleagues, as to his true intentions. The measure of success he achieved in doing so provides as outstanding example of both his shrewd understanding of his fellow-men and his 'slipperiness'.

6

Religion and Principle

Henry Parkes, who helped to perpetuate Cowper's reputation for slipperiness, also remarked perceptively that 'his church principles were accepted as of the true pattern'.[1] Cowper in power clung to his personal religious principles as consistently as he had during thirteen years in opposition. While he held the colonial secretary's office the public and parliament of New South Wales debated with heat and fury three aspects of the church and state relationship: direct state subsidies to religion, state finance for religious education and the fate of the church and school lands. In each case Cowper tried hard to settle the question in accordance with his own deeply held convictions. Believing that Christian religious training was the key to good citizenship, he saw the schools as the only adequate means of providing that training. In 1859 he told the Assembly that if they rejected religious instruction in schools, children must go without it 'since too many parents were either averse to give it, or incompetent to do so', and the clergy were too few to reach great numbers of the people.[2] He battled hard to keep for church schools an equal right to the government aid which they had shared with national schools since 1848, refusing to change course even in 1859 when the supporters of secularism included so many of his usual parliamentary supporters that their defection brought down his government. Again, as in the 1840s, his views sometimes brought him into conflict with his bishop and his church. Even in trying to preserve for Anglicans their share of the revenues of the church and school lands he did not have the unstinted backing of their leaders.

In 1860 these lands still totalled some 450 000 acres, and their worth was estimated at half a million pounds.[3] Since the demise of the Clergy and School Lands Corporation they had been managed by a government agent, who leased them out to graziers. The lease revenue was paid to the four principal Christian sects, Anglicans, Catholics, Wesleyans and Presbyterians, in proportion to their numbers, for the support of religion and education. From 1850 the money was paid in the fixed proportions of five-sevenths (of the share given each sect) for the support of religion and two-sevenths for education. Most Anglican and Catholic churchmen believed, with Cowper, that British governments considered the lands a perpetual trust for the benefit of religion. This view had been supported by three colonial judges of the Supreme Court, Forbes, Dowling and John Stephen, during the 1830s and endorsed by the British Crown Law officers in 1839: Cowper quoted their opinions extensively. [4] These weighty authorities went virtually unquestioned until the legal men of Cowper's 1856 cabinet, Martin and Lutwyche, decided that they were mistaken. They held that the church and school lands formed part of the waste lands of the Crown and, as such, fell under the control of the colonial parliament. Manning and Darvall, holders of the law posts in the Parker ministry, decided just as firmly that the legal opinions of Martin and Lutwyche were as dubious as their politics and returned the matter to its original state. Cowper conceded that the government had the power to resume and sell the land, yet he always insisted that, under the trust, the proceeds of sale must be used only for the benefit of religion and education. The revenues were small; the Anglican share in 1858, £1408 15s 4d, would hardly keep two clergymen. It was not the money, but the principle behind its use, which generated a fierce parliamentary contest over the issue between 1861 and 1863. Through it all Cowper upheld the inviolability of the trust, even when a consistent majority of the Assembly and three of his own ministers were against him.

Upon the third issue involving religion, that of direct state grants to the churches, Cowper's attitude led some, even amongst his friends, to believe that he was taking an entirely opposite line. Under Wentworth's constitution, responsible governments had inherited Schedule C of the old civil list, which reserved £28 000 yearly for the four main Christian sects. Cowper abolished the schedule in 1862, reserving only the clerical salaries paid from it to the existing incumbents for life or until they resigned their posts. On this issue, his allies and opponents in other religious matters were largely reversed. Anglicans, both clergy and laymen, split over the question, with those who believed in voluntaryism supporting Cowper. But it was the anti-clerical group in the Assembly which gave him majorities to carry his abolition bill, while the strongest opponent of the measure was Frederick Barker, Anglican bishop of Sydney. Quite wrongly the *Empire* praised Cowper for having 'sacrificed long cherished personal predilections on this matter'. [5] In fact, as he openly admitted once the bill had passed, Cowper's abolition of state aid owed much to the opinion he had held consistently for more than ten years, that since the Church of England had no chance of becoming the established church of the colony, it was better to withdraw government aid altogether than to suffer the financing of error as well as truth.[6] The *Empire's* mistake arose because Cowper dared not expose the bigotry of his motives before his bill had succeeded. Instead, he argued that Bourke's Church Act had been intended only as transitional step on the road to complete voluntaryism, that under the existing system the distribution of the money could not be controlled by the people and that none of it reached the unsettled districts where it was most needed.[7] Little wonder that even Cowper's supporters in the Assembly shook their heads in wonder and demanded to know the principles behind actions which seemed so foreign to him. They pressed him without avail. He would not be drawn until the issue was settled.

For the second time Cowper's personal religious views brought him into conflict with the head of his beloved church. The moral dilemma of his clash with Broughton recurred over the state aid question with Bishop Barker, and again the agony of it was worsened because he had previously enjoyed the trust of the person concerned. Like the Cowpers, Barker was a low churchman. When he and his wife came to New South Wales in 1855, they stayed with old Archdeacon Cowper for some time, and Barker, a man of more sociable temperament than the ascetic Broughton, quickly established a friendship with the Cowper family. In May, 1856, Barker persuaded the Donaldson ministry to appoint Charles Cowper chairman of the Denominational Schools Board. Concerned at the poor state of church finances, Barker set up, in the same year, a Church Society which he hoped would raise the money to provide more clergymen and church schools. Cowper joined the central committee of the Church Society and became patron to the Cobbitty and Narellan branch association.. Barker put aside his busy schedule to open the new branch in person and to enjoy the hospitality of Wivenhoe. Dismayed at the hedonism displayed by uncaring colonials on Sundays, Barker also organized the Society for Promoting the Observance of the Lord's Day. Cowper duly joined it, and he took a leading part in fund-raising campaigns for the completion of St Andrew's Cathedral so that (he told his fellow-Anglicans) the bishop might have a proper setting for the ministration of his office.[8]

Yet even in 1856 there were indications that Cowper would take an independent line over state aid. He avoided the issue during the 1856 elections and he would not join the impetuous Robert Campbell in promoting the interdenominational Society for the Abolition of All State Aid to Religion. But on 11 December he voted in the Assembly for a resolution moved by Jones that no money above that provided by Schedule C be allowed for the support of religion. In May 1857 he gave blunt warning to the Church Society that state aid was likely to end soon and, mindful of the dismal fate of the Lay Association, he told members not to allow the society to die. [9] His co-religionists were further confused, when, as chairman of a select committee on railways, he curtly rejected as impractical petitions from the Lord's Day Observance Society against running the trains on Sundays. From the time he gained power in 1857 he quietly dissociated himself from his more obvious church connections, appearing no longer at the meetings of the Church Society and remaining carefully neutral during the stormy debate and rejection in 1859 of a bill to regulate the temporal affairs of the Church of England. These were prudent moves for a premier who needed to live down a reputation for bigotry. Not until 1865 did he judge it safe to sponsor a bill for his church. This measure, a renewed attempt to have parliament authorize a reorganization of the Church of England's temporal affairs, owed much of its eventual success in 1866 to Cowper's careful diplomacy and seems to have re-established in full his friendship with Bishop Barker, a friendship which lasted thereafter until the end of Cowper's life.

Cowper spent only a year as chairman of the Denominational Schools Board. That was long enough to impress upon him the inefficiency of the whole schooling system, and even in 1856 he had begun to plan the reorganization of education. The Parker government tried it first. In February 1857 Manning outlined the ministry's plans for a single system of secularly based education. Cowper sprang to the defence of the denominational schools, pointing out that they had far more pupils and were cheaper to run than the national schools. Still, the frustrations of his post on the Denominational Schools Board came out in his comment that 'he never filled an office with less gratification' and he complained of ill-paid schoolmasters and the lack of funds for school buildings. [10] Thomas Holt tried to improve the position by moving that government funds be distributed to schools according to average daily attendance, but Cowper, remarking that the situation needed a more comprehensive approach, helped to defeat the proposal.

The Parker ministry fell before it could do more, and Cowper had his hands full with the lands and electoral bills until 1859. He had no wish to bring into the torrid sessions of 1857 and 1858 another contentious matter, particularly after the uproar which followed his sacking of Plunkett from the chairmanship of the National Schools Board in February of the latter year. In effect, Plunkett tried to take control of educational policy from the hands of the ministry. It was true, as T. A. Murray pointed out, that the Deas Thomson government had specifically provided, in setting up the board, that it was to run its schools without interference from the executive government, [11] but the extent of the board's powers against those of the government was ill-defined. Plunkett took advantage of this to attempt the promotion of non-vested schools, an idea adopted by the National Schools Board in 1857 at the suggestion of their chief executive officer, William Wilkins. Drawing on Irish and Victorian precedent, these schools were to be privately owned and the board planned to grant proprietors money for books and salaries in return for the teaching of the normal national schools curriculum during the hours of compulsory attendance. On 18 December 1857 Plunkett sent to Cowper, as colonial secretary, a copy of the board's proposed regulations on non-vested schools and requested him to have them inserted in the *Government Gazette*. [12] As Plunkett noted, the adoption of these regulations would have required the Assembly to approve the funding of the new schools which could be expected gradually to replace denominational ones. Cowper, very reasonably, considered that the legislature and not the board had the ultimate responsibility for educational policy and refused to promulgate the regulations without parliamentary sanction. This would not do for Plunkett. He retorted that the board could not be guided by the individual opinion of the colonial secretary. When Cowper, after consulting Martin and Campbell, repeated his stand as the 'deliberate opinion' of his government, Plunkett virtually called him a liar and accused him of personal opposition to the regulations because of his hostility to national schools. Cowper had no wish to quarrel with Plunkett. He was in the throes of a heated election campaign after the failure of his 1857 lands bill, and any move against Plunkett would surely be greeted as bigotry by the proponents of secular education and by the conservatives, who hoped to pull down the Cowper government before they could pass their projected electoral bill. At the least a Cowper-Plunkett clash was certain to damage the former's chances of passing his own contemplated education measure. Yet, as Cowper pointed out to the Executive Council, Plunkett had deliberately made the dispute public by sending the whole correspondence to the *Empire* on the same day that the colonial secretary's office received his last letter. [13] From the height of arrogance displayed in his letters, Plunkett thus blundered into crass stupidity, for no government could be expected to tolerate such open contempt of its authority. 'If such insulting conduct can be allowed, the Head of the Government cannot congratulate himself upon being the holder of a dignified office', Cowper wrote to Martin. [14] Denison agreed and the Executive Council approved Plunkett's dismissal on 27 January 1858.

Five days later Cowper offered Plunkett's place on the National

Schools Board to Daniel Cooper (who declined it), but Plunkett did
not hear of his dismissal until 6 February. No doubt the *Sydney
Morning Herald* was correct in claiming that Cowper had delayed
the announcement until the elections were over. [15] Such a move,
'peculiarly Cowperesque', as the *Goulburn Herald* called it, [16] was
a sound political tactic. A re-elected and united ministry stood against
the anticipated storm of criticism, led by the *Sydney Morning Herald,*
fuming at Cowper's 'paltry bigotry and egotism', [17] and by James
Macarthur. Marcarthur chaired a Sydney public meeting where conservative speakers spared enough time from the main business of
abusing Cowper to shed metaphorical tears over the fate of poor
Plunkett. During February and March a few country centres held
sympathy meetings for Plunkett, and when the parliamentary session
began in April, Macarthur led the conservatives into the attack by
moving that the government had misinterpreted the powers of the
National Schools Board which allowed that body to make the regulations
sought by Plunkett. This was the only possible justification for Plunkett's
high-handed conduct, but it was a weak defence, as Martin reminded
the Assembly in pointing out that such a view would deny the right
of parliament to exercise full control over education and financial
policy. [18] Although a few liberal members sympathized with Plunkett,
they dared not risk the defeat of the government and the consequent
loss of the electoral bill. They backed the government solidly to reject
Macarthur's motions by 29 votes to 22. For opposite reasons the
conservatives voted with Macarthur. With the danger of a governmernt
resignation past, five liberal members changed sides to pass a composite
amendment by Parkes and T. W. Smith which urged the reinstatement
of Plunkett and exonerated the National Schools Board from any
intention to exceed its powers. Cowper knew the strength of the
government's position. He flatly refused to act on the resolution unless
Plunkett first withdrew his offensive expressions. Macarthur, too, was well
aware that the liberal majority would not allow the government to
fall before the electoral bill was safe. Publicly he pilloried the government
and placed a censure motion on the parliamentary order paper.
Privately, he strove to mediate between Plunkett and the ministry.
Cowper and Martin wanted to end the quarrel but Plunkett stubbornly
rejected Macarthur's overtures on their behalf. [19] Disgusted, Macarthur
dropped his censure motion and, as T. L. Suttor remarks, Plunkett
found himself left with only moral support. [20] This was enough to
gain him unopposed election to the Assembly at a Cumberland by-
election a few weeks later and he became a constant thorn in the side
of the ministry.

Having firmly established the authority of the government over the education boards, Cowper promised a measure to amalgamate them. This was the obvious step to take for increased efficiency, but how was he to satisfy the partisans of secular education without sacrificing the interests of the churches? Denison may have suggested the solution he chose; certainly the governor approved when Cowper decided early in 1859 to adopt the English 'Privy Council' system, [21] under which a single board allocated government money to all schools, religious or secular, according to the enrolment of each and the amount of money raised locally for them. First, Cowper had to sell this scheme to his ministers, particularly to Robertson, who favoured secular schooling. He won them over and went on to test public opinion by praising the Privy Council system during the 1859 election campaign. He met no overt opposition, and no doubt he had noted, with the *Sydney Morning Herald,* that although most members returned to the Assembly favoured national schools, they had shown a keen eye for votes by supporting the continuation of existing denominational schools. [22] Before parliament opened on 30 August Cowper had decided to make the education issue the main business of the session. Other major measures, the lands and elective upper house bills, were held back. But with so many new members of uncertain allegiance in the Assembly, the government waited to see how the session developed before bringing on the education bill.

At first the ministry seemed headed for disaster, as the new members asserted their independence. On the first sitting day Arnold, ministerial nominee for the post of chairman of committees, was defeated by Piddington. Twenty-four hours later Parkes moved that the unpopular duties on tea and sugar be removed, and in spite of Cowper's request that the matter be postponed until the treasurer could investigate the effects of removal on government finances, the Assembly passed the motion by one vote. This was a minor matter; the convention was well established that governments resigned office only on a direct vote of no confidence or the loss of a major bill. So parliament and the public alike were startled when Cowper's ministry immediately resigned. Cowper had decided that Parkes must be deflated and new members taught a sharp lesson. T. A. Murray, commissioned by Denison to form a new ministry, failed dismally when Hay, Flood, Martin and Parkes, too shrewd to buck the power and popularity of the men who had passed the Electoral Act, all refused to join him. Bitingly, Cowper told the Assembly that his ministry would carry on only if the House rescinded Parkes's motion. A chastened Assembly repealed it by 40 votes to 21 and the ministry stayed in power. Cowper had made his point. After two quiet weeks he brought up the education bill on 22 September.

As Suttor notes, the bill lacked one prominent feature of the English system: local freedom of management.[23] Cowper's measure provided that the Executive Council control both the allocation of funds and the making of regulations for the conduct of schools. Bishop Barker, some of Sydney's leading Anglican laymen, the *Maitland Mercury* and the denominational schoolteachers supported the bill. So did such liberal Catholics as J. K. Heydon, editor of *Freeman's Journal*. But most heeded Archbishop Polding, who warned them not to support the bill because the temper of the controlling authority 'might be wholly Protestant'[24] as indeed seemed likely, since Denison, Cowper and his ministers formed the members of the Executive Council. Most dissenters, fearing the influence of the Church of England, joined the Catholic hierarchy, the *Empire* and national schools staff in opposition to Cowper's bill. More than 6000 people put their names to petitions against the measure, only 1168 petitioned for it,[25] and at the first discussion of the bill in the Assembly the government was hard-pressed to postpone the second reading for a week in order to deal with a censure motion by Martin over the appointment of the law officers. Had Cowper been less wedded to his personal viewpoint, his political sense would have told him to withdraw the bill at this stage or at least to seek the advice of his rank and file parliamentary supporters, whom he had not consulted. Instead, he drew encouragement from his triumph in the tea and sugar duties wrangle and from the decisive defeat of Martin's censure motions in a marathon sitting which lasted through the night and up to noon of the following day.

Cowper had handled these problems cleverly and he brought up the lands bills to bolster his support. But his success led him to overestimate the loyalty of his followers on a question of such fundamental importance as education. Most were willing to concede that the government should have control of financial policy and few cared to question the antecedents of their law officers so long as the job was done. As Cowper found to his cost, the education question was a different matter, touching as it did the depths of each man's conscience. He suffered one of the worst defeats of his career when the Assembly refused a second reading to his bill by 57 votes to 8. Robertson, Weekes and Attorney-General L. H. Bayley voted loyally with their chief, but Flood, newly appointed to the works portfolio, turned against him. So did some of his closest political friends: Richard Jones, George Oakes, Lang and Dalley. The *Sydney Morning Herald* said these men had meant only to hold up the progress of the bill until Cowper could be persuaded to amend it to their satisfaction. [26] The evidence suggests this may have been so. Immediately before its refusal of the second reading the Assembly had rejected, by 40 votes to 25, Murray's attempt to postpone the bill for six months, and Cowper's comments on the failure of his measure clearly implied that he did not see that alone as sufficient grounds for leaving office. [27] but if the *Sydney Morning Herald*'s view was right, Murray upset the applecart by moving successfully that the bill be discharged from the order paper, which meant it was lost for the session. Thus completely defeated in their education proposals, the ministry resigned.

The power of Cowper's name had grown great in the two years since be had won government. The liberal press voiced its belief that no successful ministry could be formed without him, [28] and Cowper seems to have believed it too. He readily agreed to join Jones when the governor commissioned him to form a ministry. But Jones failed and a few days later Forster succeeded in scraping together a heterogeneous collection of opposition oddities to follow him into government. Sadly, Cowper resigned his seat and returned to Wivenhoe, not because he was disheartened with politics, as some thought, but because he was shorn of his official salary, the prop that kept him from the verge of insolvency. At some time between 1857 and 1859 he lost control of his two Lachlan stations. Those south of the Murray River had gone years before, and all he had were Chatsbury and Wivenhoe, both in urgent need of the strict management he had not been able to provide while he spent his days in Sydney. Even when his constituents returned him unsolicited to the seat he had resigned, he did not rejoin the Assembly. Yet four months later, when first Jones and then Robertson offered him the colonial secretary's office with a seat in the upper house, he returned unhesitatingly to that position of power, prestige and not inconsiderable salary. It must have pleased him to know that Forster's brief rule had gone far to prove what the press had said, that there was no alternative to the 'eternal Charles Cowper'.

Prudently, the Robertson-Cowper ministry shelved the education question and concentrated on the lands bills. But in 1861 they found that the progress of these bills embroiled them once more in the problem of government aid to religion, since they involved the fate of the church and school lands. In turn, developments in this question led Cowper to take action on the issue of state aid to churches. Cowper carefully avoided this question while Martin remained a member of his government. Soon after their testy colleague had quit the ministry, Cowper, Robertson and Campbell clashed openly with him over his defence of state aid. [29] When the reformed Assembly of 1859 met,

Cowper brought up a state aid abolition bill, which lapsed when his
ministry fell over the education issue. Forster made a similar move.
Again, it failed at the fall of the ministry and the incoming Robertson-
Cowper government tried to put aside the whole question of state
aid while they pressed on with Crown lands legislation. But Murray,
Cowper's nemesis in the 1859 session, again upset the ministry's plans
in 1860 when he demanded and got a select committee, which
declared the church and school lands to be part of the ordinary
Crown domain — a highly embarrassing move for the ministers, since
Cowper and Attorney-General John Hargrave believed the lands were
held in trust for the churches, while Robertson, Arnold and Weekes
took Murray's view. When Martin and Lutwyche questioned his opinion
in 1856, Cowper had dodged the problem by inducing the Executive
Council to continue the existing distribution of funds until the status
of the lands had been decided by parliament. He would, no doubt, have
been pleased if that time had never come, but Murray's committee, in
recommending that an act be passed to incorporate the church and school
lands into the Crown domain, brought the matter into the open. Cowper
fell back on a timeless answer to a thorny problem: he ignored it.
But this angered the redoubtable J. B. Wilson. On 23 January 1861
he tabled a bill which defined the church and school lands as Crown
waste lands and told the House that he would act if the government
would not. Robertson, trying hard to reconcile loyalty to his leader
with his own opposing beliefs, announced that he agreed 'in abstract'
with Wilson but objected to his measure as an obstruction to the passing
of the lands bills. [30] Such fence-sitting tactics by his chief henchman
did little to help Cowper. Sensing disaster, he sent Weekes, Arnold
and his own son Charles across the floor to vote with the opposition
and thus avoided the appearance, if not the reality, of a government
defeat when the House approved the second reading of Wilson's bill
by 39 votes to 12. Alarmed at this result, Bishop Barker and Archbishop
Polding hired counsel to plead on behalf of their respective churches
at the Bar of the House. But the eloquence of barristers failed to
sway the Assembly. The bill passed its third reading with Cowper
bitterly rejoicing that the Legislative Council was certain to reject it.
They did so the next day.

Wilson was not so easily beaten. He simply changed his method
of attack, moving on 13 September that the appropriation of church
and school lands revenue without the sanction of the Assembly be
declared unconstitutional. Cowper, already unsettled by a dispute with
Bishop Barker, who had challenged his view that the government
had the power to sell the lands, saw Wilson's motion carried against

the ministry by 22 votes to 14. Weary of the endless battle for political survival and fearing that his friends might fail him at this critical moment, he wrote gloomily to Sir John Young. 'My position in the affair differs from my Colleagues — all of whom I believe concur with the Resolutions: and if I am to consult my own feelings I shall certainly retire. This will throw all our great measures back...and I confess I am perplexed.'[31] His colleagues could not move him from his stand and they could not afford to lose him. They agreed to support his views until the lands bills passed. In return Cowper made a strong appeal to the House to stop putting up embarrassing motions until the question of the lands was settled. The members heeded him, but when the lands bills, Robertson with them, went to the upper house, the relentless Wilson reintroduced his church and school lands bill to the Assembly. With rare temper, Cowper rejected Wilson's taunts that the premier's views were lies,[32] yet he could prevent neither the passing of the bill nor the defection of his ministers: Weekes voted with the overwhelming majority against him at the final reading and Arnold absented himself from the House. Only Robertson loyally spoke and voted for his leader's views as he opposed the measure in the Council. For the second time that body rejected it, the government narrowly survived Wilson's censure motion, and the session ended before Wilson could try again.

Cowper knew well that Wilson would try again. The Council could be relied upon to reject Wilson's bill as often as he liked to bring it up, but public feeling was rising against the ministry over the issue. Even before Wilson had begun his moves in 1861, Cowper had persuaded the Executive Council to approve the sale of the lands, with the intention that the proceeds should be invested for the benefit of the churches. Thus he hoped to divert public wrath because the lands were not open to selection and to placate the Assembly by allowing them to decide the distribution of revenues between the various sects. This could have been authorized by executive fiat alone, but Wilson had also to be headed off in the Assembly. When the 1862 session opened, the ministry speedily tabled a bill on the lines agreed to by the Executive Council. Robertson and Cowper bluntly advised the Assembly to accept it, since the upper house would never pass such a measure as Wilson's.[33] Members knew it. Wilson brought up his bill for a third time, the ministry delayed it while they pressed their own, and weary members passed it, but not before Robertson, unable to repress his own opinions, had split the ministry in telling the Assembly that they might allocate all the funds for education and none for religion if they chose.[34] Lang promptly tried to have the provision for support of religion removed from the bill. Robertson and Weekes supported him. Cowper and Arnold joined the majority which defeated Lang, and Cowper must have heaved a great sigh of relief — too soon, for the Council, which had twice rescued Cowper from Wilson's measure, managed in turn to rescue Wilson from Cowper's. They amended the bill to provide that the money be allocated under the existing system with any change to be approved by both houses. This move angered the Assembly's secularists by removing their right to allocate the funds and it resurrected the old and highly unpopular claim of the Council to have power over money bills. When the amended version of the measure reappeared in the lower house, John Lucas managed to pass, by 25 votes to 19, the very proposal which Lang had lost a few weeks earlier, [35] and Cowper, faced with the choice of abandoning either his principles or the bill, chose the latter.

Once more, stalemate. But the ending of other forms of state aid in 1862 took much of the heat out of the controversy over this last remnant. Furthermore the British law officers, following a request for advice from Young, laid it down that, while the colonial parliament was fully competent to deal with the question of the church and school lands, the rights of all existing individual recipients should be preserved. This gave some support to Cowper's view, though Robertson went too far in claiming that this opinion established the inviolability of the trust. The precise meaning was open to argument. Still, parliamentary attitudes had changed sufficiently to ensure that, when the tenacious Wilson again presented his well-worn bill in 1863, the House rapidly amended it to a close approximation of Cowper's 1862 bill. The matter was still not settled when the ministry fell in October 1863. The succeeding Martin ministry referred the whole matter to the Supreme Court and the judges ruled unanimously in favour of the trust. [36] This proved decisive. When Cowper returned to power in 1865 he merely passed a regulation requiring that revenues from these lands be spent in the less populous districts, and there the matter rested until Parkes ended the religious aid provisions in 1880, but Cowper did not live to know of it.

Cowper's move to abolish direct state aid in 1862 was amongst his more notable successes. His first skirmishes with Wilson had shown him the truth of what R. B. Walker has recently confirmed, that after the 1860 elections the New South Wales Assembly contained a probable majority of men who favoured the ending of state aid. [37] But only Cowper's skilled political management (or · 'corruption', as his opponents called it) enabled him to outwit those hardy defenders of the faith, the members of the Legislative Council.

The opponents of state aid were a mixed lot — atheists, agnostics, Jews — and everyone whose church did not share in the largess fell naturally into that category. But so did many adherents of the churches which did receive state money, either because they felt that such aid weakened the moral fibre of their church or, like most of the anti-state-aiders in the Assembly, because they were liberals who believed that the state should have no official connection with religion. Cowper seems to have been alone amongst parliamentarians in his bigoted reasoning or, more likely, was the only one who admitted to it. The official Anglican attitude, expressed by the *Church of England Chronicle*, was that the church accepted government aid as its right regardless of that given, in its view wrongly, to others. Schedule C was seen as part of a compact with the Imperial parliament which was not to be set aside without its consent.[38] The Catholic church hierarchy also opposed the withdrawal of state aid, fearing a reduction in their religious coverage of the colony.[39] Not all Catholics agreed; Jabez Heydon lost the editorship of the Catholic newspaper *Freeman's Journal* in 1860 partly because he accepted, and said in print, that state aid must end.[40] Cowper's loss of church support was more than compensated for in the Assembly. The issue submerged political enmities and gave him the backing of men usually his opponents. He also regained the full support of his ministers and of such faction stalwarts as John and Thomas Garrett, John Caldwell, S. W. 'Poodle' Gray, John Dickson, I. J. Blake and John Ryan, all of whom had opposed him on the church and school lands question.

In April 1861, Cowper marshalled his followers, both state-aiders and abolitionists, to defeat a private members' bill which aimed at cutting off all government aid to the churches. Most members seem to have shared Cowper's belief that the measure was inopportune and unlikely to pass the upper house. Inopportune it certainly was to the ministry, then faced with the urgent problems of passing the lands bills, reconstructing the Legislative Council and fending off Wilson's moves against the church and school lands, but it may also be suspected that Cowper did not want to lose control of the issue. As 1862 came around, Cowper judged the prospects of passing an abolition bill to be much more promising. John Robertson, the architect of free selection, rode the crest of public adulation, the Legislative Council had been reined in and Cowper could move against state aid from a position of parliamentary strength greater than he had ever known before. Still, he had to be careful. Public opinion had run counter to abolition when he had broached the question in 1859; petitions to the legislature had shown a ratio of nearly 4 to 1 against the ending of state aid. This, he knew, did not accurately reflect the feelings of the colony, since the major churches had rallied adherents to their cause with considerable success, while the abolitionists lacked organization, but the proponents of state aid in both houses could use such figures to bolster their case. A further and more serious problem stemmed from a split within the ranks of the parliamentary abolitionists. Most thought, with Cowper, that those of the clergy who drew on government money for their salaries had a moral right to continue receiving it, and the government's bill provided that aid from Schedule C should be gradually scaled down by stopping the salaries paid for particular posts as the existing holders died or retired. A smaller group, including Forster, Wilson and Piddington, demanded that all aid be cut off immediately. The danger to Cowper's bill lay in the possibility that these extremists would side with the state-aiders to vote it down. Cowper warned the extreme group that the British government would not accept the destruction of vested interests, stressing particularly the recent disallowance of a Tasmanian bill which had attempted to abolish state aid by paying off the churches with a lump sum in government debentures. [11] They saw the point, but were still aggrieved that Cowper's bill, probably as a sop to his own church, preserved the form if not the substance of Schedule C. As Cowper had feared, they joined the state-aiders to vote against the second reading of the bill. Luckily for him, one of the latter group, Isaac Shepherd, decided at the last minute that the measure was the best he was likely to get and voted with the ministry. By one vote the bill passed [42] — too close, though, to allow Cowper to risk pushing it further. Instead, he threw overboard the concession to his church by abolishing Schedule C directly and recommitting the amended bill. This move won over the recalcitrant abolitionists, Anglican opposition was swept aside, and the bill passed easily the remaining stages.

The Council still stood astride the road to success. Seven of its most influential members, led by Deas Thomson, published their protests against Cowper's bill in the columns of the *Sydney Morning Herald*. [43] Would others be swayed more by reluctance to oppose the will of the Assembly or by the flood of petitions, 12 481 signatures against, to 955 for, the bill, which poured in upon them? [44] Hargrave, representing the ministry in the Council, managed to push the bill through the second reading by one vote when he agreed, at C. K. Holden's insistence, to amend the form of the bill to restore Schedule C. Thus, as the *Church of England Chronicle* bitterly noted, the bill passed in the Council by omitting the provision which had passed it in the Assembly. [45] But Holden had also inserted a clause stipulating that the church and school lands funds should not be interfered with, and this the Assembly rejected before sending the bill back to the Council. That accursed problem again! It seemed about to bring down the entire bill. But Holden, a leading Sydney solicitor, had previously asked Cowper for a government legal post, and the wily premier chose this moment to appoint him. [46] Holden immediately withdrew from the House. In his absence his clause was lost and the bill passed by 9 votes to 8. Furiously, Martin and other state-aiders in the Assembly berated Cowper for buying off Holden in order to pass the bill. But Holden's qualifications for appointment were beyond question and Cowper could afford to treat the clamour of Martin and Co. with contempt. He refused to say a word in reply and even had the novel experience of being defended by Wilson and Lucas. [47] His only real sorrow lay in the bitter resentment directed at him by members of his own church. The *Church of England Chronicle* had no doubt that 'the ambidextrous Colonial Secretary' had engineered both Holden's defection and the complete tactical management of the bill. His balancing feats, said the editor, were comparable to those of Blondin, and both were wished 'a safe and speedy retirement from the performance of their dangerous feats'. [48] Bishop Barker made a last-ditch attempt to prevent the bill from receiving the royal assent, failed, and direct state aid came to an end in New South Wales.

R. B. Walker points out that Windeyer, Forster and others who opposed state aid were motivated by the hope of reducing the powers of the Anglican bishops. [49] In effect, this was a continuation of the process begun by Robert Lowe's attacks on Broughton in the 1840s. Cowper would never have supported this position for a moment. Ironically, his stern moral viewpoint pressed him into alliance with those who sought to tear down the very structure in which he believed, and brought him the resentment of those he most respected. Cowper cannot have been unaware of this, but he clung firmly to what he saw as his religious duty.

Of all the great questions enumerated by the liberals when they first came to power, only education awaited legislation at the end of 1862. Cowper, still anxious to settle this issue, gave it considerable thought during that year. The debacle of 1859 had taught him that no measure could pass which did not satisfy the advocates of secular education. How could this be done while still preserving the right of denominational schools to government funds? Cowper thought he saw the answer in a Victorian education bill which passed into law in 1862. He drew up a simplified version of this measure, 'but still keeping it very near to the Melbourne Model', as he told J. D. Lang. [50]

Cowper's bill provided for a single, government-appointed board which was to be responsible for regulating and administering all schools receiving government funds. Denominational schools were to retain their right to aid so long as they gave at least four hours of secular education each day. However, restrictions were placed on the growth of new schools through clauses which stated that they could receive aid only if they met prescribed minimum limits for pupil numbers and distance from other schools. The aim was to counter one of the most persistent criticisms of the denominational system, that sectarian jealousies had led to a multiplicity of tiny, inefficient schools which competed agianst one another within small areas. Another clause laid it down that no grants for school buildings or repairs could be made unless the site was vested in the Board of Education. These restrictions on the growth of church schools were the main concessions made to secularist sentiment. To balance them, the 1863 bill omitted the 1859 provisions for parliamentary control of the board in favour of direct supervision by the Executive Council. So long as Cowper headed the government, this clause would be likely to guarantee eligible church schools a significant share of state funds. He could only hope that the measure would work sufficiently well to ensure that future governments would hesitate to disturb it, and if they did try to disturb it, there was always Cowper's hand-picked Legislative Council to stop them.

Understandably Cowper put these proposals forward with great caution. In October 1862 he allowed details of them to be made public. The *Empire,* harsh critic of his 1859 bill, noted that acceptance in the sister colony of the 1862 Victorian Act had 'been such as to encourage the belief that its principles are just, and also suited both to the times and to the conditions of the community'. [51] The *Church of England Chronicle* feared that the new system might be too secular and grumbled at the lack of help for denominational schools. Yet behind the editor's complaints, there was an unspoken feeling that the church could not now expect a more favourable settlement. [52] The bill seems to have aroused no great public interest, and Cowper could draw some cautious encouragement from its first reception. Nevertheless, he had still not decided whether or not to press on with it when the 1863 parliamentary session opened in June: the governor's opening speech did not mention it. Four weeks later the decision came. The second reading debate made it clear that he had every chance of carrying the bill. The secularists accepted it. [53] So did some of the denominationalists, on the ground that it was the best obtainable. [54] The bill passed by 40 votes to 15 and survived the committee stages almost unscathed, but when the Cowper government fell from power two months later, no further progress had been made. Speaking on Parkes's education bill in 1866, Cowper implied that the 1863 bill had been lost because the pressure on his government was then too

great to allow time to proceed with it. [55] This was cant: the adoption
of the committee report and the third reading, all that remained to
complete the bill in the lower house, would have been mere formalities.
It is possible that Cowper feared an inconvenient and time-consuming
clash with the Legislative Council should the bill reach that body while the
government was struggling to survive, but his attitude to Parkes's
1866 bill suggests that he may simply have been unhappy at being
forced to place restrictions on denominational schooling. Parkes's bill
was very similar to his own, yet he opposed it strongly and extolled
the virtues of the Privy Council system which had cost him the government
in 1859. His speech showed that he believed still that religion was
essential to morality and that the state should do what parents neglected.
As the head of government in 1863 he was forced into caution. In
opposition three years later he felt free to speak his mind.

However 'slippery' Cowper may have been on most political fronts,
he could lay claim to a steadiness of personal principle on religious
matters that few could match. Tactically and strategically he deployed
his political skills to the limit to help his cause. Morally he stood fast
and his position of leadership gave him a greater influence than any
other man on the issues involved. The ending of state aid to churches
could not have been long delayed had Cowper never taken up the
question, since liberal sentiment ran strongly for it, yet it is probably
fair to claim that Cowper's adroit management significantly speeded
its coming and with a minimum of political disruption. His greatest
personal success, however, was in preserving another kind of state aid
for his church, through the outcome of the church and school lands
controversy. He and a Legislative Council which was virtually his own
creation succeeded in thwarting the will of most of his ministers and
the elected representatives of the people in defence of a principle. It was
victory by attrition, and its practical effect was to continue a form of
state aid to the churches for nearly twenty years. In contrast, Cowper's
education policy proved to be no more than continuation of the
rearguard defence of denominationalism which he had been fighting
since 1843. The failure of his 1859 bill ended his last attempt to
settle the question on terms fully acceptable to his personal conscience.
The 1863 measure served only to show perceptive secularists like Parkes
that the tide was running their way. In Cowper's comments on Parkes's
education bill there was even a hint of relief that the matter had been
taken out of his hands. He had failed, through no fault of his own,
to protect the religious education he cherished. He had not failed his own
religious conscience.

7

Working the Wires of Patronage and Power

Late in 1858, with Cowper well entrenched in government, Henry Parkes wrote to his young disciple William Windeyer, reviewing the state of the Assembly. At the head of the ministerialists, he remarked, was Cowper, 'working the wires of patronage and power, with which he is now grown pretty familiar and endeavouring to propitiate the popular appetite by the flavour of his Cabinet measures'.[1] We have seen the major measures through which Cowper managed to 'propitiate the popular appetite'. In his reference to the manipulation of men through the exercise of the powers given by office, Parkes stressed a factor of equal importance to the survival of faction governments and correctly assumed that Cowper had been quick to recognize it. But to what extent were the wires his to work? In practice, Cowper's powers were affected by the need to come to terms with four elements of the political scene: the British government, through its local representative the governor; his ministerial colleagues; the parliamentary opposition; and public opinion.

Cowper began badly with Sir William Denison. Denison's strong conservatism and his rejection of Cowper as a 'needy man' in 1856 have been noted earlier. The governor was a determined man, an efficient and experienced administrator, and in 1856 he viewed with contempt most liberal politicians. When Cowper's first ministry fell in that year, Denison remarked that 'responsibility is in fact a name, a claptrap, meaning nothing—but the right of the majority to make fools of themselves to their heart's content'.[2] He never modified his basic conservatism. Just before he left the colony in 1861 he wrote a memorandum for his successor in which he repeated his 1855 view that change was an evil of great magnitude and expressed regret at having assented to the 1858 Electoral Act because enfranchising 'the ignorant and uneducated' had brought a 'marked and objectionable change' in the composition of the Assembly.[3] Nevertheless, as Loveday and Martin have shown, Denison recognized that his political position had to appear an impartial one.[4] He was largely responsible for establishing the system used by the executive government before Cowper came to power, whereby ministerial measures were sent to him for formal submission to the Executive Council before introduction to parliament. Cowper accepted this arrangement, which gave Denison the chance to try to influence government policy—a chance which his surviving correspondence with Cowper shows he did not hesitate to use. Yet he considered that he could not reject the advice of any ministry which was backed by a majority.

In this he was not entirely right. There were two ways in which he could and did exercise an independent discretion: in the appointment of members to the Legislative Council and in cases where his Imperial instructions clashed with the advice of his ministers. But in the ordinary course of government Denison acted with a firm impartiality. Thus his dislike of Cowper's neediness and Martin's 'ignorance'[5] did not prevent him from taking an impeccably neutral attitude to the protests which greeted the latter's appointment as attorney-general in 1856. As noted earlier, he refused in 1858 to appoint fifteen new members to the upper house to help pass the electoral bill, but eventually allowed Cowper to gain thirteen more supporters in that year. Nor is he known to have rejected any of Cowper's subsequent nominations to the upper house. He declined to give the Cowper ministry a dissolution in 1856, but allowed them one in 1857, to the fury of their opponents, and he did the same in 1860. Personal relations between Cowper and Denison grew warmer with time. Cowper appreciated Denison's impartiality and in mid-1858 conceded that their early differences had been 'amicably settled'.[6] They had a common enthusiasm for railway development, similar views on state aid to churches and Denison supported Cowper's 1859 education bill. No doubt Cowper's tactful manner and his ready acceptance of the rules which Denison had down for the conduct of executive government business helped to soften the governor's early suspicion of him. The evidence suggests that Cowper sometimes allowed his actions to be influenced by Denison on what he saw as minor questions. He accepted without demur Denison's initiative in offering the presidency of the upper house to Sir William Burton in 1858, and Cowper's rejection of Victorian overtures towards federation possibly owed something to Denison's opinion that the expense of another legislature was not warranted. But in major questions, the governor was unable to move him. Denison's opposition to the successful electoral bill of 1858 has been noted. His very logical arguments against Cowper's belief in low minimum land prices were ignored,[7] as was his suggestion that the government should help the clergy by matching private endowments with land grants.[8]

Apart from Legislative Council appointments and dissolutions of the Assembly, only one instance is known of Denison having forced his will upon his ministers. This arose from the clash of Imperial and local authority, which C. H. Currey has dubbed the 'Great Seal Case'. [9] This affair began in 1845 when John Tawell, a man with landed property in New South Wales, was tried for murder and executed in England. Under British law, his property was escheated to the Crown, but in the customary manner the government decided to grant the murderer's property to his heirs, in this case Tawell's wife and children. At that time there was no legal doubt that the British government could grant the lands, but arguments over their exact status under the law, over indefinite boundaries and the rights of buyers against Tawell's heirs, who had been cheated of sale proceeds by an absconding trustee, delayed the issue of a deed of grant until after the coming of responsible government. In 1858 the secretary of state for the colonies, Newcastle, raised the issue again, and the colonial law officers sided with the local buyers against British legal opinion that Tawell's heirs were entitled to the lands. Since neither side would give way, this raised the constitutional problem of whether the British government still had the power to grant colonial lands under any conditions. The British law officers held that, in the Tawell case, they did have such power; the colonial law officers held that they did not. The matter came to a head late in 1860 when Newcastle gave Denison firm instructions to have a deed of grant prepared in favour of Tawell's heirs, stamped as the law required with the Great Seal of the colony. Denison decided to settle the issue before he was due to leave (on 22 January 1861) for his new post in Madras. Ignoring the colonial legal advisers and Lands Department, he had Billyard, the trustee's solicitor, draw up a deed, which he signed. Customarily, the Great Seal was held in the colonial secretary's office, though the governor's commission assigned its keeping to him. Denison therefore sent the deed to Cowper with the request that he stamp it with the seal. Cowper consulted his attorney-general, Hargrave, who equated the colonial secretary's position as keeper of the colonial seal with that of the lord chancellor, the sole authorized keeper of the Great Seal of England. This opinion denied the Imperial government the right to control the use of the colonial seal. Cowper therefore refused to stamp the deed, contending that 'if such a proceeding were to be in any way aided by the colonial authorities, it would be tantamount to an admission that grants of land in New South Wales may be made, by direction of the Secretary of State for the Colonies, not only irrespective of the colonial Government, but in direct opposition to the reiterated protests of the Crown Law Officers of successive Governments during a long series of years'. [10] Denison stood firm, pointing out that the case was unique and offering to collect the seal himself from Cowper's office, but Cowper, his government at the height of popularity after the 1860 election, threatened a ministerial resignation if the governor persisted. Denison responded by sending his private secretary to Cowper's office with the request that the Great Seal be given to him. Cowper gave way. He handed over the seal and with it his government's resignation. Denison stamped the deed, sent the seal back with a polite refusal of the ministerial resignation and left the country the next day, whereupon Cowper and his cabinet quietly resumed office.

'It is a case of high Colonial pretensions encountered with unusual firmness', noted the Duke of Newcastle smugly when he heard of it, [11] and Currey too implies that Cowper wavered in the face of the Imperial authority, [12] but the ministry had already demonstrated its firm grasp of political realism, and Cowper had been opposing British governments and their representatives since 1843. Cowper's explanation to the Assembly was even less convincing. He stated that because the governor's Instructions gave him power to use the Great Seal, the government 'would not, therefore, have been legally justified in refusing it to him'. [13] Yet this was the precise point which Hargrave had held was overruled by the analogous positions of the colonial secretary and the lord chancellor. It is far more likely that the finale to the Great Seal case was a good example of Cowper's preferred methods of dealing with difficult political problems. He shared local pride in political independence and was careful of the dignity of his government. Both would have suffered had he conceded the British claim. On the other hand there was little point in disturbing the harmonious constitutional balance between mother country and colony over a problem which could never occur again. He therefore conciliated local opinion and salvaged his government's pride by resignation, confident that Denison must refuse to accept it. At the same time he made sure, by handing over the Great Seal, that the matter was settled to Newcastle's satisfaction. He probably calculated that the public and the legislature were too involved with the lands question to show much interest. They were, and Cowper quietly dropped the matter.

When Denison was replaced by Sir John Young, Cowper noted that he and Lady Young were 'very affable' and seemed 'well fitted for their office'. [14] The pleasant and diplomatic Young provided a considerable contrast to the brusquely mannered Denison. He fell readily into friendship with Cowper, 'delivered bound hand and foot' to him, claimed William Macarthur, because Robert Lowe had commended the 'statesmanlike abilities' of his old ally to Young. [15] This did not prevent Cowper from taking advantage of Young's initial ignorance of local conventions to help him reconstruct the Legislative Council as he wished, but Sir John, if he resented this, did not show it and he fell in easily with the established limitations upon the governor's power. Early in 1863 he recommended Cowper for the Companionship of the Bath, a high distinction. Notations made on Young's despatch by Newcastle and by Messrs. Gairdner and Elliott, officials of the Colonial Office, show that Cowper was regarded with a good deal of suspicion in those quarters. [16] Young pointed out that Donaldson and Parker had both been knighted for their political services, which were of much shorter duration than Cowper's, and remarked that the premier's colleagues were pressing for some recognition of him. At first, Newcastle questioned the statement that Donaldson and Parker had been knighted for political services. When Gairdner confirmed it, the Colonial Office rejected Young's application by remarking that it was not the practice to recommend 'avowedly on the pressure of a Political party as in the present case'. [17] Cowper was left with good reason to suspect a conservative bias at the Colonial Office.

If the influence of the governors on Cowper's policies was small, the same cannot be said for that of his ministerial colleagues. It has been seen that differences of opinion amongst the ministers forced Cowper to bring on his lands bill in 1857 instead of the electoral reform measure, and the subsequent progress of lands legislation owed more to John Robertson than to him. In theory, the man commissioned by the governor to form a ministry had full freedom of choice in selecting his ministers. In practice, it was difficult to find men who would agree to work together under a given leader, as the abortive efforts of Murray, Hay, Cooper and Jones testified. Cowper constructed his early ministries with cool pragmatism. Martin was a necessity; Jones and Murray brought prestige and widened the ministerial appeal. Again, since all three were potential leaders, it suited Cowper to have them as colleagues instead of rivals. Robertson was needed to strengthen the government's following and to augment its popularity at a critical time. Campbell was an exception. Though widely popular, he was generally (and unjustly) thought to be poor ministerial material, a man 'remarkable for the wildness of his political ideas, and the rectitude of his purpose, and the goodness of his heart', according to the *Sydney Morning Herald,* [18] but he was Cowper's oldest and most loyal friend. To that and Cowper's shrewder estimation of his real abilities he owed his Treasury post. When Campbell died in 1859 Cowper grieved most bitterly. He was, wrote Cowper, 'my excellent friend — though we were intimately acquainted for more than Thirty years we never had an unkind word with each other'. [19] Campbell's successor, E. C. Weekes, was another successful merchant, who had turned to politics in 1856, with Cowper's help. He proved to be an unsteady supporter, but a minor figure in the House. His elevation to the Treasury suggests that the strengthening of the ministry was not a major consideration to Cowper at that time. Had it been, an approach to Forster, Piddington or Flood could have been expected, since Flood had influence on both sides of the House and the other two were fast emerging, in the absence of Parkes, as the principal nuisances to the government. Weekes's financial knowledge as a successful businessman was an asset to the ministry, but a greater asset may have been his equable temperament, which enabled him to work well with other men. At a time when the popularity of his government stood high as a result of the passing of the Electoral Act, Cowper no doubt felt that ministerial harmony was more important than questionable accretions of support. The last of Cowper's long-serving non-legal ministers, W. M. Arnold, was a Hunter Valley landowner, classed with Robertson as an 'out and out radical' in 1857.[20] He had considerable talent as a parliamentary speaker, withering his opponents with biting sarcasm; as an anonymous satirist put it, he was a man of 'bold front and a devil of a temper'.[21] He also showed considerable independence of action, at least twice to the embarrassment of Cowper.[22] In March 1858, Cowper quietened him by engineering his election to the post of chairman of committees, but he was defeated for re-election in 1859 by Piddington. Robertson brought him into the government as minister for works in March 1860. The *Northern Times* forecast accurately that 'a government salary will have a capital effect upon his somewhat hasty temper, and his uncharitable disposition'.[23] The combination of Cowper, Robertson, Weekes and Arnold, with J. F. Hargrave as attorney-general, lasted and, more than that, worked well, for three years—a term longer than that enjoyed without change of personnel by any other ministry during the period of faction government in New South Wales.

Hargrave, like all of Cowper's law officers after Martin, had little influence beyond his own department. The conservative and unco-operative attitude of the New South Wales Bar was a constant problem to the early liberal ministries. Cowper and Forster eased the difficulty of finding suitable men by downgrading the importance of the posts. There were able to do this because, as the *Maitland Mercury* said, most laymen disapproved of the barristers' opposition to a democratically elected government, and the status of the appointments concerned only lawyers.[24] Forster held the opinion that the Crown Law officers should not be political appointees and in June 1858 he brought up a motion to this effect. Robertson opposed this on behalf of the ministry by pointing out that, in the case of permanent, non-political appointees, a government might have to take the advice of law officers who were unsympathetic to it. [25] Cowper repeated this opinion in 1859 [26] and it remained the basis of his policy. Nevertheless, he acted to reduce the power and prestige of the legal officers. Lutwyche replaced Martin as attorney-general, but he remained in the upper house. His successors, L. H. Bayley and Hargrave also went to the upper house, away from the centre of power and the authority of an elected position. [27] Cowper's young protegé, W. B. Dalley, reluctantly took the solicitor-general's office when Lutwyche was promoted, holding it until February 1859. In that month, Cowper forced through the Assembly by one vote resolutions which removed the law officers from the cabinet and placed them under control of the colonial secretary. [28] The immediate purpose of this arrangement was to placate opposition to his appointment of Bayley, who had been in the colony only two months, by ensuring that his actions were subject to Cowper's control. The upper house upset his plans by refusing to sit until the government was represented there by a responsible minister and executive councillor. [29] Cowper was forced to shelve his plans and have Bayley appointed to the Executive Council. When Forster succeeded Cowper as premier he carried out his long-cherished ambition to make the law posts non-political by appointing W. M. Manning and retaining Cowper's solicitor-general, Hargrave, as purely legal officers. The Robertson ministry of 1860 restored the political basis of the law posts, but ran into difficulties when they could find only Hargrave to fill the senior post and no one at all for the solicitor-generalship. The problem was solved by simply leaving the post vacant. Cowper's reliance on men of low standing at the Bar meant that they had little influence in government beyond legal questions. In 1863 he showed that this was a forced arrangement when he persuaded the articulate and prestigious barrister J. B. Darvall to take the attorney-generalship with a seat in the Assembly, but the ministry fell a few weeks later, before Darvall could exert much personal influence on government policy.

Loveday and Martin have shown that Cowper's cabinet of 1857-8 was troubled by the refusal of James Martin to accept the principle of collective responsibility and that this was an important factor in their decision to get rid of him. [30] This principle, strongly advocated by Cowper, was never questioned within his ministries thereafter. By 1860 a definite method of dealing with questions raised at cabinet meetings had been worked out. Robertson explained that every minister had two votes when matters connected with his department came up and, once a question was settled, ministers were all bound to vote on it in the same way unless a clause or bill was specifically left open. [31] This arrangement gave Cowper, as colonial secretary, an automatic advantage, since everything that was not included in the narrow fields of works, lands and direct finance fell within his compass. In practice, he had only to gain the support of one minister to deadlock any issue connected with education, state aid, electoral reform, the Legislative Council, Chinese immigration, police, administration of justice, patronage and the many other administrative and political matters which were dealt with by his department. He could then expect that his personal influence and superior political standing within the cabinet would be enough to give him his way. There are no records of his cabinet meetings, but Cowper's pre-eminence within his governments can be inferred from other sources. The widespread press and public opinion that Cowper was virtually a dictator has been noted. At the same time sections of the press, both friendly and hostile, indirectly conceded that this was not an accurate assessment of Cowper's position by commending the skill with which he blended the various opinions within his cabinet to form a united front. [32]

Robertson, his most eminent colleague, remarked that Cowper held the ministry together by his ability and 'the force of his own character'. [33] In explaining his reasons for asking Cowper to return from retirement to take the colonial secretary's post in his 1860 ministry, Robertson acknowledged that Cowper was the only man who could hold the ministry's parliamentary followers together. [34] A year later Robertson conceded that 'a larger section of this community have confidence in the discretion, in the experience and in the sound judgement of my hon. friend the Colonial Secretary than they have in mine'. [35] Since Robertson clearly recognized the superior standing of Cowper in the cabinet, parliament and the country, it is not surprising that he voluntarily returned the premiership to his old leader at the end of 1860. At that early stage of his long career Robertson, in the words of the *Northern Times*, lacked 'that courtesy, tact and propriety of address, which are of such importance in a Prime Minister'. [36] One of the reasons why Cowper could hold a ministry together and Robertson could not was indirectly illustrated by two incidents which occurred during their country tours. In 1861 Cowper visited Deniliquin, then a hotbed of separationist and anti-government sentiment. [37] A local man, William Edmonds, who had threatened to crack 'one or two little nuts' with Cowper, was included in a deputation to him. After Cowper had dealt with the deputation's complaints in his usual urbane and tactful manner, he turned to Edmonds and remarked, 'Mr. Edmonds, I believe you are the man who said he had "some nuts to crack with me if I came up here"; would you have any objection to crack them now?'[38] 'Great laughter' immediately broke the tension. Two years later, Robertson toured southern areas of the colony. At Goulburn, when a deputation led by the mayor complained that they had not received a fair share of railway finance, Robertson interpreted one of the mayor's remarks as a slur on government integrity. This was denied, but Robertson, 'highly excited', demanded, 'Then what the devil do you mean if you don't mean that?'[39] The mayor retired insulted and the *Sydney Morning Herald* insinuated that Robertson was no gentleman.[40]

Robertson's prominence in the passing of the Land Acts does not counter the evidence that Cowper exerted much the stronger influence in the cabinet. Perhaps the most direct evidence of this point can be seen in the support Cowper's ministers gave to his 1859 education bill and to his viewpoint in the church and school lands question, though it was totally opposed to their own. On occasion, he did not hesitate to·intervene personally in areas which were the responsibility of his colleagues. During a tour of the south and west of New South Wales in 1862 he freely promised land and money grants, roads, bridges and public buildings to local deputations. Arnold's proposed tramway to Windsor was converted by Cowper to a locomotive railway, and in 1863 he bluntly contradicted the gloomy financial picture presented to the Assembly by his new treasurer, T. W. Smart, forcing him to recant. Cowper was no dictator but his ministerial leadership was never in doubt.

Personal friendships helped to consolidate Cowper's position. The editor of the *Maitland Mercury* remarked in 1859 that his early impression that Cowper was insincere had dissolved when he 'found that man after man who joined him in public life for a time, and thus became really qualified to judge, spoke far more highly of him after they had had this personal experience than they had ever done previously'.[41] Cowper's reputation for making and keeping friends extended to his ministers. He and Robertson enjoyed probably the. longest of personal and political friendships during the period of faction government in New South Wales. Richard Jones remained Cowper's warm friend for life and, with Robertson, administered his estate at his death. Weekes remained a loyal supporter after he left the Treasury in 1863. The most direct evidence of the affection which Cowper could inspire in his associates was provided by Hargrave when he agreed to step down from the senior to the junior law post to make way for Darvall. He wrote to Cowper, 'What I have done is only the least return I could make for the unvaried kindness and consideration I have met with from you and your colleagues. I...trust it will strengthen

your hand for the good work before you; and enable you to...govern
this Colony with a firm and happy Government for the rest of your
life'. [42]

Cowper's greatest problems in the exercise of political management
arose within parliament. His reconstruction of the Legislative Council in
1861 turned an obstructionist body into one reasonably responsive to
the will of the government, but management of the Assembly, where
his steady supporters were always a minority, was a constant problem. He
quickly developed a variety of methods to cope with it. The failure
of his first lands and education bills showed clearly that his personal
standing and that of his ministers was not sufficient to force legislation
through the House. Greater subtlety was needed and Cowper developed
appropriate techniques. One was to dangle the carrot of popular legislation, as in the case of the electoral and lands bills. Another, bargaining
and compromise to satisfy the demands of individual members was
most evident in the electoral bill. The education bill of 1863 was a
compromise between the views of various groups within parliament, and
in the case of the church and school lands Cowper successfully postponed
the issue until his successors removed it from parliament to the courts.
In this case too, and in that of the Assembly's attempts to lower the
governor's salary he could be sure that unwelcome legislation would
be rejected by the Legislative Council. In desperate cases Cowper was
prepared to use shock tactics, as in the resignation and reinstatement
of his ministry over Parkes's tea and sugar duties motions. In other
instances he ignored the demands of the majority and used the procedures
of the House to delay embarrassing issues until he felt the government
was strong enough to make a stand.

A notable example of this approach occurred over the duty on the
export of gold. This duty, set at 2s 6d per ounce, was imposed by the
Parker government in 1857 as a replacement for the hated licence
fee. Cowper and most liberals voted against its introduction, and his
ministry did not oppose goldfields member J. D. Wilson when he moved a
resolution for its abolition in 1860. However, the Cowper-Robertson
ministry, wedded as it was to a 'free trade' policy, had few sources of
revenue to replace the duty. [43] Their first attempt to remove it was
blocked by the upper house. When the government also lost in the
upper house a proposal to increase the duty on imported spirits, Weekes
announced that they would have to retain the gold duty for that year. [44]
Wilson replied with a motion that the duty ought not to be levied after.
1861. It passed by 29 votes to 3, with the ministers joining the majority, [45]
but when Cowper's proposal to replace the duty by doubling the 10s
annual fee for a miner's right was rejected by the Assembly, the ministry

was in a dilemma. They had either to accept the loss of badly needed revenue or to renege on their own vote in the face of the great majority of the Assembly. They decided that the duty must stay and took no action. The tireless Wilson returned to the attack on the last day of the year. Weekes's protestations that the government had always been against the duty and would remove it as soon as possible were greeted with cheers and laughter, but the attendance was thin in the Assembly that day and the government managed to withdraw enough of its supporters to have the House counted out before the matter came to a vote. [46] Wilson, unable to have the motion restored to the order paper before the end of the session, withdrew it in disgust.

The ministry knew Wilson would not give up, but the need for the money was imperative. With their popularity at its greatest after the passing of the lands bills, they met Wilson's renewed attempt to abolish the duty in September 1862 with a firm insistence that the money was needed. At the same time, they introduced a bill to reduce the impost gradually to the Victorian level of 1s 6d per ounce. This compromise narrowly won the Assembly's approval, [47] and there the matter rested. The ministry had gained two extra years of the full tax and had managed to establish permanently a source of revenue that they had been committed to abolish.

One of Cowper's most difficult parliamentary problems arose from the need to satisfy the strong anti-Chinese feeling within the colony which came to a head at the Burrangong goldfields in 1861. [48] Cowper did not share this prejudice, but most of the Assembly, including his closest colleague, Robertson, did. Given the state of public feeling, Cowper would have placed his government in jeopardy had he treated the Chinese fairly, as he wished to do. Again, the problem was solved by compromise. Cowper restricted both the intake of Chinese and their freedom of movement on the goldfields. Yet eventually, with the help of his reconstructed Legislative Council, he managed to defeat the more extreme demands of public prejudice.

In response to public uneasiness at the sudden influx of Chinese to New South Wales goldfields in 1858, over 10 000 compared to a mere 220 in 1857, Cowper introduced a very moderate bill imposing a limit of one passenger for every 2 ton displacement of ships which brought Chinese to New South Wales and a landing tax of £3 per head. In doing so he made it clear that he did not intend his measure to be prohibitive and he praised Chinese habits of industry, cleanliness and discipline. [49] Opposition led by Parkes, who demanded a complete ban, forced Cowper to compromise by raising the landing tax to £10 per head. In this form the bill passed the Assembly, only to be rejected by the upper house. Cowper was pleased to let the matter drop and he even sought Chinese support in the 1859 election campaign.[50] The ministry did not oppose John Lucas's abortive attempt to carry a similar bill in 1860, but took no decisive action themselves until they were forced to by the violent Burrangong goldfields riots of February 1861. The cabinet acted firmly and probably wisely in sending a military force to calm the situation and by placing it under the direct control of Cowper.[51] The premier handled the miners with a skilful blend of tact and firmness, agreeing to examine their grievances while insisting that the law must be upheld and the Chinese protected.[52] They gave him a good hearing and he returned to Sydney amid commendation from all sides. 'Even "the enemy", anxious as they are to find fault, find themselves in difficulty', Robertson told him delightedly.[53] But his success at Burrangong led Cowper to overestimate the willingness of the miners to await the slow progress of the law in settling the Chinese problem. In spite of further rumblings of discontent,[54] Cowper recommended within two months of his visit to the Burrangong field that the Executive Council approve the withdrawal of the troops on the ground of expense. Robertson, as the responsible minister, agreed to bring in a bill to confine the Europeans and Chinese to different areas on goldfields, and the Executive Council ordered the troops withdrawn.

Cowper also realized that he must act to curtail further Chinese immigration into New South Wales. Reversing his previous praise of their industry he criticized the Chinese for failing to help develop the country or to supply the labour market, though he declined to join other politicians in abusing them personally.[55] Unluckily for his personal influence, both his immigration restriction bill and goldfields management bill failed in the upper house and the Burrangong miners reacted with renewed attacks on the Chinese. Again the ministry had to send troops and police to restore order. The agitation spread to Sydney where, at two packed meetings, a number of parliamentarians spoke bitterly against the Chinese.[56] At this time Cowper was attending an intercolonial conference in Melbourne, where he learned the details of Victoria's Chinese immigration bill. When the new parliamentary session began in September, he adopted this measure almost unchanged and passed it through the Assembly. The bill aimed to make the carriage of Chinese unprofitable to shipowners and prohibited their naturalization in the colony.[57] Cowper's reconstructed Council approved the measure without major amendments and it duly passed into law, with immediate effect. The numbers of Chinese entering New South Wales dropped from 10 138 in 1858, to 2572 in the following year.

A greater problem was the fate of the Chinese already in New South

Wales. When J. B. Wilson moved to have them excluded from goldfields, Cowper pointed out that such a move was entirely unreasonable and declared that 'it was unmanly in the extreme to treat them in the cruel manner [in which] they had been'. [58] He refused to go further In preparing the bill, Robertson had inserted a clause denying a miner's the segregation of 'aliens' at the discretion of the gold commissioners. [59] In preparing the bill, Robertson had inserted a clause denying a minor's right to all Chinese who entered the colony after 31 July 1862. At Cowper's insistence this provision was removed, but S. W. Gray, usually one of Cowper's supporters, moved successfully to have the Assembly reinstate it. Again the councillors came to Cowper's aid by objecting to the clause, and the Assembly bowed to their wishes. [60] The Chinese continued to work on New South Wales goldfields and for this relatively favourable outcome they owed much to Cowper's social conscience.

However, when faced with strong public prejudice upon issues which involved him in no deep social commitment Cowper was much more ready to give way even at considerable cost to the efficient economic management of the country. This can be seen in the part he played in the passing of the lands bills. The ministry's railway policy provides another example. Cowper never lost his enthusiasm for railways as a vital means of developing the country, or his personal interest in their administration. In 1858 he stressed the 'development' argument in several strong public speeches which made it clear that he was also vitally concerned to maintain Sydney's position as the hub of New South Wales and 'the first city in the Southern Hemisphere'. [61] Denison fully shared his premier's views on railway development, and by late 1858 both were convinced that the construction of the southern line to Albury should be given urgent priority in order to counter the threat of economic and perhaps political dominance of the southern districts by Victoria, then rapidly developing road, rail and Murray River transport links with the Riverina. Nevertheless, as Cowper admitted in 1860, pressure from Assembly members representing electorates in northern and western districts forced the government to allot the large sum raised for railway works equally to the continuation of the northern, western and southern lines. [62] The result was slow construction and falling rail profits. In addition, Victoria had captured so much of the southern trade of New South Wales that, in 1860, Weekes threatened to establish customs houses on the Murray, which led to renewed talk of secession in the affected districts. Faced with this situation, Cowper's ministry decided in 1861 to slow the northern and western railways works and concentrate on the southern line. This decision, promoted by Cowper and Arnold, was opposed by Robertson who claimed that the southern railway 'would only benefit Melbourne'.[63] It was also opposed, furiously, by the western and northern members. Two of them, Henry Rotton and William Cummings, incited their constituents to hold protest meetings, which demanded 'as a matter of common justice mile for mile in the construction of railways, with the other great districts of the colony'.[64] Strengthened by the timely passing of the lands bills, the ministry was able to withstand Rotton's motions condemning them for not continuing this policy, but the continued agitation from the western districts alarmed them. When Cummings moved that £250 000 each should be placed on the supplementary estimates for extension of the northern and western lines, Cowper, Weekes and Robertson all supported it.[65] Arnold's opposition could not prevent the motion from passing, by 23 votes to 7. The government's surrender returned them to the uneconomic three-lines policy and they were forced to seek another £500 000 to finance it.

Of all the methods used by Cowper's government to manage the Assembly, patronage was the one which aroused greatest controversy amongst his contemporaries. The *Sydney Morning Herald* saw patronage as the 'great bond' that held Cowper's supporters together.[66] Between 1856 and 1871, ministries had the power to control all appointments to the public service. In practice, as Loveday suggests, this power was limited by the readiness of the parliamentary and press opponents of the government to raise the cry of corruption.[67] Of necessity, the Donaldson and Parker ministries had to deal with patronage. Supporters pressed them for favours to friends and con-stituents,[68] but there is no evidence that the conservative ministries used patronage to influence a particular parliamentary vote; nor are they known to have 'bought off' enemies in this way. The refinement of patronage as a political tool was left to Cowper. In 1863 he frankly told the Assembly, 'What was the object of placing parliamentary patronage in the hands of a Ministry if it was not that they should bestow it upon their friends...A Ministry could not keep their friends together if it were not for their patronage. So long as they made good appointments to the offices, the Government had a right to consider their friends before others'.[69] The Assembly received this statement with equanimity. The principle stated in the last sentence was well recognized by members, though it did not prevent the opposition from seeking to make political capital out of government appointments.

Cowper's opponents found their strongest case for criticism in his use of patronage to remove potential opponents. This could involve the judicious timing of an offer to affect a particular vote, as in the case of G. K. Holden's appointment to the Titles Office. At times an alert opposition could greatly embarrass the government over such opportunistic manoeuvres. In February 1859 Cowper was trying to pass through the Assembly a bill to reconstitute the ministry. At the same time, after meeting with four refusals from other men, Cowper had decided to offer a vacant district judgeship to Robert Owen, a solicitor and M.L.A. for East Camden. Owen usually opposed the ministry. Knowing that the Assembly was fairly evenly divided on the proposed reconstruction of the ministry, the premier let Owen know on the night before the vote was due that he was being considered for the position though, 'not wishing to compromise Owen in the House', he claimed, Cowper did not actually offer it to him. [70] Owen, thoroughly compromised, voted with the ministry. This might have passed unnoticed had not the alert and vindictive J. H. Plunkett induced Owen to deny, prior to the vote, that such an offer had been made to him, and had not the government won the division by a single vote. When Owen's elevation to the judgeship was announced a few days later, Plunkett moved for a select committee to examine the matter. Backed by the conservatives and a group of liberals dismayed at the suggestion of government corruption, he had his way. Most of the committee were Cowper's enemies. 'He could hardly believe himself in the company of gentlemen', fumed Cowper when they questioned him. [71] Their report implied that both Cowper and Owen had lied in giving evidence, and condemned their course as 'highly dangerous to the integrity and independence of this House, and to the liberties of the people'. [72] Cowper, his popularity high after the passing of the Electoral Act, mustered his supporters and defeated Plunkett's attempt to have the Assembly adopt the report, but the incident damaged his political reputation.

On a broader level than was involved in the Holden and Owen cases, there were opportunities to remove opponents who felt the financial pinch of being unpaid members. Henry Parkes was the most notable of these. His co-operation with Cowper lasted until the latter was firmly established in office in late 1857. Thereafter the close bond between the two men began to dissolve. By the time Parkes returned to the Assembly as one of Cowper's fellow-members for East Sydney in June 1859, he was prepared to oppose the ministry openly. Two days after the session opened, his tea and sugar duties motions brought Cowper temporarily down. The estrangement from his old political friend probably owed much to Parkes's ambition. Cowper's attitude in forming his 1856 government had shown Parkes that the new premier was not willing to consider him for a place in the ministry. He may have believed unfounded rumours spread by Martin, W. B. Allen and others that Cowper wanted to keep him from regaining control of the *Empire,* and the death of Robert Campbell broke a long-lasting link in the chain of friendsḥip. When the ministry offered him the post oí collector of customs at £1200 a year, at a time in 1858 when he was bankrupt and living on borrowed money, Parkes refused in the belief that Cowper and Robertson were trying to remove him from political life. [73] By 1861 the ministry had greater cause to wish him out of the way. By then he had clearly shown himself to be the most able man amongst the troublesome 'ultra-liberals'. Parkes made his own removal easy. Financially pressed and wishing to revisit his homeland, he moved, in May 1861, for two immigration lecturers to be sent to England. His obvious hope of being appointed to one of these posts was realized. [74] Cowper and Robertson were delighted to send him off with a salary of £1000 a year and he did not reappear in the Assembly until mid-1864.

Loveday has noted that Joseph Chambers, elected as an anti-ministerial candidate at the 1859 elections, was bought off by Cowper with the appointment of crown prosecutor shortly afterwards. [75] The case of James Hoskins, M.L.A. for Goldfields North from 1859 to 1863, provides an example of a friend bought off when he turned to an enemy. Hoskins, a miner, supported Cowper until he was antagonized by the reconstruction of the Legislative Council in 1861. As an opponent thereafter he made a nuisance of himself during the 1862 session, but he had no financial resources of his own, relying on the promise of his constituents to pay him a salary, and such payment proved to be highly irregular. In February 1863 he accepted from Cowper a post as superintendent of minor roads at a salary of £350 a year. [76]

As Cowper so bluntly stated in 1863, the ministry used patronage extensively to keep its friends together. Loveday has estimated that between 1856 and 1870, twenty-two men who had held Assembly seats accepted offices of profit under the Crown. [77] Cowper's ministers appointed the majority of these, on a scale which varied according to the social and political standing of each man and the services he had rendered. Lutwyche and Hargrave were each appointed judges of the Supreme Court, in 1859 and 1865 respectively. Dalley received his reward for loyal service by joining Parkes as immigration lecturer in England. Between 1860 and 1863 at least nine other Cowper-Robertson supporters in the Assembly resigned to take government appointments. Not all were needy men. Barrister I. J. Blake, who became a district court judge in 1861, and A. Dick, appointed solicitor to the examiner of titles in 1862, took advantage of the chance to better themselves in their professions, but some were in desperate need. In 1861 it was said that David Buchanan had begged a government post of Arnold, minister for works, and that when Arnold could not find one for him, the irrepressible Buchanan had refused to leave the minister's office until given a shilling to go on with. [78] The tale is probably apocryphal, but Buchanan was bankrupt when Cowper gave him a minor works position in 1863.

Legal appointments, police, lands and works provided the posts, and most were awarded in 1862 and early 1863, [79] when the ministry felt that its position in the House was secure. Other ways could be found to reward followers who remained in the Assembly. The Parker ministry in 1857 had appointed barristers to act as crown prosecutors at country circuit courts, on occasions when neither the attorney-general nor the solicitor-general could be present. Cowper, with only one legal officer for much of the time, expanded this system. He had little chance to favour his friends, since, apart from the official law officers, Dalley was possibly the only barrister who supported him, but Dalley's junior status at the bar did not prevent him from obtaining a share of this lucrative government business. [80] In the preparation of criminal prosecutions, Cowper exercised a more direct influence, since, as the *Empire* pointed out, he had ultimate control over the selection of solicitors who were given this work by the inspector-general of police. This newspaper claimed that R. H. M. Forster, who 'invariably' voted with the government, had received all of this work from November 1862 to July 1863. 'The manipulation of members of Parliament has almost arrived at the dignity of science', commented the editor with glum resignation. [81] Cowper easily defeated opposition attempts to deprive Forster of his seat for taking government employment, but he did not deny the exercise of patronage.

In addition to salaried posts the government had under its control appointments to the unpaid magistracy. The position of justice of the peace was then one of considerable distinction and was keenly sought after. Cowper made full use of the ministry's powers of appointment to garner support amongst the legislators and the electors. When he came to office in 1857 there were 813 names on the Register of Justices. By October 1863 he had added 791 new men, [82] including at least 15 parliamentarians, nearly all of whom were Cowper supporters at the time of the appointment.

A well-placed supporter of the Cowper ministry could hope to gain favours for friends and relatives. Cowper himself led the way by appointing his son Charles in 1861 as clerk of the Executive Council at £600 a year, and he was suspected of helping his half-brother, W. M. Cowper, to obtain the sinecure appointment of dean of St Andrew's Cathedral. [83] Robertson, Weekes and Arnold all used their influence to aid relatives in the public service. [84] Loveday records the intercession of Parkes with Cowper in 1857 on behalf of E. J. Hawksley and veteran liberal journalist E. S. Hall. [85] Cowper found government posts for both. A letter of Arnold's shows that he was willing to find a position in the Works Department for a man recommended by R. T. Jamison, [86] and William, brother of one of Cowper's strongest supporters, Joseph Eckford, was appointed a justice of the peace, allegedly at the latter's request. [87] Cowper's opponents claimed that over-generous compensation for land taken from his parliamentary supporters for railways and public works was paid and that members were bribed by promises of various public works for their districts. This was the 'Gospel of St. Cowper' according to the *Border Post,* [88] but firm evidence is lacking.

It is clear that Cowper made considerable political use of the variety of patronage open to him, but the experience of his governments bears out Loveday's contention that his contemporaries did not think inefficiencies in the public service were caused by patronage. [89] Opposition attempts to censure him on the issue were defeated decisively. The press grumbled at 'corruption' but did not impute inefficiency. In all the controversy over Owen, no one suggested that he was not suitable for a judge's position. Conservative objections to Lutwyche's appointment to the Supreme Court were based, not on his legal standing, but on the unsuitability of his wife for life in the upper strata of society: she was said to have been his mistress and to have borne him children out of wedlock. [90] In 1859 the *Empire* complained that Cowper had appointed so many justices of the peace that 'one could scarcely throw a stone in the street, without knocking down a Justice', [91] but when he first took office, there was a constant chorus of complaint from the country press that existing magistrates failed to attend to their duties. Cowper sent out a circular demanding that justices either attend the courts or resign. [92] When this had little effect he appointed a flood of new men. The liberal press found little to grumble at in his appointments and recorded their satisfaction that Cowper had broken the hold of the large landowners on the magistracy by appointing professional men and tradespeople to the posts. [93] In 1861 the *Sydney Morning Herald* remarked that, 'reckless as he [Cowper] may have seemed in... patronage ...we have heard of convenient appointments he has absolutely refused to make', [94] and two years later the same paper considered that his government would not have fallen had he not refused patronage pressed on him by his supporters. [95]

In spite of the political uses of patronage, most appointees to the magistracy and to minor government posts were not relatives or friends of politicians, simply because of the numbers involved. Surviving records of the colonial secretary's office bear out the contention of the *Southern Cross* that 'every Minister will bear testimony that his application book [for public service appointments] is full to overflowing'.[96] In some instances local opinion provided a guide in sifting the mass of applications, but the lack of a coherent political organization to support the ministry in country areas meant that many appointments were distributed haphazardly.

Cowper was sharply conscious of the government's lack of direct political influence in the outer districts of the colony, and to counter this, he began a series of ministerial tours of these areas in 1861, during the parliamentary recess. His visit to the southwest of the colony in that year has been noted. In 1862 he undertook a long and exhausting tour of the southern and western areas, which was followed up by Robertson and Charles Cowper Jnr in 1863. Wherever they went, the ministers met local deputations, listened to their grievances, promised to rectify them and granted public lands and works as freely as they dared. To a people who measured their support for the government by the amount of public money spent in the district, this form of ministerial patronage was very acceptable. As a Deniliquin citizen told his fellow-townsmen in 1862, Cowper's politics were immaterial: 'All they had to think of was to get the most out of him that they could.'[97] The only problem was, as the *Goulburn Herald* remarked, that in trying to propitiate the country districts with public works the government allowed its expenditure to exceed its income. Thus, said the editor, 'we take the revenue as far as it will go, and then make up the deficiency by borrowing'.[98] This remark virtually summarized government financial policy during Cowper's years of power, and the result of it provided the main impetus to his fall in 1863.

As proclaimed free-traders, Cowper's ministers were in no position to expand customs dues, the main source of government income, and few parliamentarians approved of direct taxation. The leading secondary source of government income, land sales, fell below expectations each year from 1859 to 1861. Weekes was probably right in attributing this to public uncertainty while the struggle for the lands bills was in progress,[99] but the passing of this legislation did not help to fill the Treasury as the ministry had hoped. After a rise in receipts with the first rush of selectors to the land in 1862, a steep fall took place in 1863,[1] when the ministry's need was greatest. The railways provided another major problem. They were the source of the government's greatest capital expenditure, were urgently demanded by the people and, as Cowper recognized, good communications were essential to the success of land selection.[2] Yet the uneconomic three-lines policy meant that returns from them remained low while capital expenditure soared. [3] The Cowper ministries filled the gap in revenue by turning to the London capital market. They were lucky in finding there buoyant conditions and ready acceptance of New South Wales debentures from 1858 to 1864. Even so, Weekes as treasurer became notorious for filling budget deficits by counting unspent votes from previous years as 'savings' and adding them to current receipts. Some newspapers expressed uneasiness at the growing public debt, [4] but the financial issue was submerged until 1863 by the tide of popular legislation.

Paradoxically, the ministry's financial and political difficulties were increased by moves they made in 1861 and 1862 for greater administrative efficiency. Before this time they had been too occupied with politics to pay much attention to the functioning of the public service. Late in 1861 the pressure of urgent legislation began to ease and Cowper, as the responsible minister, moved to reorganize the New South Wales police force on a centralized basis. In 1852 he had supported the retention of the old police system whereby local magistrates controlled the appointment of constables for their areas. [5] When he introduced his bill in November 1861 he admitted a change of mind, declaring his belief that central control would give greater efficiency. He also conceded that it meant greater expense. [6] His measure proposed to divide the colony into nine police districts with a hierarchy of foot and mounted police in each. Opposition speakers objected on the grounds that there was no public demand for the change, that it would put more patronage in the hands of the ministry and that it would increase the expense of law enforcement. But the great majority of members felt, with the *Sydney Morning Herald,* that it was a much-needed reform [7] and they paid no heed to what Cowper called 'the ravings of 2 or 3 noisy Members who did not know what they were talking about'. [8] The bill passed with ease. Thus in 1862 the basis of the modern New South Wales police force came into being. Unfortunately for Cowper, its formation coincided with a new and prolonged upsurge in bushranging offences, which the new force failed to suppress. It was unlikely that the old force could have done better, but the issue was useful to the opposition in their attempts to undermine government support.

Cowper was more fortunate in another important reform which he undertook at that time, the introduction of the South Australian Torrens system of registering land titles. Registration under the old laws was so costly and complicated that it presented a barrier to selectors under the Land Acts. Cowper had foreseen this problem and early in 1862 chaired a select committee which considered the matter. Torrens himself came to Sydney at Cowper's invitation and outlined his system to the committee. Cowper and his fellow-members were instant converts and few objected when Torrens titles entered the law of New South Wales in August 1862. The system was a great success, but the government's enemies were able to cry 'corruption' over the appointment of Holden and Dick to the legal posts in the new Titles Office.

The 1862 session had gone well for the ministry. 'The power of the Government in the Assembly is now...great & is extending so that we could always command support on reasonable laws', [9] boasted Cowper to James Macarthur in October of that year. The looming problems of public finance and bushranging seemed to be more than offset by the continuing disunity of the parliamentary oppositionists. Of their potential leaders, Parkes was in England, Murray had gone to the presidency of the Legislative Council, Hay, with no conservative party to back him, had abandoned active opposition for the speakership of the Assembly, and men like Wilson and Piddington, most active against the ministry in 1861 and 1862, had no following. Forster, well described by the *Empire* as 'hard-grained and knotty like a piece of wrinkled red-gum that will splinter rather than unbend', [10] had demonstrated during 1859—60 that he could not hold followers together. Only Martin remained. In 1859 he had recognized the need to build a coherent group as an alternative to the Cowper government, [11] but his declared intention to form one was frustrated by his own personality. During the early years of responsible government Martin was, in the words of his biographer, 'too confident in his own judgement, too direct and uncompromising to gather any great following'. [12] He openly opposed free trade, manhood suffrage, the ballot, the ending of state aid to religion, and free selection before survey. The last of these lost him his seat in the Assembly at the 1860 election and he was not able to return to parliamentary life until June 1862.

Martin gained an important ally when Geoffrey Eager, once Forster's minister for works, won a West Sydney seat in January 1863. The opposition to Cowper gathered further strength when two avowed opponents of the ministry, James Buchanan and Allan MacPherson, gained seats a few months later. It is difficult to estimate what success Martin had achieved in building the nucleus of a new faction before the 1863 session opened in June, but it could not have been great. In July, when he and Eager tried to censure the ministry over crime and the use of patronage, their motions were rejected by two-thirds majorities. The *Sydney Morning Herald* commented sardonically that the result was known before the debate started [13] and that Cowper was safe 'while the opposition is but an array of resentments and antipathies, adverse to him, but not less adverse to each other'. [14]

Cowper's new treasurer, T. W. Smart, gave the opposition a new
chance to pull together when he made his first financial statement
on 3 September. Smart, a wealthy businessman, had been an associate of
Cowper in politics, the church and the Sydney Railway Company in the
early 1850s. When Weekes, afflicted with failing eyesight, resigned the
Treasury in March 1863, Cowper induced Smart to replace him in the
hope that his high reputation as a financier would strengthen the
ministry. The appointment was indeed greeted with general approval, [15]
but Smart was an orthodox financier, not a politician, and he was
horrified at the deficit financing of his predecessor. Cowper made the
mistake of allowing him a free hand in his financial proposals. To the
consternation of his colleagues he told the Assembly that a deficit of
£440 000 existed in the public accounts and outlined plans to cover
this debt with a wide rantge of increased customs duties and a doubling of
the rate of postage of letters. [16] The press was shocked at the staggering
size of the public debt thus suddenly revealed. [17] So were uncommitted
members of the Assembly, and Eager seized the chance to bring down a
censure motion on finance. In a hasty attempt to mend his fences,
Cowper virtually contradicted his treasurer by claiming that, as in
previous years, the actual deficit would be negligible because of 'savings'
from unused votes. Smart's later remarks on the budget showed that
Cowper had made him toe the standard ministerial line. He assured the
Assembly that 'savings' and underestimation of receipts would reduce
the deficit to the point where he could afford to abandon the proposed
new duties. [18] He may well have been right. For all the furore over
the issue, no clear picture of the state of public finances ever emerged,
but public and parliamentary confidence in the ministry's financial
management had been badly shaken.

There were other issues which helped to sap Cowper's strength. The
opposition fired criticism at the police, magisterial appointments,
government patronage and Cowper's failure to settle the matter of
border duties with Victoria. [19] Cowper was so shaken by the attacks
on his new police force that he temporarily lost his usual common
sense, in reading to the Assembly a telegram he had sent to
Inspector-General McLerie, accusing his men of drunkenness and
cowardice and threatening to organize another force to supersede
them. [20] The acquisition of Darvall by the ministry in August, meant
to strengthen the government, may have weakened it instead, by
increasing suspicions that Cowper was moving towards conservatism.
Darvall publicly blamed the Land Acts for the ministry's financial
problems; Robertson contradicted him, and this did not help matters
either. [21] The *Sydney Morning Herald* also suggested that some members

of the Assembly were disgruntled at Cowper's refusal of patronage. [22]
Here, as in other matters, he was caught in that trap between public
demands for expenditure and public resentment of taxation which
troubled all faction governments in New South Wales.

Eager's finance motion was rejected by one vote, but Thomas Garrett,
the ministry's unofficial 'whipper-in' then allowed a government
supporter, E. C. Close, to leave the chamber without arranging a
'pair' for the vote which followed on the first item of the estimates,
traditionally a test of government support in the House. Consequently
the division was equal and the chairman of committees, Robert
Wisdom gave his casting vote against the ministry, [23] ironically for
Cowper, who had procured for Wisdom the chairman's appointment
two years earlier as a reward for his support of the government. The
next day the ministry resigned. Thus came to an end the six-year period
during which, in Forster's words, Cowper was the most powerful man in
the country and the only one able to form a party. [24]

8

Troubled Years 1864–1870

From the fall of his ministry in 1863, Cowper's political fortunes began to decline. Twice more he headed governments, but never again was he thought to be unchallenged as the colony's leader. In part this was due to the rise of rival factions ably led by Parkes and Martin. Declining revenues and an untimely shrinkage of the British capital market hindered him and he lost the services of his most tried and able colleagues at critical times, in some cases, ironically, because of the system of patronage which he had done so much to promote. He paid the penalty, too, for decades of concentration upon politics to the detriment of his property interests; for a time, near-bankruptcy forced him out of parliament altogether. Lastly he seems to have become less flexible with increasing age, less able to adapt his policies to the new situations he faced during the 1860s.

Cowper and his ministers were furious at their 1863 defeat. Arnold harangued the pleasure-seekers at Sydney's mayoral picnic on the iniquities of his political opponents, threatening to retaliate in full for the obstructionism which had plagued the outgoing ministry. Outwardly Cowper and Robertson accepted their defeat more graciously; inwardly they seethed. Their first chance at revenge came when Martin, the new premier, returned to his constituency of Orange for ministerial re-election. At that time the Cowper faction had a strong political organization in the area and Charles Cowper Jnr was quickly persuaded to resign his Tumut seat and contest Orange with Martin. Young Cowper won, but his action displeased the forsaken electors of Tumut. Martin immediately stood for and won the vacant seat. Balked in their attempt to deprive the incoming administration of its head, the Cowper faction settled down to the tactics of harassment and attrition which were fast becoming the standard procedure of the 'outs' under faction government.

Martin's appointment of the pompous 'Betsy' Eagar as finance minister gave his opponents scope for ridicule. Cowper revealed that Eagar, without consulting his colleagues, had offered him a post in a coalition ministry, and Cowperite wit J. A. Cunneen told the Assembly how Eagar, passing a flower garden tended by a girl, had asked for a flower and her name. When she replied 'Miss Smith', Eagar (according to Cunneen) said, 'perhaps you would desire to know in return upon whom you have bestowed the favour — I will tell you. I am not a Mr. Brown, a Mr. Jones, or a Mr. Smith — I am the Finance minister of New South Wales'.[1] The whole House roared but, as Robertson had discovered when he lost a censure motion against Eagar's financial statement by 27 votes to 11,[2] most members were determined to give the ministers a chance to develop their policies before passing judgement on them.

The formation of the Martin ministry confused the previous tendency of the more conservative elements in the Assembly to move closer to Cowper and of the 'radicals' to oppose him. Martin, his solicitor-general Faucett and secretary for public works Holroyd were considered to be conservatives, but the colonial secretary Forster and secretary for lands J. B. Wilson clearly belonged to the 'radical' section of the Assembly. In addition, Martin and Eagar had strong protectionist leanings, while Wilson and Forster were proclaimed free-traders. This coalition held together for fifteen months and in doing so undercut the basis on which new parties might have formed, either on liberal/conservative or protectionist/free-trade lines. Moreover, Martin, for all his earlier horror at Cowper's 'corrupt' political management, found himself obliged to govern by precisely the same methods. Personal loyalties and interests remained the basis of politics.

Impressed by the urgency of the colony's financial problem, Eagar persuaded his reluctant free-trade colleagues to sanction a wide range of new tax levies, including a system of *ad valorem* duties on imports. This step towards protectionism alarmed the merchants and, backed by almost the whole colonial press, they formed a Free Trade Association to whip up public sentiment against Eagar's proposals. Some sections of working-men saw protection for their jobs in taxing imports and they turned out to disrupt association meetings — to no avail. Sentiment in the Assembly, where it counted most, ran strongly for free trade. Cowper and those who had formed his ministry were free-traders to a man and they used the issue as a rallying point against Eagar in the Assembly. Daunted by the outcry, Eagar watered down his proposals and put the bill to the Assembly. Cowper's exuberant follower Thomas Garrett tried to have the legislation entitled 'A bill to cripple the commerce of the city, and transfer its trade to Victoria and Queenland', only to be drowned out by concerted roars of 'fire' and 'hear, hear' from the government benches.[3] Weeks of wrangling followed, until the upper house rejected almost the entire bill. Desperately, the government turned to retrenchment and the raising of more overseas loans. Still the financial position continued to grow worse: in May 1864 it was freely said that the government accounts were £48 000 overdrawn. [4] Yet the general feeling persisted that the Martin government had not been fairly tried, and the opposition leaders knew it. Parliament had been in session since June 1863 and Cowper and Robertson could neglect their property interests no longer. Weeks before the session ended in April 1864 both had abandoned the Assembly's acrimonious debates to attend to their personal affairs. Almost Cowper's last act of the session was to push through his superannuation bill for public servants.

Public dissatisfaction with the Martin ministry grew sharply during the parliamentary recess. The deficit continued to grow. Mad Morgan, Ben Hall and Co. still robbed the mails and roamed the back country at will. 'Corruption!' cried the newspapers and speakers at public meetings when the government revised the magisterial lists and appointed its friends to the public service, [5] and the press complained that Martin's ministers were mere puppets in the hands of their leader. [6] Cowper must surely have spared a wry smile at the familiarity of all this, but he made the most of the chance thus presented by moving a censure motion on the first day of the new session in October. The ensuing wrangle showed the growing dissatisfaction of members with the government's performance, and Arnold, with his usual mastery of invective, whipped up such an atmosphere of suspicion against Holroyd on an unproved corruption charge that the humiliated minister resigned his office. The ministry went to its doom when Henry Parkes, newly re-elected to the House, and his infant faction joined the Cowper group and dissident independents to pass censure on the government. As Martin sourly noted, eight men who had voted to oust Cowper only a year earlier, voted in turn to oust him (Martin). [7]

Instead of resigning, the ministry adjourned the House while Martin cautiously explored the possibilities of coalition with either Parkes or Cowper. The *Empire* speculated hopefully on the prospect of a Cowper-Parkes combination, a revival of 'the old liberal party', as a correspondent put it. [8] It seems that Parkes did contemplate that prospect and that Robertson favoured it, [9] but Cowper felt he did not need either Parkes or Martin and held aloof, whereupon Martin, choosing the alternative to resignation, persuaded Sir John Young to grant him a dissolution.

The public saw the Martin ministry as protectionist; the opposition took a free-trade stance and the tariff issue dominated the election campaign. The result was complete triumph for the Cowper faction.

Cowper topped the East Sydney poll, Robertson that of West Sydney, and all eight Sydney seats went to their faction, to the exclusion of Martin, Forster and Eagar. Martin's supporters barely managed to win enough   seats outside Sydney to preserve their faction core in the Assembly. [10] The premier himself tried a second time for Tumut, only to be soundly beaten by his old nemesis, Charles Cowper Jnr. He eventually scrambled home in a pastoral seat, Forster in another, but Eagar failed dismally to take Arnold's seat of Paterson and remained outside the Assembly. On the first day of the new session, 27 January 1865, Cowper forced the resignation of the ministry, and Young commissioned him to form a new one. Superficially, Cowper appeared to be in a strong position. Upon the election results, opponents of Martin in the Assembly outnumbered supporters by nearly 2 to 1, [11] yet the balance of power still lay with 'independents', and Cowper well knew the fickleness of their support. In reality his prospects in 1865 were distinctly unpromising. The bushranging problem was unresolved. Cowper had bequeathed a difficult financial problem to Martin, and Martin had returned it, worsened, to him. The early rush of selectors to the land had subsided and with it the land revenues. Customs revenue too was down and Eagar had panicked the shaky London loan market by dumping upon it £230 000 worth of government debentures which had failed to sell in New South Wales. Cowper knew he would have to resort to greater taxes or severe retrenchment, both of which were certain to be highly unpopular. Moreover, he had not the funds to support liberal distribution of patronage, or the promise of popular social legislation to divert public attention as in former years. Most important of all, Martin had used a year in power to build a firm faction core which would form the basis of a stronger opposition than any Cowper had previously encountered.

Given his urgent need to build a strong ministry, press assumptions that Cowper would invite Parkes to join [12] seemed logical, but, after hesitating for a week, he finally re-entered office with his old team intact. The distrust which Cowper and Parkes felt for one another had re-emerged when Parkes returned from England in 1863. Cowper hoped to buy his ever-impecunious rival out of politics with the inspectorate of prisons and, according to Parkes, tried through inter-mediaries to induce him to ask for the post. Parkes in turn tried to have Cowper offer it to him directly, with the. obvious hope of crying 'bribery' as he refused it. Each was too shrewd to fall into the other's trap. This was part farce, but real bitterness followed in August 1863 when Parkes stood against Darvall at his ministerial re-election for the East Maitland seat. Darvall was outragged, for he had generously helped Parkes with his law studies. The campaign was bitter and Cowper, whose attitude to Parkes had never previously exceeded exasperation, denounced his conduct as 'black ingratitude to those who have so long and so persistently befriended him'. [13] The miscreant himself admitted in later years that he had been 'indiscreet' in opposing Darvall. [14] Even had Cowper not allowed past quarrels to stand in the way of political advantage, it would have been difficult to seat Parkes and Darvall in the same cabinet. Still, in failing to negotiate with Parkes, Cowper showed that he underestimated the calibre of the man and the extent of his following.

Apart from neglect of Parkes, Cowper's cabinet choice was prudent. Robertson, his trusted friend, still rode the wave of popularity created by the Land Acts. Arnold, arrogant and casual as he sometimes appeared in his ministerial role, was still, in the words of Sir John Young, 'one of the ablest if not the ablest minister and most powerful debater in the State'. [15] In his legal appointments Cowper simply had no choice and was glad to reappoint Darvall and Hargrave. The reasons for Smart's restoration to the Treasury were less obvious. He had shown little political sense, less speaking ability and he carried a suspected taint of protectionism. But competent financiers were scarce in parliament. Furthermore, Cowper had found, as Robertson, Parkes and other faction leaders were later to do, that penury was the price they paid for power. The demands of government left little time for personal affairs. Weekends with his family at Wivenhoe became a rarity for Cowper, and seldom indeed could be visit his more distant lands. His official salary kept him barely solvent until he lost office in 1863. A year later Wivenhoe was mortgaged for more than £4000, Cowper could not pay the interest, and in December 1864 the mortgager moved to sell the estate. Cowper's friends tried to save the home for his family by opening a subscription list, but time was short and Smart stepped in, paying out the mortgage personally on the understanding that he would be reimbursed from the proceeds of the public appeal. Thus matters stood when Cowper formed his government two months later. In the circumstances it is hardly surprising that Smart again received the Treasury.

The new ministry began well. Their nominee, Thomas Garrett, deposed Robert Wisdom (whose turncoat vote in 1863 had lost them office), from the chairmanship of committees. They tackled boldly the chronic problem of bushranging. Martin, critic though he had been of Cowper's centralized police force, had recognized its potential superiority over the old system by retaining it virtually unchanged when he came to power, but his shilly-shallying half-measures, concentrating more police in disturbed districts and increasing rewards, had little effect on bushranging. When Cowper resumed the government, all the well-known gangs (those of Ben Hall, Connell and the Clarke brothers) were still free, as was the bloodthirsty lone hand Morgan. Within a few days of the Assembly's meeting, Darvall brought up a felon's apprehension bill which authorized blood money rewards and the shooting on sight of declared outlaws. More important, perhaps, the bill provided for draconian penalties against those who harboured or abetted them — confiscation of all property and up to fifteen years in gaol. Aghast, Martin, Forster and J. B. Wilson protested that such measures were inimical to British law and civil liberties, but the mood of parliament and people matched that expressed by the *Sydney Morning Herald:* 'We do not like such a law, but we prefer it to crime triumphant.'[16] The bill, limited in its operation to one year, passed easily into law. Within twelve. months Morgan, Hall and his chief henchmen, Gilbert and Dunn, had all been shot or hanged. Luck and the increasing efficiency of the police bore heavily on this result, but Cowper claimed and received much credit for checking the bushranging menace. Significantly, Martin renewed the Felon's Apprehension Act for a further year when he came to power in 1866.

It was the government's misfortune that Cowper failed to be equally decisive in dealing with his main problem, the colony's financial deficit. Sir John Young advised him to bring in a 'firm and full' financial policy immediately and stake his ministry's existence on it. [17] With land revenues sagging, the loan market weak, and extensive resort to customs duties ruled out by his free-trade stance, Cowper had, it seemed, no alternative to direct taxation if he was to reverse the plunge into public debt. Parliamentarians, overwhelmingly representative of the middle classes upon whom the main burden of direct taxation could be expected to fall, detested the thought of it. Twice in 1864 the Assembly had emphatically rejected proposals by Darvall which aimed at endorsing the principle of an income tax.[18] Yet Cowper might well have carried it a year later. The electorate had voted decisively against Martin's tinkering with the Custom House; press and public were shocked by Smart's revelation that the deficit had doubled under the Martin regime;[19] even the Assembly members showed clear signs that old attitudes were changing under the threat of insolvency. When the ever-bumptious David Buchanan tried in May 1865 to pass again the motion rescinding the duty on gold, which had caused Cowper so much trouble in 1861 and 1862, it was rejected, at the instance of Parkes, by an overwhelming majority.[20] Parliament would have found it difficult to refuse at least a temporary measure of

direct taxation, and Cowper did, at first, plan for an income tax.
Yet finally, as Young remarked acidly, he 'chose to temporise'. [21]
Apart from a small rise in stamp duties and some modest pruning of the
previous year's estimates, Smart's budget proposed only to cast more
debentures on the London market. As Cowper had intended, these
measures offended no one very greatly, but they did not solve the
financial problem either, being based on highly optimistic revenue
estimates. Though land revenues rose as the selectors of 1862 made
the final payments on their land, other revenues languished. The
government's overdraft soared at the Bank of New South Wales, the
bank demanded an immediate reduction and, to make matters worse,
the stubborn parochialism of the Assembly members brought about
the rejection of a financially advantageous plan for sharing Murray
River revenues which Cowper, Darvall and Smart had laboriously
worked out with the Victorian ministers. There was no alternative
to new revenue-raising measures and, within two months of his first
budget, Cowper introduced a second one. Had he tried direct taxation,
even at this stage, he might have kept the initiative in the Assembly.
Instead, he raised some levies on imports. Possibly he hoped that the
limited scale of the measures proposed would make them widely
acceptable, as his earlier budget had been. Almost certainly a majority
of his ministers disliked direct taxation. But to take up what was virtually
the policy of his opponents was a mistake surprising in a politician
of Cowper's experience and shrewdness. In this case his penchant for
compromise and conciliation, so often a source of strength to his
governments, brought disaster. The Martin faction, delighted at the
turn of events, patronizingly allowed the measures to pass and the
government staggered to the end of the parliamentary session under an
avalanche of abuse from former friends.

Tired and ill, Darvall resigned his seat and left for England. His
loss, enough of a blow to Cowper, was worsened when Fagar won the
resultant by-election for East Sydney after campaigning on the premier's
alleged desertion of his principles. At the same time a Supreme Court
judgeship fell vacant and Hargrave prudently decided that the time
was right for him to leave politics for a safer field. He asked for the
post and, considering the long and loyal service he had given, Cowper
could not deny it to him. Bereft of both his law officers and berated
for his 'petty and shifting course of policy', [22] Cowper strove urgently
to strengthen his position during the parliamentary recess. His name
was still anathema to the senior members of the Bar. Both Edward
Butler and W. M. Manning refused the attorney-generalship, and this
vital post was filled only when Young, allowing his friendship with

Cowper to override his vice-regal impartiality, persuaded Plunkett to take it. Thus were old enemies publicly reconciled, but, as Plunkett told a surprised James Macarthur, his feud with Cowper had died years before [23] — which says much for the tolerance of both men. Cowper next induced Martin's formidable colleague, Peter Faucett, to leave politics in favour of a judgeship. 'We may congratulate the country on the appointment of a really .competent judge', commented the *Freeman's Journal* ironically, 'and Mr. Cowper on having satisfactorily disposed of an opponent.' [24] However, a bid to lure W. C. Windeyer away from Parkes by offering him the solicitor-generalship failed and, more seriously, so did renewed efforts to neutralize the growing menace of Parkes himself. He refused first the still-vacant inspectorate of prisons and then Cowper's offer of cabinet rank as postmaster-general. Robertson, still eager for alliance with Parkes, pressed Cowper to offer him 'something better', [25] for the popular lands minister, sliding towards bankruptcy through a wild venture into stocking Queensland's gulf country with sheep, had to resign from parliament to salvage what he could of his personal fortunes. Immediately his electors renominated and re-elected him unopposed, but he was too hard-pressed to re-enter the ministry. Still, Cowper does not seem to have appreciated the value of Parkes's support and made no overtures to him. Instead he reshuffled the ministerial offices. Smart moved to the works portfolio and Arnold to lands. Saul Samuel, treasurer in Forster's ministry of 1859-60, became treasurer to his old enemy Cowper, Plunkett retained the senior law post, and the postmaster-generalship went to J. A. Cunneen. 'Bill Cunning' [26] had been an undistinguished follower of Cowper for some years, but he was a Catholic and Cowper probably hoped his appointment to the ministry would attract support from his co-religionists. Some of them however made it clear that they thought Cunneen a fool. [27]

The reconstituted cabinet faced the Assembly for the first time on 24 October. Within a week the speaker John Hay, in ill-health, resigned the chair and Arnold stood for the post. As with Hargrave, Cowper could not deny his colleague the reward of faithful service. Even the opposition helped vote Arnold into the chair, thus tacitly acknowledging both his fitness for the position and their pleasure at the prospect of being no longer flayed by his tongue. Rather than weaken the ministry further by placing a new man in the lands post, Cowper decided to add the duties to his own until Robertson could settle his affairs and return to the ministry.

The financial problem was now worse than ever. Debenture sales were slow and government revenue ran £200 000 below expectations at the end of September. Cowper, returning to an old dream, cautiously floated a suggestion that remote Crown lands of poor quality might be sold at a cheap price to aid the revenues. A section of the liberal press cried in outrage at this attempt to overthrow those bastions of liberty, the Land Acts, [28] and no more was heard of cheap land. Cowper, it seemed, could not win whatever he did. He tried to economize by postponing public works, and the Assembly forced him to reinstate deferred items in the current estimates, whereupon he was immediately attacked for abandoning his financial policy. [29]

Samuel proposed to the Assembly an increase in customs duties and a new system of trading licences. These plans were greeted with guarded approval by the Chamber of Commerce and condemned by rowdy meetings of working-men, who demanded their replacement with property and income taxes. [30] Parkes moved to have the Assembly reject Samuel's measures as unjust and inequitable and was defeated only because most members, hopelessly divided as they were over the best course to follow, still balked at the obvious alternative to the treasurer's proposals, direct taxation. The ministry's victory was fleeting, since the Assembly promptly emasuculated the bill during detailed examination. To Cowper's consternation, the frustrated treasurer at once resigned his office, and the government's position became desperate when their new bankers, the Oriental Bank, refused to grant them more credit. [31]

Cowper was cornered. He had to have more revenue immediately, yet, as the *Sydney Morning Herald* pointed out, the Assembly's attitude and the slowness of collection inherent in direct taxation left him virtually no alternative to *ad valorem* duties, [32] which he knew he could pass with the support of the Martin faction. To adopt the opposition's policy would be humiliating and would shatter the last of the free-trade pretensions which had led him to power less than a year earlier, but the choice was humiliation or resignation. For once, Cowper's usual decisiveness failed him. Probably he had begun to realize belatedly that his old autocratic style of decision-making, consulting perhaps his ministers but rarely the bulk of his followers, was no longer appropriate in the face of a formidable new opposition professing the same liberal principles as he did. He called a meeting of his followers to advise him, and they almost unanimously urged him to stay in office. Thus encouraged, he added the treasury portfolio temporarily to his other duties and proposed public service retrenchment and a 5 per cent *ad valorem* duty. With Martin's help these measures passed the Assembly just before the Christmas recess and the financial problem appeared at last to be on the way to a solution.

By then it was apparent that the unrelenting pressure of political life had worn Cowper down. Age had added to his air of urbane dignity but his once-dark hair was now a sparse grey fringe and his pleasant face lined. Persistent ill-health troubled him during 1865 and by the year's end he badly needed rest. Yet he could not rest, since he alone could hold his faction together. He prolonged the Christmas parliamentary recess as long as he could. Partly rested and greatly cheered by the news that John Robertson was now ready to resume the lands ministry, Cowper recalled the Assembly on 9 January 1866. Rumours spread that he was quietly trying to negotiate a coalition with Martin. Parkes, who had been steadily building up his faction strength all year, probably heard of this and, judging the ministry to be sufficiently unpopular, he decided that they must be toppled. In this aim, two government actions greatly helped him: the declaration of extensive water reserves on squatting runs and the choice of Marshall Burdekin as the new treasurer. The first move was a reasonable step towards ensuring that water rights were equitably shared between squatters and land buyers on western runs, many of which were due to be opened to selectors in 1866. Water, especially in the dry inland plains of New South Wales, was the key to economic survival; a squatter who could arrange by means of 'dummying' to buy up all the water-frontage on his run effectively kept selectors off the whole property; a selector who took up a squatter's waterhole might virtually hold him to ransom for the use of it.

Bitter squatter-selector conflict during the early years of Robertson's Land Acts had shown how necessary it was to have some form of arbitration between them. The idea of declaring water reserves, conceived by the surveyor-general in 1864, had been approved by the Martin ministry, and Cowper's intention to proclaim these reserves, openly stated months before the end of 1865, had drawn no public reaction. But when a list of reserves was gazetted on 23 December, the *Empire* accused Cowper of trying to strangle free selection in the interests of the squatters. [33] Much of the country press followed the *Empire*'s lead, and Parkes, with superb skill, used the emotional hubbub so generated to bring about an unexpected political coup. He drafted his popular young friend W. C. Windeyer into the contest against Robertson at his ministerial re-election for West Sydney and, in spite of Windeyer's refusal to stand, swept him to victory on the tide of anti-squatter feelings. [34] Robertson, author of the Land Acts and only weeks before the most popular man in the country, found himself with neither seat nor portfolio and reviled as the lackey of the squatters.

Cowper's motives in appointing Burdekin to the Treasury are far from clear. Burdekin was, as Sir John Young observed, 'a young man of good character and fair abilities' [35] who certainly did not deserve to have *Sydney Punch* compare his appointment to the Treasury of New South Wales with the appointment of the emperor Caligula's horse as a consul of Rome. [36] But, as Young also noted, he appeared to have no particular qualification for the Treasury. [37] There was never a shortage of applicants for vacant cabinet posts; Cowper implied that he was positively besieged by them and would only say he chose Burdekin because he was able and well educated. [38] No member of the Cowper-Robertson faction, apart from Samuel, was an experienced financier; it is likely that the *Maitland Mercury* was right in implying that Cowper felt free to choose a pliable nonentity as treasurer in order to keep control of finance in his own hands. [39] However, the appointment was a serious error of judgement on Cowper's part, for it antagonized many of his own supporters and gave Parkes the opportunity to bring down the government.

Plunkett, visiting Melbourne, did not know of Burdekin's appointment until his return, whereupon he resigned his office in protest. Thus embarrassed, Cowper had to propose Burdekin's seat vacant, as the law required, in preparation for his ministerial re-election. Many of Cowper's usual supporters stayed away from the Assembly that day in token of their own disapproval and Parkes saw his chance. Condemning Burdekin as 'barren of mind and feeble of character' he moved an amendment of censure on Cowper's motion. [40] Thirty men had promised support to Cowper at the faction meeting less than three weeks before, but Parkes's amendment passed by 25 votes to 10. Putting a bold front to disaster, Cowper demanded a dissolution from the governor. Young refused and the ministry, relieved at not having to face the electors, quietly resigned.

Parkes had demonstrated that the two major factions had now become three. It was clear that the only prospect of forming a stable government lay in a coalition of two of them. Plunkett, holding to his persistent dream of a ministry of all the talents, tried to persuade Martin, Parkes and Cowper to combine in office. An all-party coalition was not so visionary as it seemed at the time, since the Parkes-Robertson combination twelve years later virtually accomplished that object, but given the problems and personalities involved in 1866, Plunkett advocated a lost cause. Martin had the governor's commission to form a ministry. When Plunkett's efforts had failed, Cowper and Parkes were virtually in competition for Martin's favour. Martin himself preferred Cowper. Parkes countered by reminding Martin of Cowper's low standing with the electorate and subtly suggested that a Parkes-Cowper combination would be much easier to accomplish than a Martin-Cowper grouping because, he implied with bland effrontery, most of the new Parkes faction members had been filched from Cowper and would the more readily agree to coalesce with their old comrades. [41] Undecided, Martin consulted his supporters and they almost unanimously opted for Parkes. Martin bowed to the majority and Cowper found himself leading the opposition.

With the loss of his official position and salary, Cowper's financial problems again became critical. The Wivenhoe appeal of 1864 had petered out with only £672 in hand, and Smart, hoping to stir Cowper's friends into action, advertised the property for sale by auction. Immediately, the *Sydney Morning Herald* said, 'a very numerous and influential meeting of gentlemen of all shades of political opinions' [42] gathered, with Cowper's old friend Richard Jones in the chair, to reactivate the appeal. His old political allies turned out in force to join the appeal committee: ex-members of Cowper ministries, Saul Samuel, Edward Flood, E. C. Weekes; Catholic supporters Daniel Egan and Thomas Donaghy; and men such as J. D. Lang, William Speer, J. T. Neale, B. James and J. D. Gordon who had long stood with Cowper in parliament or on the hustings. Thomas Garrett, coarse-grained and fun-loving, leader of a drunken water fight at one of Cowper's ministerial picnics, yet an able and energetic organizer, took over the secretaryship of the appeal, and within two months the debt was paid. The strain of many difficult years seeped through the formal words of Mrs Cowper's letter of thanks to the appeal committee. 'There is no one better acquainted than I am with the sacrifices made by my husband', she wrote. 'I feel constrained to confess that, however he may have been borne up by a sense of duty...I have often been disposed to complain that he was placed in a position which seemed to require that sacrifices so serious should be made by him and his family'. [43] Cowper himself said nothing. He had taken ship for a visit to New Zealand. He must have felt keenly the blow to his much-valued dignity and standing in the community in having to rely on the charity of friends, though he may have drawn consolation from the unanimous support of the press and the wide range of people who subscribed: Bishop Barker, political friends and opponents, merchants, public servants, Sydney working-men and those from the remotest parts of the colony. Last of all, long after the appeal had closed, W. C. Wentworth heard of it in England and sent £100. However, as Roger Therry wrote, 'it was certainly not very kind of Cowper's friends to...make a present of Wivenhoe to Mrs. Cowper', [44] thus implying that he might be trusted to run the affairs of the country, but not his own. Recalling the famous remark of Sir James Dowling that his land 'would not depasture a bandicoot', Therry added, 'The Wivenhoe land is certainly not so bad as this; but I pity the family that has to depend on the crops it will ever yield, for a comfortable maintenance'. [45] Therry was right. Cowper clung to his parliamentary seat for a few months longer until, near destitute, he resigned on 23 February 1867 and joined the mercantile firm of Towns and Co.

The year between Cowper's fall from power and his retirement was an exceptionally quiet one politically. The Martin-Parkes ministry appeared to govern as it pleased and the liberal press decided that Cowper's political touch was slipping. He must have seen the wry humour of the situation when only the Catholic organ, *Freeman's Journal,* regretted his retirement. [46] Still, the press was less than fair to Cowper. He held his faction core together until Robertson, who returned to the Assembly in August 1866, could be groomed to take over the leadership and he continued to probe for government weaknesses. The main reason for the decline of party strife in 1866 was simply lack of opportunity. So long as Parkes and Martin kept their alliance intact and their followers behind them, they were sure of outvoting the opposition. That they were able to do both was partly due to Cowper himself. The financial measures which had helped to topple him from power solved the budgetary problem for his successors. 'It is impossible', said the *Sydney Morning Herald* drily, 'not to admire the good fortune of the Ministers who have succeeded Mr. Cowper in the possession, through him, of a magnificent revenue, collected upon principles substantially their own, and in opposition to his'. [47] 'The dirty work was done for us by our predecessors', admitted Parkes candidly. [48] He and Martin were able to avoid clashes over their fiscal differences by simply accepting the status quo.

Another reason for their strength in 1866 was that the main issues of the session transcended normal faction loyalties. Cowper sided with Parkes against Martin to defeat a prolonged and determined effort to restore state aid to churches, and the only major government legislation was Parkes's education bill. This measure followed the broad outlines of Cowper's 1863 bill except that it imposed more specific restrictions on the growth of denominational schools, thus polarizing the issue around personal conscience to a greater extent than in 1869. Cowper's strong pleas for the continuance of church schools went unheeded by the Assembly. [49] Forcefully, Robertson followed with opposing views. He had, he said, supported Cowper's education bills of 1859, 1862 and 1863 as steps towards lessening the power of the clergy over the colony's funds and he now supported Parkes's bill as a greater step in that direction. The bill passed on the personal views of members and the skilful management of Parkes. Not until October 1868, twenty months after Cowper's retirement, did internal strains upon the Martin-Parkes ministry allow Robertson to oust them from government.

The firm of Towns and Co. had extensive interests in coal, whaling,

Queensland cotton-growing, meat packing and importing. The senior partner, Robert Towns, who owed to Cowper his seat in the Legislative Council, was the archtype, almost the caricature of a successful nineteenth-century businessman — brusque, ruthlessly intent on maximum profit, and a rather unpleasant person. By contrast the firm's junior partner, Alexander Stuart, was a man of some culture and wider horizons, who eventually entered politics and became premier of New South Wales. He was Cowper's good friend and it was he who arranged for the impecunious ex-premier to enter the firm. Towns at first objected to the employment of a man with personal debts and no capital, giving his reluctant consent only when Stuart agreed to pay Cowper a small salary from his own resources until the firm's profits should expand sufficiently to allow Cowper a share. The price that Cowper paid was acceptance of Towns's decree that he give up all political activity.[50] During the next two-and-a-half years he broke this rule only once, in nominating William, son of his old friend Robert Campbell, for the West Sydney seat at a by-election in December 1868. Cowper spent much of the intervening time in Queensland, looking to the firm's interests there.

Early in 1869 Cowper received his first Imperial honour, the C.M.G., lowest of the three grades of the Order of St Michael and St George. Far from being grateful, he was highly indignant, for at the same time James Martin and T. A. Murray received awards which conferred knighthood on them. He felt, with some justice, that he had done more for New South Wales than either of them. He knew too that Young had recommended him for the higher award of C.B. in 1862 and 1863. He probably did not know that Young had lowered his recommendation to C.M.G. in 1865, when their normally good working relationship was under strain from Cowper's refusal to heed the governor's financial advice and his pin-pricking insistence upon observing even the most minor rights of the colonial secretary's office, which led Young to comment sharply on Cowper's love of 'the show as well as the reality of management and power'.[51] Yet Young's irritation was only temporary. On the point of departure from New South Wales in 1867 he warmly praised Cowper's courtesy and ability before the whole of the Martin-Parkes ministry and, by his own account, believed he had succeeded in persuading the Colonial Office to sponsor Cowper for the higher award before he left London to become governor-general of Canada.[52] Probably Young was right in attributing the eventual result to British horror at Cowper's swamping of the Legislative Council in 1861.[53] 'The go to the bottom of an inferior Order is going very low', lamented Cowper,[54] but his appeals to everyone who might help him gain the coveted knighthood had no effect.

Towards the end of 1869 Cowper moved to re-enter politics. Two overt considerations impelled him: Towns and Co. were, in Stuart's words, 'on the verge of insolvency'[55] at that time, and Robertson, then premier, needed Cowper's help. Like his old chief, Robertson had proved himself a better politician than he was a businessman. In 1869 he again neared bankruptcy and needed time to attend to his personal affairs. Their political opponents later suspected that Robertson and Cowper had struck a bargain: Cowper was to re-enter politics and assume the premiership on a caretaker basis until Robertson could settle his affairs; in return, Robertson was to appoint Cowper to the post of colonial agent-general in London when he himself resumed the premiership. The opposition may well have been right. The agent-general's position fell vacant in October 1869, but neither Robertson nor, later, Cowper when he took over as premier, made any move to fill the position until Cowper himself took it fourteen months later. Nor did Cowper's actions during his 1870 term as premier suggest that he was anything more than a seat-warmer for Robertson.

Cowper's first attempt to re-enter the Assembly ended disastrously. He stood with two other government candidates for his old seat East Sydney at the general election of December 1869, only to be defeated heavily by Parkes, Martin, Buchanan and an independent, George King. The press attributed Cowper's defeat to sectarianism, for Parkes and his supporters were then riding a wave of anti-Catholicism, the aftermath of O'Farrell's attempt to assassinate the Duke of Edinburgh in 1868, and the Robertson faction was seen to have Catholic connections. Daniel Egan, a Catholic, was Robertson's postmaster-general, in succession to his co-religionist, Cunneen of Cowper's 1865 ministry. Robertson himself had, in 1864, become the first president of the Sydney branch of the Irish National League, a body set up to press for an independent Irish legislature. What crowning irony for Cowper, to be rejected by the electorate because of his Catholic sympathies! However, there were additional reasons for his defeat. His opposition to the 1866 education bill, his disastrous government of 1865, his long absence from politics and, above all, the great rise in stature of Robertson as a faction leader in his own right, all helped to down him. In the words of the *Sydney Morning Herald,* Cowper's name 'did not charm as it was wont to do'.[56] Utterly humiliated, Cowper would not appear at the declaration of the poll. But, in time-honoured fashion, government supporters found in the country a refuge from the wrath of Sydney, and Cowper was returned as the member for Liverpool Plains. The overall results of the elections left party strengths in the Assembly much as they had been, with the balance of power held by independents.[57]

Robertson's financial affairs had now reached an alarming state.

According to the governor, the Earl of Belmore, one of his partnership ventures owed £140 000. [58] Belmore showed no surprise when Robertson resigned the premiership a few days after the elections and recommended Cowper as his successor. The governor did nothing to dispel his reputation for snobbery when he gladly agreed, with the remark that 'it was so very desirable in my opinion that a person of his social position should be added to the government'. [59] Nevertheless Belmore had his doubts about the stability of the arrangement, for only Samuel, the treasurer, had worked with Cowper before and two of the ministers, Manning (attorney-general) and Forster (lands) were old oppoents of the new premier. Forster, the governor decided, would give the most trouble. 'From what I can make out', noted Belmore perceptively, 'he seems to be nearly as formidable as a colleague as in opposition, and moreover he does not care about remaining in office'. [60]

Belmore's fears were well-founded. Cowper had to exert all his powers of conciliation to hold the ministry together until the end of a difficult session. Robertson, harassed by a strong opposition under Martin and Parkes, had ended the 1869 parliamentary session without passing the estimates for 1870. The opposition was no less aggressive when Cowper took over. He successfully brushed aside a charge made by Martin that Belmore had acted inconsistently in issuing a writ for his ministerial re-election only three days after the return of the first one. But when Martin's nominee, John Lackey, beat Garrett, the government candidate, for the chairmanship of committees, Cowper took alarm and jettisoned the legislative programme he had inherited from Robertson to concentrate on keeping the ministry in power. The vital 1870 estimates became the only government business of the sesson and, by simply accepting opposition amendments which he could not prevent, Cowper managed to close the parliamentary proceedings on 7 May without losing his precarious hold on the premiership. The price he paid was a familiar one to him: overwork and indisposition, deepening into series illness in early June.

Cowper's own ministers were amongst his greatest burdens. Forster, prickly as ever, resigned from the Lands Office in April when a minor vote went against the government. With difficulty Cowper persuaded him to stay on till the session's end. The premier then found himself in the same position as in 1865: holding the Lands Office himself in hopes of Robertson's return to it. Unfortunately, ministerial differences were not confined to Forster. Robert Owen's position as government spokesman in the Legislative Council carried neither portfolio nor pay and, not unnaturally, he thought himself entitled to both. Since Daniel Egan was in poor health, Cowper asked him to resign the postmaster-

generalship so that Owen could have his portfolio and salary,
but Egan refused to go voluntarily and Cowper could not risk splitting
the government ranks by sacking him. Egan remained in the post
until his death in October 1870. With the problem of Owen unsolved,
Cowper had to contend with strife between his law officers, Manning
and Solicitor-General J. W. Salomons and with the latter's failure to
gain election to the Assembly. In August, both problems were solved.
Owen resigned and Cowper pacified Salomons by installing him as leader
of the upper house.

Cowper's correspondence with Belmore shows that he quickly
established a good working relationship with the aristocratic young
governor, as he had with Denison and Young. Belmore thought
Cowper a good administrator and was pleased by his polished manner,
so much at variance with the bluntness of John Robertson or the
uncouthness of such fellows as Garrett and Egan. In turn, Cowper's
affability towards the governor was increased by the knowledge that
Belmore usually left his ministers to run the colony with a minimum
of interference. The only known tension between them arose when
Belmore felt his dignity threatened by Cowper's insistence that
correspondence from foreign consuls, formally addressed to the
governor, should pass through the colonial secretary's office.

Ill as he was in June, Cowper could not rest. An intercolonial
conference was to be held in Melbourne late in the month to attempt
the construction of a common tariff. This was too important an issue
to leave to others so, faced with the journey to Melbourne, Cowper
tried to persuade Robertson to rejoin the ministry immediately and
take charge of the government in his absence. Robertson was not
yet clear of the Insolvency Court and reluctantly had to refuse, whereupon
Cowper left Owen in charge and took ship to Melbourne with Samuel.
The conference was a failure. Protectionist Victoria and free-trade
New South Wales could not agree on a uniform policy. The only
concession Cowper would make to intercolonial co-operation was his
admission that, sooner or later, the Australian colonies must federate.
However, as a modern historian has noted, 'he obviously preferred
later'. [61] As usual, he was more interested in practical administration
than in visionary schemes for the future.

Cowper returned to Sydney knowing that his government would face
serious problems when parliament resumed in August. He could not
hope to have another 'estimates only' session. Yet to bring on any
major legislation would be to invite defeat, since his ministry continued
to lose support, as the *Sydney Morning Herald* said, in the manner
usual to governments in New South Wales 'because they cannot satisfy

everyone'. [62] By miserable ill-fortune too Cowper once more faced a financial deficit, due to a business recession and declining land revenues. At sixty-three years of age, worn and ill, Cowper could see no better prospect than yet another exhausting session of parliament. It is little wonder that his letters to Belmore expressed a deep despondency [63] or that his thoughts turned towards the haven of the London agency-generalship. The opposition had voiced its suspicions on that score in May, when Cowper's son Charles received the appointment of water police magistrate. *Lictor* suspected that ' "Old Charley" was poking his fun/To manage snug billets for him and his son.' [64]

When the session opened on 11 August, Cowper openly admitted his interest in the agency-generalship. Since Robertson rejoined the ministry two days later, the way seemed clear for Cowper to take up the post immediately, yet he did not do so. It was probably true, as the *Maitland Mercury* suggested, that Robertson still wanted Cowper's help in government and that Cowper would have received the agency position as soon as his parliamentary position became untenable. [65] But Cowper knew well that it was not enough to gain the post; he also had to keep it. For security of tenure he needed at least the tacit consent of the opposition leaders, and the most effective way to gain it was to keep them out of power until they were glad to be rid of him.

Thus he battled on against increasing difficulties. Martin failed by only two votes to unseat the ministry on opening day and scored his first success within twenty-four hours when Garrett, put up by Robertson against Cowper's advice for the chairmanship of committees, lost heavily to Lackey, a costly loss for the ministry, since Lackey promptly used his casting vote in committee to defeat their first financial measure of the session, a bill to fund the colony's external loan debt. When Martin's next censure motion, disapproving the recent issue of £450 000 in government debentures, was defeated narrowly after an all-night sitting, the *Sydney Morning Herald* justly remarked that the ministry was strong enough to prevent defeat but not strong enough to carry out its policy. [66] 'Our friends seem very lukewarm — but we must make the best fight we can', Cowper wrote to Belmore. [67] Well aware that Martin and Parkes were reserving their main attack for the government's financial proposals, the ministry held back the budget until 20 October. The government hoped to fulfil Robertson's long-standing promise to abolish ` *ad valorem* duties, replacing them with new fiscal duties, an amended Stamp Act and a tax of 6d in the pound on incomes over £200. Cowper had at last been driven to sanction direct taxation and he undoubtedly feared that the income tax proposal would prove to be

the ministry's main danger point. Instead their fate was decided by the
Stamp Act. This act, one of Cowper's 1865 measures, was due to expire
at the end of 1870, and by the time the Assembly had finished cutting
back the government's proposed customs duties, it was clear that only
renewal of the act could secure the country's finances and the ministry's
survival. On 30 November, Samuel tried to suspend standing orders
and rush the renewal through in one evening. He failed and Cowper
adjourned the House in order to consult his followers at a conference on
2 December. Four days later, Cowper's appointment to London was
gazetted. Robertson announced it to the Assembly, with the news of the
government's intended resignation, the next day.

At first sight, Cowper's position as the nominee of a defeated ministry
seemed to be alarmingly unsafe, but gradually the public discovered
that Cowper, in a last demonstration of his 'slipperiness', had connived
with Robertson and Martin to gain what he wanted. The key to this
situation was the exit of Parkes from parliament late in the year as
he neared his second bankruptcy. Rumours that Martin and Robertson
were contemplating alliance had circulated since July 1870. Such a move,
if Cowper went off to London, seemed a feasible way of ending the
conditions of near-stalemate which had hampered the Robertson-
Cowper government since 1868 and which could be expected to dog
Martin similarly if he took office without Robertson. The formidable
Parkes, still ostensibly Martin's ally, and the only other parliamentary
leader of stature, stood in the way. When he went, Martin and Robertson
felt free to conclude their alliance. The colonial press rightly suspected
that Martin had agreed to Cowper's appointment before it was made, [68]
and Cowper, in gaining the support of both the remaining faction
leaders in the Assembly, had every reason to believe he could look forward
to a comfortable old age in London. His long career in colonial
politics was over.

9

Retrospect

On 13 February 1871 the Martin-Robertson ministry farewelled Cowper at a public dinner well attended by his old political friends. They turned out again two days later to see him sail for England with his wife and youngest daughter, Rose. His active political life was over. Under Cowper's predecessors, E. W. F. Hamilton and W. C. Mayne, the colonial agent's office had dealt mainly with routine details of immigration and the buying of goods for the New South Wales government. With Cowper's appointment a change occurred. To his comrade J. D. Lang, Cowper conceded that his duties were 'not closely defined', but, he added with a touch of pomposity, 'there is one portion that is diplomatic—and that is decidedly confidential'.[1] It seems that Cowper's diplomacy was exercised mainly in raising colonial loans on the London Stock Exchange,[2] but his duties were not too onerous. He slid easily into the social world of expatriate Australians in England, renewing old friendships with Charles Nicholson, Daniel Cooper, W. C. Wentworth, T. W. Smart, Robert Lowe, E. W. F. Hamilton, and others. 'I cannot tell you how pleased I was with him', wrote Hamilton to William Macarthur after a visit from Cowper. 'So thoroughly amiable about all...not an unkind word...His manners are singularly good.'[3] Early in 1872 the British government awarded him the knighthood he had sought for so long. 'I am not C.M.G. & Sir Charles Cowper but Sir Charles Cowper K.C.M.G.—a Very [sic] different thing', he told Alexander Stuart with almost childish delight.[4] He had finally lived down the 'swamping of 1861.

Cowper's halcyon days did not last long. Even before he gained his knighthood the Martin-Robertson ministry was tottering. 'Poor Robertson—I fear he has wasted his opportunity. Champagne has been his enemy', Cowper lamented in March 1872[5] with concern for an old friend and his own future. Two months later Parkes displaced the ministry and formed his first government. Later in 1872 Cowper's fears were confirmed when Parkes reduced his salary. At the same time, suffering severely from the cold and damp of the English climate,

Cowper fell into the grip of a chronic illness. Steadily his health grew worse and much of his work passed into the hands of his small staff, his daughter and his old political associate Daniel Cooper. He lived in fear of recall, [6] but Parkes proved to be unexpectedly generous. Cooper and Donald Lanarck, London manager for the Bank of New South Wales, repeatedly urged Parkes to retire the sick man. [7] Parkes ignored their advice, assured Charles Cowper Jnr that his father's job was safe and wrote in kindly fashion to Lady Cowper. [8] In 1874 he appointed Cowper Jnr sheriff of New South Wales. Altogether, the Cowper family had good cause to feel the gratitude which Charles Jnr expressed in his letters to the man whose intentions they had so feared. [9] Parkes's actions reflected both his own creditable personal qualities and the lingering warmth which he, like many others who had worked with Cowper in earlier days, felt for his old colleague. Under Parkes and the succeeding Robertson ministry of 1875, Cowper remained in his post as his illness deepened until, on 19 October 1875, he died. He lies beside his younger son, dead nineteen years before him, in Highgate Cemetery.

Cowper has few memorials: a street in Sydney, an electorate in New South Wales, not much more His name is not a household word as is that of Parkes, and historians have not paid attention to him as they have to John Robertson. Yet if his worth is to be measured by the value of his contribution to the building of a stable, democratic society in New South Wales, he ranks with these men. His twenty-seven years in the legislature of that colony spanned a period of great change in government and in the shape of society. The stain of convictism which overshadowed the whole colony in 1843 had vanished by 1870, submerged by time and a new generation, partly immigrant, partly native-born, all free men and women. When Cowper first entered the Legislative Council, that body represented a privileged minority of the 164 000 people in New South Wales, and real power lay with the governor and his British masters. When he left the colonial parliament, half a million people lived under the rule of a parliament as democratic in nature as almost any in the world. Cowper himself had headed the government of the new democracy for nine of its fifteen years of existence, but had he retired at its birth, he would still have left an impressive record behind him. He had been an outstanding leader of the anti-transportation movement not only within his own colony but throughout the whole of eastern Australia, and the success of the movement, vital as it was to the evolution of a self-governing community, owed much to him. His social activism extended further, into a rare concern for the outcasts of the Victorian era — orphans and the insane. He fully earned the credit given him by contemporaries for his work on their behalf. On another level, he had the vision to see the great need for railways as a key factor in the economic development of New South Wales. A Birch has commented, justly, that up to 1848 he, more than anyone, kept the idea of railways alive.[10] He also nursed the first rail project through its most difficult years, and it was his government which boldly borrowed millions to push the iron rails far out from Sydney, setting the example for others to follow, and touching off great changes in the pattern of inland settlement, for development followed the railways. These alone were notable achievements. But greater in the eyes of his contemporaries were achievements related to the major political movements which occurred between 1857 and 1863, when Cowper was unquestionably the most powerful politician in New South Wales. The Electoral Act of 1858, the Land Acts of 1861, the reconstruction of the Legislative Council and the ending of state aid to churches all had significant long-term effects, not always those intended, upon the form and direction of New South Wales society. The Electoral Act tipped the balance permanently against the old colonial conservative group, leading rapidly to their political extinction and to thirty years of faction government. Cowper's preservation of a nominee Council, paradoxically, proved to be a greater aid to democratic government than was the elected Council of Victoria, and his basic settlement lasted until 1934. The termination of state aid was a great step towards placing all the churches of Australia, for the first time, on an equal footing under the law, and Cowper's 1863 education bill showed Parkes the way to the settlements he imposed in 1866 and 1880, settlements disturbed only in recent years. The Land Acts changed the pattern of ownership and rural debt in ways not fully foreseen by their originators, but they did give to thousands a chance to try for their version of the Australian dream — independence on the land. Rightly, John Robertson's name looms largest here, but the passing of his land bills owed much to the tactical skill of his chief.

Most of these measures were the legislative realization of political trends beyond the power of any individual to alter, and Cowper owed much of his success in government to his early recognition of and willingness to follow existing currents of political thought. He was not a creator of liberal trends, but during his years of power he did more than any other individual to hasten their coming and to shape them during a critical period in the development of Australian government. Nevertheless, his greatest achievement may well have been simply to provide an orderly administration. His temperament and talents were ideally suited to the task of fashioning the basis of faction government. He was patient, tactful, adaptive and incredibly hard-working and it is difficult to see who else could have provided New South Wales with an equal degree of continuity in administration during the first years of independent government. As an administrator he built mainly upon the foundations laid by earlier governments, though he saw more clearly than did most of his contemporaries that basic job security was a necessary aid to efficiency in the public service. Thus he tried in 1836 and 1854 to compensate government officers for gold-caused inflation, [11] and ten years later he gave them their first superannuation scheme. [12] He introduced on his own initiative two major measures of administrative reform, the police reorganization and the torrens titles system. Both have stood the test of time.

Possibly the best assessment of Cowper's role in the political world of New South Wales was that made by the most eminent of the men who knew his work at first hand. 'He was', said Henry Parkes when he knew of Cowper's death, 'as valuable a public servant as we ever had in this colony'. [13]

Abbreviations

Archives	Archives Office of New South Wales
Despatches	Despatches from the Governors of New South Wales to the Secretary of State
H.R.A.	*Historical Records of Australia*
J.R.A.H.S.	*Journal of the Royal Australian Historical Society*
M.L.	Mitchell Library, Sxdney
S.M.H.	*Sydney Morning Herald*
V. & P. L.A.	Legislative Assembly of New South Wales, *Votes and Proceedings*
V. & P. L.C.	Legislative Council of New South Wales, *Votes and Proceedings*

Notes

1 THE SHAPING OF A COLONIAL CONSERVATIVE

1 Cowper Autobiography, ch. 1, pp. 1-2.
2 Ibid.
3 *Lachlan Macquarie* (Sydney, 1973), p. 148.
4 Broughton to Rev. Edward Coleridge, 14 February 1842, Broughton Letters, FM4/225.
5 Ibid.
6 Cowper Autobiography, ch. 6, p. 1.
7 Ibid., ch. 6, p. 15.
8 Ibid., ch. 2, p. 19.
9 Scott to Darling, 19 April 1829, *H.R.A.*, ser. 1, vol. 15, pp. 119-20.
10 See Turney, 'A History of Education in New South Wales 1788-1900' (Ph.D. thesis), p. 363, and Cleverley, 'The Administration of State-assisted Elementary Education in Mainland New South Wales 1789-1855' (Ph.D. thesis), pp. 194-5, 237-9, 253.
11 Bourke to Lord Stanley, 16 February 1834, *H.R.A.*, ser. 1, vol. 17, p. 372.
12 Land Board report of 16 August 1827, Letters from individuals re land, Colonial Secretary's Dept, Archives 2/7967.
13 *H.R.A.*, ser. 1, vol. 19, pp. 268-9.
14 Cowper's obituary, *Town and Country Journal*, 30 October 1875, p. 694.
15 31 July 1843.
16 MacAlister, *Old Pioneering Days in the Sunny South*, p. 121.
17 List of signatures, Indian Labour, New South Wales, 1842, A2029.
18 27 November 1842, Despatches, 1842-59, vol. 41.
19 *Australian*, 12 October 1842, p. 2.
20 Gipps to La Trobe, 8 October 1842, Gipps-La Trobe Correspondence.
21 11 October 1842, p. 2.
22 *S.M.H.*, 28 December 1842, p. 2; Broughton to Coleridge, 14 January 1843, Broughton Letters, FM4/225.
23 12 October 1842.
24 Not all such tenants were excluded. James Macarthur indicated that 15 of his tenants had voted in the Camden election (*Australian*, 1 July 1843).
25 17 September 1842.
26 12 July, 30 September 1842.
27 Molony, 'John Hubert Plunkett in New South Wales 1823-1869' (Ph.D. thesis), p. 126.
28 *Port Phillip Patriot*, 10 July 1843.
29 See *Colonial Observer*, 9, 12, 16 November, 28 December 1842, 11, 21 January, 18 February 1843; *Australasian Chronicle*, 3, 5, 7, 14 January 1843; *Port Phillip Patriot*, 30 January, 20 February, 10, 27 July 1843.
30 *Colonial Observer*, 7 October 1841 (first issue).
31 *S.M.H.*, 11 October 1842; *Colonial Observer*, 19 October 1842.
32 *Australian*, 12 October 1842; *Australasian chronicle*, 3 January 1843.
33 *S.M.H.* 27 December 1842, 24, 26 May 1843; *Colonial Observer*, 11 January 1843.
34 *Colonial Observer*, 9 November, 28 December 1842; *Port Phillip Patriot*, 9 March 1843.
35 *S.M.H.*, 4 January 1843.
36 *Australasian Chronicle*, 17 January 1843.

[37] *S.M.H.*, 3 April 1843.
[38] *S.M.H.*, 23 May 1843.
[39] *S.M.H.*, 5 January 1843; *Australian*, 20 January 1843.
[40] *S.M.H.*, 7 January 1843.
[41] 24 May 1843.
[42] See the exchange of correspondence between Macarthur and Wentworth, *S.M.H.*, 1, 3 July 1843.
[43] William Macarthur to James Macarthur, 28 December 1842, Macarthur Papers, 1st ser., vol. 38.
[44] *S.M.H.*, 8 February 1843, p. 3; see also James Macarthur's speech, *S.M.H.*, 8 February 1843.
[45] Waldersee, *Catholic Society in New South Wales 1788-1860*, p. 220.
[46] *S.M.H.*, 8 February 1843.
[47] *S.M.H.*, 13 May 1843.
[48] *Australian*, 18 January 1843.
[49] Broughton to Coleridge, 14 January 1843, Broughton Letters, FM4/225.
[50] *Australasian Chronicle*, 21 January 1843.
[51] *Colonial Observer*, 18 February 1843.
[52] See letter of 'R.W.C.', *S.M.H.*, 18 January 1843.
[53] See Nadel, *Australia's Colonial Culture*, pp. 244-5.
[54] *S.M.H.*, 28 March 1843.
[55] 30 May 1843; see also correspondence, *Australian Chronicle*, 1, 8, 13 June 1843.
[56] *Australian*, 28 June 1843.
[57] Gipps so informed Lord Stanley, 18 July 1843, Despatches, 1842-59, vol. 42.
[58] See the speeches of James Macarthur, A. Murray and Edward Flood at the Cumberland nomination, *S.M.H.*, 28 June 1843.
[59] Rusden, *History of Australia*, vol. 2, p. 306.
[60] 28 June, 3 July 1843.
[61] *S.M.H.*, 28 June 1843.
[62] *S.M.H.*, 3 July 1843.
[63] *History of Australia*, vol. 2, p. 306.
[64] *S.M.H.*, 11 July 1843.
[65] Cowper gained, at these two polling places, 265 votes, compared to Lawson's 116 and Macarthur's 147 (*S.M.H.*, 4 July 1843).
[66] J. L. Templar, reported in *S.M.H.*, 2 August 1843.

2   PRINCIPLES AND POPULARITY 1843 1848

[1] *S.M.H.*, 30 October 1845.
[2] *Colonial Observer*, 24 October 1844.
[3] Gipps to Stanley, 19 August 1843, Despatches, 1842-59, vol. 41.
[4] *S.M.H.*, 28 June 1843.
[5] *S.M.H.*, 7 July, 3 August 1843.
[6] *Australian*, 20 January 1843; *S.M.H.*, 20 January 1843.
[7] 23 October 1843.
[8] *S.M.H.*, 6 October 1843.
[9] *S.M.H.*, 23 November 1843.
[10] *S.M.H.*, 2 October 1843.
[11] *S.M.H.*, 19 August 1843.
[12] Gipps to Stanley, 18 October 1843, Despatches, 1842-59, vol. 41.
[13] Gipps to La Trobe, 30 December 1843, Gipps-La Trobe Correspondence.
[14] *Quest for Authority in Eastern Australia 1835-1851*, p.22.
[15] *S.M.H.*, 17 November 1843.
[16] See Cowper's remarks, *S.M.H.*, 11 September 1844.
[17] 'Report of the Select Committee on Education', *V. & P.* L.C., 1844, vol. 2, p. 451.
[18] *Sentinel*, 12 March 1845.
[19] *S.M.H.*, 14 August 1845.
[20] *S.M.H.*, 23 September 1846.

21 Entry of 22 July 1847, Kemp Diary. A2063.

22 *S.M.H.*, 16 July 1847.

23 This is shown by Cable in his article 'Religious controversies in New South Wales in the Mid-Nineteenth Century—1. Aspects of Anglicanism'.

24 See Cowper Autobiography, ch. 5, p. 3.

25 Ibid., ch. 5, p. 5.

26 *S.M.H.*, 2 August 1848.

27 Quoted in Knight, *Illiberal Liberal*, pp. 26-7. Lowe made this remark in 1850, after his return to England.

28 Details of these regulations are given in Buckley's article 'Gipps and the Graziers of New South Wales'.

29 8 February 1844.

30 *S.M.H.*, 31 May 1844.

31 Ibid.

32 *Weekly Register*, 30 November 1844.

33 *S.M.H.*, 23 October 1845.

34 *Atlas*, 7 February 1846. The term 'constitutionalists' is not a strictly accurate title for this group, with the exception of Lowe, but is preferable to their other common designation as 'landowners', since men like Lowe, Bland and Lamb had primarily, or solely, urban interests.

35 *S.M.H.*, 5 August 1848.

36 *S.M.H.*, 26 September 1846.

37 Ibid.

38 *S.M.H.*, 14 October 1846.

39 16 October 1846.

40 *S.M.H.*, 23 October 1846.

41 *Australian*, 27 July 1848.

42 *S.M.H.*, 19 May 1847.

43 *S.M.H.*, 16 September 1847.

44 22 March 1848.

45 'Exiles' was a euphemistic term for men pardoned before leaving England on condition that they were not to return before the due date of expiry of their original sentences. They had been sent to the Port Phillip district, but not to New South Wales proper, during Lord Stanley's tenure of the Colonial Office.

46 10 April 1848.

47 Ibid.

48 21 January 1848.

49 Fitzroy to Grey, 11 August 1848, Despatches, 1842-59, vol. 57.

50 11 October 1847.

51 *Heads of the People*, 4 September 1847; *Australian*, 9 May 1846.

52 *Australian*, 9 May 1846.

53 20 May 1848

54 *S.M.H.*, 9 August 1844. Road maintenance had been carried out by the Colonial Engineer's Department, abolished in 1843 at Cowper's instance.

3 THE EVOLUTION OF A LIBERAL 1848—1856

1 L. Meredith, *Notes and Sketches of New South Wales* (Sydney, 1973), p.38.

2 *Atlas*, 29 July 1848.

3 Fitzroy to Grey, 20 January 1848, Despatches, 1842-59, vol. 56; Fitzroy to Grey, 30 April 1847, Governor of New South Wales, Transcripts of Missing Despatches, 1844-55, No. 100.

4 *S.M.H.*, 27 July 1848.

5 *S.M.H.*, 5 August 1848.

6 Irving. 'The Development of Liberal Politics in New South Wales 1843-1855' (Ph.D. thesis), pp. 226-7, points out that the commerce-trading-manufacturing-professional group of those gainfully employed in Sydney grew from about 31 per cent in 1846 to 45 per cent in 1851.

7 *S.M.H.*, 22 December 1848.
8 Ibid.
9 *S.M.H.*, 24 August 1844.
10 Hamilton to George Clive, 8 March 1849, Collaroy Station Papers, vol. 1
11 The name 'liberal' did not come into general use for this group for another two or three years. It is used here for convenience.
12 *Empire*, 7 October 1851.
13 Report by the Chairman of the New South Wales Association for Preventing the Revival of Transportation, *S.M.H.*, 11 January 1851.
14 *S.M.H.*, 31 July 1851.
15 *S.M.H.*, 8 April 1852.
16 *S.M.H.*, 10 April 1852.
17 *S.M.H.*, 9 January 1850.
18 Percy Simpson, a disappointed candidate for the post of engineer to the Sydney Railway Company, *Empire*, 26 June 1852.
19 *S.M.H.*, 21 September 1853; Cowper to the Board of the Sydney Railway Company, Minute Book, 1852-5, pp. 214-16.
20 *Empire*, 25 November 1854.
21 *Empire*, 30 August 1851.
22 Cowper to Parkes, 22 December 1854, Parkes Correspondence, vol. 6, pp. 378-85.
23 Ibid.
24 *Empire*, 30 August 1851.
25 In Pike (ed.), *Australian Dictionary of Biography 1851-1890*, vol. 3, p. 477.
26 22 May 1852. This newspaper was, at that time, a strong supporter of Wentworth and the squatters.
27 *Empire*, 28 October 1851.
28 *S.M.H.*, 29 June, 2 July 1849.
29 *S.M.H.*, 8 August 1849.
30 1 January 1852.
31 1 January 1853.
32 24 September 1853.
33 21 May 1853.
34 A concise account of the composition, aims and proceedings of this body is given by Loveday, 'Democracy' in New South Wales: the Constitution Committee of 1853', *J.R.A.H.S.*, vol. 42, pt 4 (1956).
35 Irving, 'The Development of Liberal Politics' (Ph.D. thesis), pp. 360-1.
36 *S.M.H.*, 9 December 1853.
37 Macleay to W. Macarthur, 29 December 1854, Macarthur Papers, 1st ser., vol. 58.
38 'Sarsfield O'Sullivan', in *Freeman's Journal*, 25 September 1855.
39 See vols 6 and 7 passim.
40 Cowper to Parkes, 29 May 1855, Parkes Correspondence, vol. 7.
41 *Our Antipodes*, vol. 1, p. 90.
42 *Daily Telegraph*, 6 June 1906. Charles Cowper Jnr was reminiscing to a reporter of events fifty years earlier.
43 *S.M.H.*, 8 December 1853.
44 17 December 1853. Hawksley, editor of this newspaper, was then a close associate of the more radical politicians.
45 Cowper to Parkes, 22 December 1854, Parkes Correspondence, vol. 6.
46 Cowper to Parkes, 10 January 1855, Parkes Correspondence, vol. 6.
47 17 December 1853.
48 13 September 1854.
49 See particularly Cowper to Parkes, 20 August 1854, Parkes Correspondence, vol. 6; see also *S.M.H.*, 23 September 1854.
50 Cowper to Parkes, 27 January 1855, Parkes Correspondence, vol. 6.
51 Denison, *Varieties of Vice-Regal Life*, vol. 1, p. 304.
52 Ibid., pp. 312-13.
53 Cowper to Parkes, 9 May 1855, Parkes Correspondence, vol. 6.
54 *S.M.H.*, 19 September 1853.

[55] 24 September 1851, Lang Papers, vol. 6.
[56] See Cowper's remarks, *S.M.H.*, 24 July 1851; also his electoral advertisement, *S.M.H.*, 9 August 1851.
[57] *S.M.H.*, 8 July 1853.
[58] *Empire*, 7 October 1854.
[59] Letter signed 'A Schoolmaster', *Empire*, 16 October 1854.
[60] *Empire*, 7 October, 29 November 1854.
[61] See Cowper to Parkes, 22, 27 December 1854, 10 January 1855, Parkes Correspondence, vol. 6.
[62] *Parliament, Factions and Parties*, p.23.
[63] Cowper to Parkes, 22 December 1854, Parkes Correspondence, vol. 6.
[64] *S.M.H.*, 28, 29 April, 2 May 1854.
[65] 24 February 1855.
[66] 3 March 1853, Parkes Correspondence, vol. 6.
[67] Cowper to Parkes, 10 January 1855, Parkes Correspondence, vol. 6. Several others of Cowper's letters to Parkes, dated from 1853 to 1855, express similar sentiments.
[68] Cowper to Parkes, 5 May 1854, Autograph Letters of Notable Australians, A70.

4   THE QUEST FOR POWER 1856 1857

[1] Deniehy to Parkes, 30 January 1856, Autograph Letters to Sir Henry Parkes, A71.
[2] Cowper to Parkes, 12 January 1856, Parkes Correspondence, vol. 6.
[3] *S.M.H.*, 11 February 1856.
[4] 15 July 1848.
[5] *S.M.H.*, 6 June 1855.
[6] *S.M.H.*, 16 February 1856.
[7] *S.M.H.*, 27 May 1856.
[8] Denison to Labouchere, 12 June 1856, Denison Correspondence, FM3/795.
[9] 22 February 1856.
[10] Denison to Labouchere, 12 June 1856, Denison Correspondence, FM3/795.
[11] See Loveday, 'The Development of Parliamentary Government in New South Wales 1856-1870' (Ph.D. thesis), p. 75.
[12] Circular letter of 19 August 1856, signed by Cowper, and notifying liberal members of a meeting, Parkes Correspondence, vol. 6.
[13] Cowper to Parkes, 5 July 1856, Parkes Correspondence, vol. 6.
[14] Cowper to Lang, 12 July 1856, Lang Papers, vol. 7.
[15] 9 August 1856.
[16] *S.M.H.*, 21 August 1856.
[17] 22 August 1856.
[18] 22 August 1856.
[19] T.W. Smith, chairman at an anti-Cowper meeting; *S.M.H.*, 30 August 1856.
[20] *S.M.H.*, 4 September 1856. Stephen emphasized that, while he saw nothing derogatory to the Bar in appointing Martin as attorney general, he was not thereby approving of the appointment.
[21] Denison to Donaldson, 15 February 1859, Donaldson Ministry Letters.
[22] Cowper to Parkes, 11 May 1857, Parkes Correspondence, vol. 50.
[23] *Maitland Mercury*, 24 March 1857. *The Maitland Mercury*, like the great majority of country newspapers, usually supported the liberals.
[24] Cowper to Parkes, 31 March 1857, Parkes Correspondence, vol. 6.
[25] See for instance Cowper to Jamison, 27 April, 4 August 1857, Jamison Papers, vol. 3; Cowper to Arnold, 27 July 1857, Arnold Correspondence, MSS 901; Cowper to Parkes, 22 June 1857, Parkes Correspondence, vol. 6.
[26] *Empire*, 26 January 1857.
[27] Cowper to Parkes, 22 June 1857, Parkes Correspondence, vol. 6.
[28] Cowper to Parkes, 22 December 1856, Parkes Correspondence, vol. 7.
[29] *S.M.H.*, 26 January, 3 February 1857.
[30] Cowper to Parkes, 11 May 1857, Parkes Correspondence, vol. 50.
[31] Cowper to Parkes, undated, Parkes Correspondence, vol. 6.

32 Cowper to Parkes, 30 July 1857, Parkes Correspondence, vol. 6.
33 Cowper to Parkes, 22 June, 30 July 1857, Parkes Correspondence, vol. 6. At first, Jones had wanted to allow the conservatives to rule unhindered until the liberals could evolve a more coherent party organization and policy.
34 Cowper to Parkes, 30 July 1857, Parkes Correspondence, vol. 6.
35 17 August 1857.
36 Quoted in Loveday and Martin, *Parliament, Factions and Parties,* p. 34.

5 'SLIPPERY CHARLIE'

1 See Parkes, *Fifty Years in the Making of Australian History,* vol. 1, pp. 116-17.
2 Windeyer, 'Responsible Government—Highlights, Sidelights and Reflections', *J.R.A.H.S.,* vol. 42, pt 6 (1957), p. 298.
3 16 June 1858.
4 18 October 1859.
5 *S.M.H.,* begun in 1831, was then (and still is) the longest-surviving Australian newspaper. Even in the 1850s it was irreverently called 'the Old Lady' or 'Grannie'.
6 *S.M.H.,* 5 September 1861.
7 *Political Portraits, p.5.*
8 3 October 1859.
9 9 October 1863.
10 *S.M.H.,* 22 December 1860.
11 Forster to Parkes, 5 May 1859, Parkes Correspondence, vol. 52.
12 *S.M.H.,* 29 October 1863.
13 29 October 1856.
14 26 May 1859.
15 *S.M.H.,* 17 November 1860.
16 29 August 1863.
17 Gavan Duffy to Parkes, 1 September 1856, Parkes Correspondence, vol. 51.
18 *Empire,* 16 December 1851, 6 January 1858. This newspaper had earlier implied (9 September 1857) that Cowper had no fixed political principles.
19 Letter of 'An Electoral Atom', *S.M.H.,* 10 March 1860.
20 Piddington to Parkes (then in England), 21 October 1862, Parkes Correspondence, vol. 30.
21 Parkes Papers, Miscellaneous Correspondence, A1050-1.
22 *Parliament, Factions and Parties,* pp. 57-63.
23 *Political Portraits,* p. 5.
24 Ibid., p. 7.
25 *S.M.H.,* 11 January 1858.
26 *S.M.H.,* 14 October 1864.
27 19 November 1857.
28 29 October 1857.
29 *S.M.H.,* 4 May 1857. Robertson attributed the leadership of the 'consistent' liberals to Jones, but, as the lands debate showed, Jones was more closely in sympathy with Cowper, and Robertson led the more extreme liberal group.
30 *S.M.H.,* 26 November 1857.
31 When Donaldson accused Cowper of making such a compact, he denied it, but Moreton Bay member Henry Buckley later admitted that Donaldson was right (*see S.M.H.,* 15 December 1858.).
32 *S.M.H.,* 10 December 1857.
33 16 January 1858.
34 6 January 1858.
35 Loveday and Martin, *Parliament, Factions and Parties,* p. 29, show that of 23 liberals who stood for re-election in January 1858, 22 were returned, as against only 8 out of 15 conservatives, but, as they point out, 6 independents retained their seats and 17 new members of then uncertain allegiance had been elected.
36 *S.M.H.,* 15 January 1858.
37 3 April 1858.

[38] *S.M.H.*, 3 December 1860.
[39] *S.M.H.*, 6 August 1858.
[40] Cowper to Jamison, 21 August 1858, Jamison Papers, vol. 3.
[41] *S.M.H.*, 13 November 1858.
[42] Cowper to Jamison, 6 January 1859, Jamison Papers, vol. 3.
[43] *S.M.H.*, 7 December 1858.
[44] See *S.M.H.*, 16 June 1858, 26 May, 2, 13 June 1859.
[45] 30 October 1860.
[46] See Cowper's answer to a question on this issue, *S.M.H.*, 3 December 1860.
[47] Cowper first openly admitted this motive for his change of front in his election speeches for the 1860 election, at which time he and his government were wildly popular (see *S.M.H.*, 6 December 1860).
[48] 2 June 1859.
[49] Cowper to Parkes (in England), 23 November 1861, Parkes Correspondence, vol. 6.
[50] See Loveday, "The Legislative Council in New South Wales 1856-1870', *Historical Studies*, vol. 2 no. 44 (April 1965), pp. 489-91; Currey, 'The First Proposed Swamping of the Legislative Council of New South Wales', *J.R.A.H.S.*, vol. 15, pt 5 (1929), pp. 286-91; Graham, 'The Role of the Governor of New South Wales under Responsible Government 1861-1890' (Ph.D. thesis), pp. 61-9
[51] *S.M.H.*, 31 August 1853, 10 May 1861. For Campbell's views, see *S.M.H.*, 1 September, 8 December 1853.
[52] *S.M.H.*, 18 August 1858, 26 May 1859, 22 March, 9 July 1860.
[53] See Robertson's interjection to Cowper's speech at a ministerial banquet, *S.M.H.*, 18 August 1859.
[54] *S.M.H.*, 30 August 1856.
[55] *S.M.H.*, 18 August 1858.
[56] See Robertson's speech in the Assembly, *S.M.H.*, 17 October 1860.
[57] *S.M.H.*, 26 May 1859.
[58] See the election speeches of Cowper and Arnold, *S.M.H.*, 3 December 1860.
[59] *S.M.H.*, 12 April 1861.
[60] *S.M.H.*, 4 April 1860. Loveday's article 'The Legislative Council' gives a concise account of these incidents.
[61] See Loveday, loc. cit., p. 488. Since the Assembly had not then passed the 1860 estimates, the ministry needed to pass an indemnity bill to cover funds already spent.
[62] Young to the Duke of Newcastle, 19 April 1861, Despatches, 1860-71, P.R.O. 1806.
[63] Loveday, loc. cit., p. 487.
[64] *S.M.H.*, 17 March 1860. See also Robertson's speech, *S.M.H.*, 22 March 1860.
[65] *S.M.H.*, 20 October 1860.
[66] Quoted in Currey, 'The First Proposed Swamping', loc. cit., p. 285.
[67] *S.M.H.*, 10 May 1861.
[68] Quoted in Currey, loc. cit., pp. 286-7.
[69] Graham, 'The Role of the Governor' (Ph.D. thesis), p. 61.
[70] Young's comment, quoted in Currey, loc. cit., p. 285.
[71] Graham, op.cit., p. 62.
[72] See Young to Cowper, 7, 10 June 1861, Cowper to Young, 8 June 1861 Cowper Correspondence, vol. 1; Wentworth to Young, 14 June 1861, Wentworth Papers.
[73] Cowper to Young, 8 June 1861, Cowper Correspondence, vol. 1.
[74] Deas Thomson, Manning, Macarthur, G. K. Holden, R. Fitzgerald and Charles Kemp are known to have accepted Cowper's conditions. See Thomson to Young, 7 June 1861, Thomson Papers, vol. 2; Manning to Young, 14 June 1861, Manning Papers, vol. 4; Fitzgerald to Cowper, 15 June 1861, Kemp to Cowper (dated 'Tuesday' only), Cowper Correspondence, vol. 2.
[75] Wentworth to Young, 14 June 1861, Wentworth Papers.
[76] Cowper to Parkes, 23 November 1861, Parkes Correspondence, vol. 6. Parkes was then in England as one of the government's immigration commissioners.
[77] 23 April 1861, Macarthur Papers, 1st ser., vol. 38.
[78] William Macarthur to James Macarthur, 15 May 1861, Macarthur Papers, 1st ser., vol. 38.
[79] 22 June 1861, Macarthur Papers, 1st ser., vol. 28.

80 Macarthur to C. Campbell, 2 November 1861, Macarthur Papers, 1st ser., vol. 24.
81 Young to Newcastle, 19 July 1861, Despatches, 1860-71, P.R.O. 1807
82 Comment written by Newcastle on Young's despatch of 21 May 1861, Despatches, 1860-71, P.R.O. 1807.
83 *S.M.H.*, 18 September 1861.
84 24 June 1861. The *Border Post* (Albury), 26 June 1861, made a similar point.
85 Piddington to Parkes, 20 August 1861, Parkes Correspondence, vol. 43.
86 *S.M.H.*, 18 January 1862.
87 Cowper to Parkes, 23 November 1861, Parkes Correspondence, vol. 6.
88 Cowper to Parkes, 21 December 1861, Parkes Correspondence, vol. 7.
89 21 November 1862.
90 'The Legislative Council', loc. cit., p. 498.
91 Ward to Macarthur, 19 October 1862, Macarthur Papers, 1st ser., vol. 29.
92 W. Macarthur to J. Macarthur, 15 May 1861, Macarthur Papers, 1st ser., vol. 38.

6 RELIGION AND PRINCIPLE

1 *Fifty Years in the Making of Australian History*, vol. 1, pp. 116-17.
2 *S.M.H.*, 20 October 1859.
3 See the report of the select committee on church and school lands, published in the *Empire*, 3 May 1860.
4 See Cowper's Assembly speech, *S.M.H.*, 14 September 1861.
5 30 June 1863.
6 *S.M.H.*, 19 August 1863.
7 See Cowper's speeches, *S.M.H.*, 16 September 1859, 17 July 1862.
8 *Church of England Chronicle*, 15 May 1857.
9 Ibid.
10 *S.M.H.*, 12 February 1857.
11 See Murray's comments, *S.M.H.*, 28 April 1858.
12 This letter and the subsequent correspondence between Cowper's office and Plunkett was published in *S.M.H.*, 11 January 1858.
13 See Cowper's minute to the Executive Council, 27 January 1858, Colonial Secretary's Dept Correspondence, Archives 4/7176·1.
14 13 January 1858, Colonial Secretary's Dept Correspondence, Archives 4/7176·1.
15 *S.M.H.* 10 February 1858.
16 13 February 1858.
17 10 February 1858.
18 *S.M.H.*, 28 April 1858.
19 See Martin to Cowper, 8 July 1858, Macarthur to Cowper, 16 July 1858, Colonial Secretary's Dept Correspondence, Archives 4/7176·1.
20 Suttor, *Hierarchy and Democracy in Australia 1788-1870*, p. 170.
21 Denison to Cowper, 6 January 1859, Cowper Correspondence, vol. 1. This system had been recommended for use in England by a committee of the Privy Council in 1859.
22 13 July 1859.
23 *Hierarchy and Democracy*, p. 266.
24 *Freeman's Journal*, 19 October 1859, printed the letter which Polding had requested should be read in Catholic churches.
25 See *V. & P.* L.A., 1859-60, vol. 1, pp. 935-7, for petitions for and against the bill.
26 24, 27 October 1859.
27 *S.M.H.*, 27 October 1859; *Empire*, 27 October 1859.
28 See *Empire*, 21 October 1859; *Northern Times*, 14 September 1859; *Bathurst Free Press*, 7 September 1859; *Maitland Mercury*, 1 November 1859.
29 *S.M.H.*, 15 December 1858, 5. 6, 7 January 1859.
30 *S.M.H.*, 24 January 1861.
31 Cowper to Young, 14 September 1861, Cowper Correspondence, vol. 1.
32 *S.M.H.*, 12 October 1861.
33 *S.M.H.*, 6 June 1862.

34 *S.M.H.*, 6, 26 June, 3 July 1862.
35 *S.M.H.*, 20 November 1862.
36 Graham, 'The Role of the Governor' (Ph.D. thesis), pp. 85-6.
37 'The Abolition of State Aid to Religion in New South Wales', *Historical Studies, Australia and New Zealand*, vol. 10, no. 38 (May 1962), pp. 168-9. Walker divides the post-1860 Assembly into 36 voluntaryists, 24 state-aiders and 13 'unknowns'.
38 *Church of England Chronicle*, 1 April 1859. This journal closely reflected the views of Bishop Barker and the upper church hierarchy.
39 *Freeman's Journal*, 8 February, 20 August 1862.
40 See Heydon's editorials, *Freeman's Journal*, 29 December 1858, 8 January 1859.
41 *S.M.H.*, 17 July 1862.
42 *S.M.H.*, 25 July 1862. Voting was 29 to 28.
43 *S.M.H.*, 6 November 1862.
44 Ibid.
45 21 October 1862.
46 Holden was appointed principal solicitor in the Titles Office under the new Torrens Act, at a salary of £1200 a year.
47 *S.M.H.*, 5 December 1862.
48 21 October 1862.
49 'The Abolition of State Aid', pp. 169-70.
50 Cowper to Lang, 2 October 1862, Lang Papers, vol. 7.
51 24 October 1862.
52 7 November 1862.
53 Piddington, Lang, Dalgleish and Wilson supported the bill as affirming the principle of secular education. Of those who voted against the second reading, only William Forster was a known supporter of secular education (*S.M.H.*, 24 July 1863).
54 Ibid., particularly the speech of James Hart.
55 *S.M.H.*, 27 September, 11 October 1866.

7   WORKING THE WIRES OF PATRONAGE AND POWER

1 Letter of 1 December 1858, quoted Windeyer, 'Responsible Government — Highlights, Sidelights and Reflections', *J.R.A.H.S.*, vol. 42. pt 6 (1957), P. 306.
2 Denison to Labouchere, 22 September 1856, Denison Correspondence, FM3/795.
3 Enclosure to Denison to Newcastle, 18 January 1861, Despatches, 1860-71, P.R.O. 1806.
4 *Parliament, Factions and Parties*, p. 107.
5 On 5 August 1856 Denison remarked to Donaldson on 'a committee of ignorant persons like Martin & Co.'. Denison Letters, B 205, No. 28.
6 Report of Cowper's speech at the Queen's birthday ball, *Empire*, 26 May 1858.
7 Denison to Cowper, 2 November 1857, Cowper Correspondence, vol. 1.
8 Denison to Cower, 13 January 1859, Cowper Correspondence, vol. 1.
9 The circumspection of British governments and the Colonial Office ensured that clashes of authority were rare. The 'Great Seal' case was the only notable one in Cowper's time. Currey, 'The Great Seal Case', *J.R.A.H.S.*, vol. 15, 5 (1929), pp. 267-82, gives a comprehensive factual account of the issue.
10 Cowper to Denison, 16 January 1861, quoted by Currey, loc. cit., p. 278.
11 Note by Newcastle, added to margin of Denison to Newcastle, 21 January 1861, Despatches, 1860-71, P.R.O. 1806.
12 Currey, loc. cit., pp. 280-1.
13 Quoted by Currey, loc. cit., p. 281. See also Cowper's speech to the Assembly, *S.M.H.*, 24 January 1861.
14 Cowper to James Macarthur, 22 June 1861, Macarthur Papers, 1st ser., vol. 28.
15 W. Macarthur to J. Macarthur, 15 May 1861, Macarthur Papers, 1st ser., vol. 38.
16 See notations on Young to Newcastle, 19 March 1863, Despatches, 1860-71, P.R.O. 1812.
17 Ibid., for Gairdner's note on the attached draft reply. Gairdner noted that 'I have always heard he [Cowper] was a clever politician', but that his real merits were little known.
18 28 August 1856.
19 Cowper to Lang, 27 April 1859, Lang Papers, vol. 7.·

20 Editorial, *Maitland Mercury*, 19 February 1857. Arnold first entered politics by winning the Durham seat in 1856.

21 'Our Celebrities', *Goulburn Herald*, 17 July 1861. The *Empire*, 16 March 1860, assessed Arnold as a bold, satirical speaker, clear-headed and possessing a keen sense of humour.

22 Arnold disregarded Cowper's intention to move a censure motion against the Parker government on 18 March 1857, by moving one of his own on the previous day. It was counted out when only 11 members remained in the House as he finished speaking. A quorum was 20 (*S.M.H.*, 18, 19 March 1857) Arnold forcefully opposed Cowper's 1857 lands bill (see *S.M.H.*, 20 November 1857).

23 14 March 1860.

24 18 October 1859.

25 *S.M.H.*, 23 June 1858.

26 *S.M.H.*, 24 February 1859.

27 Bayley spent his first four months as attorney-general (January to April 1859) in the Council. He then won the Mudgee seat in the Assembly and remained there until Cowper's government was defeated in October. Hargrave began his ministerial career as solicitor-general with a seat in the Assembly in 1859. The whole period of his attorney-generalship (April 1860 to July 1863) was spent in the upper house.

28 *S.M.H.*, 24 February 1859.

29 *S.M.H.*, 3 March 1859, p. 3. Deas Thomson withdrew his motions to this effect, but George Allen succeeded in adjourning the House until the government should decide the question, thus putting pressure on Cowper to accede to the majority wish, as expressed by the motion.

30 *Parliament, Factions and Parties*, pp. 112-13.

31 See Robertson's speech at Scone, *S.M.H.*, 14 December 1860.

32 *S.M.H.*, 30 August 1859; *Empire*, 21 October 1859, 6 July, 21 May 1860; *Maitland Mercury*, 1 November 1859; *Goulburn Herald*, 23 February 1859; *Southern Cross*, 10 March 1860.

33 *S.M.H.*, 18 August 1859.

34 *S.M.H.*, 22 March 1860.

35 *S.M.H.*, 1 March 1861, p. 3. Robertson was explaining to the Assembly the reason for Cowper having handled the issue of the Lambing Flat anti-Chinese riots instead of him (Robertson's portfolio gave him control of goldfields).

36 14 March 1860.

37 A local complaint was that the government spent little money in the area, and the pastoralists resented the lands bills. Deniliquin was then the centre of the Riverina separationist movement.

38 *Southern Courier*, 9 August 1861; *Empire*, 3 September 1861.

39 *S.M.H.*, 6 June 1863.

40 *S.M.H.*, 8 June 1863.

41 *Maitland Mercury*, 1 November 1859.

42 Hargrave to Cowper (date indecipherable, follows an earlier letter of 20 July 1863), Cowper Correspondence, vol. 2.

43 P.N. Lamb has pointed out that a free trade policy meant that the government could not readily expand customs duties without causing a political crisis, and the strong feeling against land and income taxes postponed their introduction until the 1890s. See Lamb, 'Crown Land Policy and Government Finance in New South Wales 1856-1900', *Australian Economic History Review*, vol. 7, no. 1 (March 1967), p. 38.

44 *S.M.H.*, 12 April 1861.

45 *S.M.H.*, 20 April 1861.

46 *S.M.H.*, 1 January 1862.

47 *S.M.H.*, 4 September 1862. Voting was 18 for and 22 against abolition.

48 The Burrangong anti-Chinese riots, with their antecedents and results, including Cowper's part in them, have been comprehensively examined in two recent articles: Carrington, 'Riots at Lambing Flat 1860-1861', and Walker, 'Another Look at the Lambing Flat Riots 1860-1861'.

49 *S.M.H.*, 10 April, 19 June 1858.

50 *Empire*, 23 May 1859.

51 Cowper became, at Lambing Flat, a special commissioner of the government, 'under whose instructions the Force both Civil and Military will act'. Executive Council Minute Books, 4/1540, vol. 24, pp. 299-308, no. 60/9, 25 February 1861, no. 60/00, 4 March 1861.

52 Carrington loc. cit., pp. 231-2; Walker, loc. cit., p. 197. For Cowper's speeches and actions at Burrangong, see *S.M.H.*, 9, 11, 12 March 1861.

53 Robertson to Cowper (date indecipherable), Cowper Correspondence, vol. 3.

54 The miners' complained that Cowper, while on the goldfields, had sympathized with their grievances but had denied that they had any legitimate ones when he reported to the Assembly (see *S.M.H.*, 9 April 1861). As *S.M.H.* pointed out, this was not true of his reported speeches: he took a similar 'law and order' line in both (*S.M.H.*, 3 April 1861).

55 *S.M.H.*, 13, 20 April 1861.

56 *S.M.H.*, 1, 6 August 1861.

57 See Cowper's comments, *S.M.H.*, 26 September 1861, p. 3. The bill allowed only one passenger per 10 tons of ship. Shipowners had to pay £10 for each Chinese before landing. A poll tax of the same amount was to be levied on Chinese arriving overland from other colonies.

58 *S.M.H.*, 11 September 1861.

59 This bill was a close copy of that which had lapsed in the Council earlier in the year. Leary's move to have the word 'Chinese' substituted for 'aliens' was defeated only by the casting vote of the chairman of committees (S.M.H., 12 September 1861, p. 5).

60 *S.M.H.*, 19 September, 18, 24 October, 14 November 1861.

61 See Cowper's speech when turning the first sod on the Great Western Railway, *S.M.H.*, *S.M.H.*, 21 October 1858. See also his speeches at the banquet following the opening of the Campbelltown line, *S.M.H.*, 5 May 1858, and in the Assembly, *S.M.H.*, 15 July 1858.

62 See Cowper's speech on the East Sydney hustings, *S.M.H.*, 6 December 1860. His government passed a railway extension vote of £712 000 in 1858. Much of this money was raised by loan on the London market. A vote of £1 700 000 to be raised similarly, was passed in 1861.

63 See *S.M.H.*, 23 October, 5 December 1861.

64 Resolution passed at a Bathurst meeting (*S.M.H.*, 28 October 1861).

65 *S.M.H.*, 30 November, 5 December 1861.

66 *S.M.H.*, 26 September 1863, quoted in P. Loveday, 'Patronage and Politics in New south Wales 1856-1870', *Public Administration* (Sydney), no. 4 (December 1959), p.341.

67 Ibid., p. 343.

68 For examples, see Donaldson Ministry Letters, A731, pp. 214-18, 265, 288-90, 354-5.

69 *S.M.H.*, 19 August 1863.

70 See Cowper's and Murray's evidence before the select committee on Owen's case, *V. & P.* L.A., 1858-9, vol. 1, pp. 396, 418-20.

71 *S.M.H.*, 30 March 1859.

72 Select committee on Owen's case, Report, *V & P.* L. A., 1858-9, vol. 1, p. 385.

73 Loveday, 'Patronage and Politics', p. 356. The ministerial motives cannot be assessed with any certainty. Probably Parkes was partly correct in his assumption, but at that time Cowper and Robertson were still appreciative of his past services.

74 For Parkes's wish to obtain an immigration post, see Parkes to Sarah Parkes, 13 February 1860, Parkes Papers, A1044, and Parkes Diary, A1011, entry for 5 to 15 December 1858. These entries show that Parkes had been contemplating such a move for more than two years before he brought up his motions on 1 May 1861.

75 'Patronage and Politics', p.355. A ministerial supporter, James Dickson, gained the seat when Chambers resigned from it.

76 *S.M.H.*, 20 February 1863.

77 'Patronage and Politics', p. 354.

78 J. Chisholm to J. Macarthur, 31 January 1861, Hassall Correspondence, vol. 1.

79 The Cowper-Robertson ministry's other appointments were: F. A. Cooper, gold

commissioner, 1860; S. B. Daniel, commissioner of Crown lands, 1862; J. Garrett, police magistrate, 1862; G. Markham and J. Garland, superintendents of police in 1862 and 1863 respectively; and T. Lewis, inspector of mines, 1863.

80 Executive Council Minutes, 4/1540, vol. 24, p. 292, no. 60/8, 1 February 1861. Prosecutors were paid £80 a day plus £2 travelling expenses. Holroyd, Driver and Windeyer, who sometimes supported Cowper, also took government legal briefs. *S.M.H.*, 14 August 1863.

81 *Empire*, 18 September 1863. The colonial secretary controlled the police and his office had to approve payments for legal work in connection with prosecutions.

82 These statistics are drawn from Colonial Secretary's Correspondence, Register of Justices of the Peace, 1857-64, Archives 3250. It should be noted that, while Cowper was adding 791 new men, 292 justices of the peace died, resigned or left the colony.

83 For details see *V. & P.* L.A., 1859-60, vol. 3, pp. 1206-9, 1230; Denison to Bishop Barker, 26 July 1858, Government House, Miscellaneous Correspondence, 4/1665; Executive Council Minute Books, 4/1537, vol. 21, pp. 76-7, no. 31, 2 August 1858.

84 Robertson's nephew, who was also his son-in-law, was appointed inspector of police by the Cowper-Robertson ministry (*S.M.H.*, 19, 21, 28 August 1863). Arnold's attempt to promote his brother-in-law, a clerk in the surveyor-general's office, was prevented by the ministry's fall in 1863 (*S.M.H.*, 31 October 1863). Dalgleish accused Weekes of creating the post of inspector of sugar refineries for his son (*S.M.H.*, 20 August 1863).

85 'Patronage and Politics', pp. 352-3.

86 Arnold to Jamison, 3 May 1860, Jamison Papers, vol. 3.

87 See D.C. Dalgleish's speech, *S.M.H.*, 20 August 1863. See also Martin's speech, *S.M.H.*, 19 August 1863.

88 20 October 1859.

89 'Patronage and Politics', pp. 346-7.

90 Nicholson to Manning, 29 May 1860, Manning Papers, vol. 3.

91 7 November 1859.

92 This circular was reproduced in the *Bathurst Free Press*, 3 April 1858.

93 The *Empire*, 7 March 1860, claimed that Cowper's appointments 'broke down a system of caste which had become hateful and dangerous'. For similar comment, see *Northern Times*, 21 January, 21 March 1860; editorials, *Maitland Mercury*, 5 November, 20 December 1859.

94 4 March 1861.

95 9 October 1863.

96 31 December 1859. The Colonial Secretary's Correspondence, Archives 4/751·1, lists ninety written applications to the Forster ministry for government posts, between 24 October 1859 and 3 March 1860.

97 *Pastoral Times*, 7 January 1862, reporting a speech by a local magistrate, Kelly.

98 16 November 1861.

99 See Weekes's budget speech, *S.M.H.*, 19 October 1860.

1 Land revenue for 1863-4 fell from £400 000 to £300 000 (Lamb, 'Crown Land Policy and Government Finance,' p.48) Final payments from the 1862 selectors were not due till 1865.

2 See Cowper's speech on the hustings, *S.M.H.* 6 December 1860.

3 In 1860 and 1861, Weekes admitted in his budget speeches that railway revenue had fallen below government estimates (see *S.M.H.*, 19 October 1860, 1 February 1861). *S.M.H.* noted in 1862 that a rise in rail receipts had taken place (editorial, 9 August 1862). This apparently ended government plans to lease out the railways to private enterprise (see Arnold's comments, *S.M.H.*, 7 June, 20 October 1862).

4 *S.M.H.*, 21 October 1861, 29 July 1862; *Maitland Mercury*, 23 January, 27 February 1862; *Goulburn Herald*, 16 November 1861.

5 *Empire*, 25 September 1861, gave the background to Cowper's new police bill, including Cowper's part in earlier moves to change the organizational basis.

6 *S.M.H.* 28 November 1861.

7 28 November, 4 December 1861.

8 Cowper to Parkes, 22 January 1862, Parkes Correspondence, vol. 6.
9 Cowper to Macarthur, 22 October 1862, Macarthur Papers, 1st ser., vol. 29.
10 'Portraits in Parliament', *Empire*, 12 July 1860.
11 See Martin's speeches, *S.M.H.*, 20 May, 2 June 1859.
12 Doyle, 'The Political Career of Sir James Martin' (B. A. thesis), p. 27.
13 28 August 1863.
14 29 August 1863.
15 See *S.M.H.*, 2 May 1863.
16 *S.M.H.*, 4 September 1863.
17 See *Empire*, 4, 5 September 1863; *S.M.H.*, 5 September 1863; *Goulburn Herald*, 10 September 1863.
18 *S.M.H.*, 24 September 1863.
19 No definite agreement on this issue had resulted from Cowper's visit to Melbourne during the parliamentary recess. Forster moved an unsuccessful censure motion over the matter, (*S.M.H.*, 2 September 1863).
20 *S.M.H.*, 1 October 1863.
21 See *Empire*, 21 September 1863.
22 9 October 1863.
23 *S.M.H.*, 8 October 1863.
24 *S.M.H.*, 29 October 1863.

8 TROUBLED YEARS 1864 1870

1 *Maitland Mercury*, 5 January 1864.
2 *S.M.H.*, 24 December 1863.
3 *S.M.H.*, 4 February 1864.
4 *S.M.H.*, 23 May 1864.
5 See *Empire*, 11 June, 29 July 1844; *S.M.H.*, 21 May, 20 August, 14 October 1864; *Maitland Mercury*, 30 July, 29 September 1864; *Freeman's Journal*, 5 March 1864. See also editoral comment from the *Yass Courier, Goulburn Argus, Illawarra Mercury*, reprinted in *Empire*, 2 August, 11 August 1864.
6 *Empire*, 19 January 1864; cartoon, *Sydney Punch*, 1 October 1864.
7 *S.M.H.*, 3, 9 November 1864.
8 *Empire*, 5, 15 November 1864; letter of 'A Cowperite and a Parkesite', *Empire*, 14 November 1864.
9 *S.M.H.*, 5 November 1864; *Empire*, 15 November 1864. See also Robertson's interjection to Martin's speech, *S.M.H.*, 9 November 1864.
10 Of 36 men who voted for Cowper's censure motion, 27 were re-elected. Of 29 who had supported the government, only 12 were re-elected (*S.M.H.*, 20 January 1865).
11 *S.M.H.*, 20 January 1865, estimated that Martin supporters numbered 24 in the new Assembly, white their opponents numbered 45. Loveday and Martin, *Parliament, Factions and Parties*, p. 44, indicate that in 1865 the Cowper-Robertson faction had 29 steady supporters to Martin's 11 and Parkes's 13, with independents holding the balance of power.
12 *Empire*, 15 November, 6 December 1864; *S.M.H.*, 20 January 1865.
13 Cowper to Lang, 'Confidential', 4 August 1863, Lang Papers, vol. 7, pp. 362-5.
14 Parkes, *Fifty Years in the Making of Australian History*, vol. 1, p. 181.
15 Young to Cardwell, 22 January 1866, Despatches to the Secretary of State, C.O. 201/538.
16 18 March 1865.
17 Young to Cardwell, 22 January 1866, Despatches to the Secretary of State, 1860-71, C.O. 201/538.
18 *S.M.H.*, 6 January ,31 March 1864. Darvall contended that the lower classes bore a disproportionate part of the tax burden under the existing system of indirect taxation, but his proposal for a tax on incomes of more than £200 a year was defeated by 30 votes to 7. Cowper appears not to have been in the House at the time.
19 *S.M.H.*, 30 March 1865; *Empire*, 31 March 1865.
20 *S.M.H.*, 17 May 1865. Parkes, as an opponent of Cowper's government could normally

have been expected to make political capital out of the issue by supporting the demand for abolition. Instead he moved 'the previous question', which passed by 38 votes to 7.

21 Young to Cardwell, 22 January 1866.
22 *Empire*, 29 May, 13 June 1865.
23 Plunkett to Macarthur, 2 September 1865, Macarthur Papers, 1st ser., vol. 30. Plunkett explained that he accepted the post temporarily 'for the honour of the Bar, and for the credit of the country'.
24 7 October 1865.
25 *S.M.H.*, 4 July 1867.
26 *Lictor*, 22 July 1869.
27 Editorial on Cunneen's appointment, *Freeman's Journal*, 14 October 1865.
28 *Empire*, 25 October 1865; editorial, *Newcastle Chronicle*, reprinted by *Empire*, 7 November 1865; editorial, *Goulburn Herald*, reprinted by *Empire*, 31 October 1865.
29 *S.M.H.*, 18, 25, 30 November 1865.
30 *S.M.H.* and the Sydney Chamber of Commerce supported Samuel's proposals; two public meetings condemned them as unjust to working-men. *S.M.H.*, 30 November, 2, 4, 5, 6, 12 December 1865.
31 *S.M.H.*, 18 December 1865, said that the bank took this stand because the Assembly had slashed Samuel's budget proposals.
32 20 December 1865.
33 28, 29, 30 December 1865.
34 See Loveday and Martin, *Parliament, Factions and Parties*, p. 48, for a concise account of this incident and comment upon Parkes's motives.
35 Young to Cardwell, 19 January 1866, Despatches to the Secretary of State, C.O. 201/538. Burdekin was then 28 years of age.
36 Cartoons, 13 January 1866.
37 Young to Cardwell, 19 January 1866, Despatches to the Secretary of State, C.O. 201/538.
38 *S.M.H.*, 17 January 1866.
39 13 January 1866.
40 *S.M.H.*, 10 January 1866.
41 Parkes to Martin, 8, 14 January 1866, Parkes Correspondence, vol. 62, pp. 14-25.
42 3 May 1866.
43 *S.M.H.*, 4 September 1866.
44 Therry to J. Macarthur, 24 September 1866, Macarthur Papers, 1st ser., vol. 34.
45 Ibid.
46 *Freeman's Journal*, 2 March 1867.
47 5 July 1866.
48 *S.M.H.*, 7 February 1866.
49 *S.M.H.*, 11 October 1866, noted that, of 31 members present while Cowper spoke, 25 were carrying on conversations in groups of two or three, while Cunneen read a book.
50 Towns to Stuart, 18 February 1867, Towns and Co. Papers, vol. 3.
51 Young to Cardwell, 21 July 1865, Despatches to the Secretary of State, C.O. 201/534.
52 Young to Cowper, 3 March 1869, Cowper Correspondence, vol. 2.
53 Young to Cowper, 19 April 1870, Cowper Correspondence, vol. 3.
54 Cowper to Rt Hon. Robert Lowe, 26 February 1869, Cowper Correspondence, vol. 2.
55 Memorandum by Stuart, 16 December 1875, Towns and Co. Papers, vol. 4.
56 4 December 1869.
57 See Loveday and Martin, *Parliament, Factions and Parties*, p.40; *S.M.H.*, 31 December 1869.
58 Belmore to Granville, 25 January 1870, Despatches to the Secretary of State, C.O. 201/557.
59 Ibid.
60 Ibid.
61 Ward, 'Charles Gavan Duffy and the Australian Federation Movement 1856-70', *J.R.A.H.S.*, vol. 47, pt 1 (1961), p. 18.
62 27 August 1870.
63 Cowper to Belmore, 12, 25 August 1870, Letters to the Earl of Belmore, vol. 1.
64 12 May 1870.

65 8 December 1870.
66 7 October 1870.
67 Cowper to Belmore, 25 August 1870, Letters to the Earl of Belmore, vol. 1.
68 See *Freeman's Journal*, 7 January 1871; *Goulburn Herald*, 22 February 1871.

9   RETROSPECT

1 Cowper to Lang, 3 November 1871, Lang Papers, vol. 7.
2 MacMillan, 'The Australians in London', *J.R.A.H.S.*, vol. 44, pt 3 (1959), p. 171.
3 30 November 1871, Macarthur Papers, 1st ser., vol. 43.
4 Cowper to Stuart, 17 March 1872, Towns and Co. Papers, vol. 16.
5 Ibid.
6 See Rose Cowper to Alex Stuart, 11 June 1875, Towns and Co. Papers, vol. 17.
7 Lanarck to Parkes, 20 October, 15 December 1874, 12 January 1875, Parkes Correspondence, vol. 54; Cooper to Parkes, 16 September 1873, 26 November 1874, 4 August 1875, Parkes Correspondence, vol. 7.
8 See report of an interview with Charles Cowper Jnr. *Daily Telegraph*, 6 June 1906. See also C. Cowper Jnr to Parkes, 18 November 1874, 3 April 1875, Parkes Correspondence, vol. 7.
9 Ibid.
10 'The Sydney Railway Company 1848-1855', *J.R.A.H.S.*, vol. 43, pt 2 (1957), p. 58.
11 See *S.M.H.*, 27 May 1853, 2, 21 July, 2 August 1854.
12 See *S.M.H.*, 7 December 1863, 8, 21 April 1864.
13 *S.M.H.*, 26 November 1875.

Bibliography

CONTEMPORARY SOURCES

OFFICIAL

Colonial Secretary's Department, Correspondence. Archives.
  Letters from individuals re land. 2/7833, 2/7967.
  Indices and registers, letters received. 2454-2461.
  Applications for government posts, 1859-60. 4/751.1.
  Removal from office of the chairman of the National Schools Board
  (J. H. Plunkett), 1858. 4/7176.1.
  Register of justices of the peace, 1857-64. 3250.
  Registers of grants and leases, 1836-56. 7/518-7/662.
  In-letters, 1860-3, 4/3425, 4/3540, 4/3475, 4/505.
  Index and registers to letters received. 2497, 2498.
  Registers of minutes, 1855-81. 4/1079, 4/1080.
Denominational Schools Board, In-letters, Archives 4/3701.
Electoral Roll for Northumberland, 1848-9. 324.91N, M.L.
Executive Council of New South Wales. Minute Books. Archives 4 — 1527-
  4/1559 (1856-71).
_____Registers of Minutes. Archives 4/1458, 4/1459, 4/1460, 4/1461,
  4/1462.
Governor of New South Wales. Despatches to the Secretary of State,
  1860-71. P.R.O. Microfilms 1806-38, M.L.
_____Transcripts of Missing Despatches, 1844-55. A1267-9, M.L.
Governors of New South Wales. Autograph Letters, 1866-73. A968-
  A970, M.L.
_____Despatches to the Secretary of State, 1842-59. Bound into
  volumes, M.L.
_____Miscellaneous Correspondence, 1856-70. Archives 4/1665,
  4/1666, 4/1667.
Historical Records of Australia, Ser. 1, vols 13, 15-19, 22, 25.
Lands Department. MSS A282, M.L.
Letters to the Earl of Belmore. Archives A2542-3.
New South Wales Legislative Assembly. *Votes and Proceedings,* 1856-71.
New South Wales Legislative Council. *Votes and Proceedings,* 1843-71.

178

NON-OFFICIAL

Manuscripts

Held at Mitchell Library, Sydney, except where otherwise stated
Arnold, W. M. Correspondence. MSS 901.
Autograph Letters. A63.
Autograph Letters Collected by Sir Henry Parkes. A990.
Autograph Letters of Notable Australians. A69, A70.
Autograph Letters to Sir Henry Parkes. A71.
Barker, Thomas. Papers. A5398.
Berry, A. Papers, Uncat. MSS 315.
Broughton, Bishop W. G. Letters. Microfilm, FM4/225-6.
Campbell Jnr, Robert. Papers, 1828-52. MSS 2129.
Collaroy Station. Papers. Vols 1, 18, 24. A2383, A2401, A2407.
Cowper, Dean. Autobiography. A679.
Cowper, William. Correspondence. A676-8.
_____Letters. AC16.
_____Letters. A3315.
_____Papers. D60.
Cunninghame Papers. A3180.
Darvall, J. B. Papers. Vol. 1. A5436.
Deniehy, D. H., Letters to Parkes, 1854-7. A709.
Denison, Sir W. Correspondence. Microfilm, FM3/795.
_____Letters. B205.
Donaldson, S. A. Letters, 1844-8. A730.
Donaldson Ministry. Letters. A731.
Duncan, W.A. Autobiography. A2877.
Gipps-La Trobe Correspondence. Public Library of Victoria.
Hassall Correspondence. Vols 1, 4. A1677.
Henty Letters, 1838-50. A1975.
Holroyd, A. T. Papers. Doc. 1029.
Indian Labour, New South Wales, 1842. A2029.
Jamison, R. T. Papers. Vols 3, 8. D38.
Kemp, Charles. Diary. A2063.
Kerr, William. Papers. MSS 981/2.
King Papers. Vol. 2 A1977.
Lang, Rev. J. D. Papers. A2221-A2244.
Macarthur Papers. First series. A2917-A2983.
_____Papers. Second series. A4304, A4348.
MacNally, M. J. 'Wivenhoe, Cobbitty'. VIB.
Manning, W. M. Papers. MSS 1107, 246/3, 246/4.
Morehead,E. My Recollections. Typescript.
Mowle, S. M. Retrospective Journal, 1836-51. A3942.
Nichols, R. Papers. MSS 375.
O'Sullivan, E. W. From Colony to Commonwealth. B595.

Parkes, H. Diary. A1011.
Parkes Correspondence. Vols 6-62. A876-A932.
Parkes Papers. A1044.
Parkes Papers. Miscellaneous Correspondence. A1051
Public Men of Australia, A68.
Rusden, G. W. Papers. Vol. 36. Leeper Library, Trinity College, University of Melbourne.
Sydney Railway Company. Minute Books, 1848-55. Archives 7/2666, 7/2667.
Thomson, Edward Deas. Papers, Vols 1, 2, 3 A1531.
Towns and Co. Papers MSS 1279.
Walker, William. Papers. Uncat. MSS 501.
Walker Family. Papers. Uncat. MSS 462.
Wentworth, W. C. Papers. A756.
Wild Family. Papers. Doc. 1050.
Windeyer, W. C. Letters. AW77.
_____Papers. Uncat. MSS 186.

Books and Pamphlets

Baker's Australian Atlas, 1843, 6 X980-11/2 (M.L.).
Barton, G. B. (ed.) *The Poets and Prose Writers of New South Wales.* Gibbs, Shallard Co., Sydney, 1866.
Byrne, J. C. *Emigrant's Guide to New South Wales Proper, Australia Felix, and South Australia* Effingham Wilson, London, 1848.
_____*Twelve Years' Wanderings in the British Colonies from 1835 to 1847.* 2 vols. Richard Bentley, London, 1848.
Buchanan, D. *Political Portraits of Some of the Members of the Parliament of New South Wales.* Davies & Co., Sydney, 1863.
Denison, Sir W. T. *Varieties of Vice-Regal Life.* 2 vols. Longmans, Green & Co., London. 1870.
Electoral Rolls for the City of Sydney, 1842-3, 1848-9 (M.L.).
Hassall, J.S. *In Old Australia.* R. S. Hews & Co., Brisbane, 1902.
Huntingdon, H.W.H. *'A Historical Account of Campbell's Wharf.* Typescript, 1918. M.L. B1364.
Lang, J.D. *Brief Sketch of My Parliamentary Life & Times.* John L. Sherriff, Sydney, 1870.
Low, F. *The City of Sydney Directory for MDCCCXLIV-V.* E. Alcock, Sydney, 1844 (M.L.).
_____*Low's Directory of the City and District of Sydney for MDCCCXLVII.* Alonzo Grucott, Sydney, 1847.
MacAlister, C. *Old Pioneering Days in the Sunny South.* Chas. MacAlister Book Publication Committee, Goulburn, 1907.
Macarthur, J., and Therry, R. *Election for the County of Camden: the Speeches of James Macarthur and Roger Therry, Esquires.* Kemp & Fairfax, Sydney, 1843.

Mansfield, R. *Analytical View of the Census of New South Wales for the Year 1841,* Kemp & Fairfax, Sydney, 1841.
_____*Analytical View of the Census of New South Wales for Year 1846.* Kemp & Fairfax, Sydney, 1847.
Mundy, G. C. *Our Antipodes: or, Residence and Rambles in the Australasian Colonies.* Richard Bentley, London. 1852.
Parkes, Sir H. *Fifty Years in the Making of Australian History.*, 2 vols. Longmans, Green & Co., London, 1892.
Reports of the Society for Promoting Christian Knowledge, 1826-63. M.L. 206/3.
Rusden, G.W. *History of Australia.* 3 vols. Chapman Hall Ltd, London, 1883.
Ryan, J. T. *Reminiscences of Australia.* George Robertson & Co., Sydney, 1895.
Therry, R. *Reminiscences of Thirty Years' Residence in New South Wales and Victoria.* Sampson Low, Son & Co., London, 1863.
Walker, W. *Reminiscences of a Fifty Years' Residence at Windsor, on the Hawkesbury.* Turner & Henderson, Sydney, 1890.

Newspapers and Periodicals

Athenaeum
Armidale Express
Atlas
Australasian Chronicle (later *Sydney Chronicle*)
Australian
Australian Churchman
Bathurst Free Press
Bell's Life in Sydney
Border Post(Albury)
Church of England Chronicle
Colonial Observer
Colonial Times and Tasmanian
Era
Freeman's Journal
Guam
Goulburn Herald
Guardian
Heads of the People
Laughing Jackass
Lictor
Maitland Mercury
Melbourne Argus
New South Wales Railway and Tramway Magazine
Newspaper Cuttings, Vol. 1 (M.L.)
Northern Times

Old Times
People's Advocate
Port Phillip Gazette
Port Phillip Herald
Port Phillip Patriot and Melbourne Advertiser
Sentinel
Southern Courier
Southern Cross
Southern Queen
Star and Working Man's Guardian
Sydney Daily Advertiser
Sydney Morning Herald
Sydney Punch
Town and Country Journal
Voice in the Wilderness
Weekly Register

SECONDARY SOURCES

Books and Pamphlets

Andrews, A. *The First Settlement of the Upper Murray, 1835 to 1845; with a short account of over two hundred runs, 1835 to 1880.* D. S. Ford, Sydney, 1920.

Austin, A. G. *Australian Education 1788-1900: Church, State and Public Education in Colonial Australia.* Pitman, Melbourne, 1961.

Barcan, A. *A Short History of Education in New South Wales.* Martindale Press, Sydney, 1965.

Barnard, A. *Visions and Profits: Studies in the Business Career of Thomas Sutcliffe Mort.* Melbourne University Press, Melbourne, 1961.

Barrett, J. *That Better Country: the Religious Aspect of Life in Eastern Australia 1835-1850.* Melbourne University Press, Melbourne, 1966.

Bartley, N. *Australian Pioneers and Reminiscences...* Gordon & Gotch, Brisbane, 1896.

Blainey, G. *The Tyranny of Distance: How Distance Shapes Australia's History.* Sun Books, Melbourne, 1966.

Clark, C. M. H. *Select Documents in Australian History 1788-1850.* Angus & Robertson, Sydney, 1970.

_____*Select Documents in Australian History 1851-1900.* Angus & Robertson, Sydney, 1965.

Coghlan, T.A. *Labour and Industry in Australia.* 4 vols. Oxford University Press, 1918.

Dickey, B. *Politics in New South Wales 1856-1900.* Cassell Ltd, Melbourne, 1969.

Dunsdorfs, E. *The Australian Wheat-Growing Industry 1788-1948.* Melbourne University Press, Melbourne, 1956.

Fairfax, J.F. *The Story of John Fairfax: Commemorating the Centenary of the Fairfax Proprietary of the Sydney Morning Herald 1841-1941.* John Fairfax Sydney, 1941.

Fawcett, J. W. *Life and Labours of the Right Reverend William Grant Broughton, D.D.* R. Woodcock, Brisbane, 1897.

Fitzpatrick, B. C. *The British Empire in Australia: an Economic History 1834-1939.* Macmillan, Melbourne, 1969.

Fogarty, R. *Catholic Education in Australia 1806-1950.* Vol. 1. Melbourne University Press, Melbourne, 1959.

Gilchrist, A. *John Dunmore Lang.* Jedgarm Publications, Melbourne, 1951.

Gollan, R. *Radical and Working Class Politics: a Study of Eastern Australia 1850-1910.* Melbourne University Press, Melbourne. 1967.

Grainger, E. *Martin of Martin Place: a Biography of Sir James Martin 1820-1886.* Alpha Books, Sydney, 1970.

Hawker, G. N. *The Parliament of New South Wales 1856-1965.* Government Printer, Sydney, 1971.

Hoban, L. E. *A Centenary History of the New South Wales Police Force 1862-1962.* Centenary Committee, Police Department, Sydney, 1962.

Johns, F. *An Australian Biographical Dictionary.* Macmillan, Melbourne, 1934.

Knight, R. *Illiberal Liberal: Robert Lowe in New South Wales 1842-1850.* Melbourne University Press, Melbourne, 1966.

Loveday P., and Martin, A. W. *Parliament, Factions and Parties: the First Thirty Years of Responsible Government in New South Wales 1856-1889.* Melbourne University Press, Melbourne, 1966.

Martin, A. W., and Wardle, P. *Members of the Legislative Assembly of New South Wales 1856-1900.* Australian National University Press, Canberra, 1959.

Melbourne, A. C. V. *Early Constitutional Development in Australia.* University of Queensland Press, Brisbane, 1963.

———— *William Charles Wentworth.* Biggs and Co. Ltd, Brisbane, 1934.

Molony, J. N. *An Architect of Freedom: John Hubert Plunkett in New South Wales 1832-1869.* Australian National University Press, Canberra, 1973.

Mowle, P. C. *A Genealogical History of Pioneer Families of Australia.* Angus & Robertson, Sydney, 1969.

Nadel, G. H. *Australia's Colonial Culture: Ideas, Men and Institutions in Mid-Nineteenth Century Eastern Australia.* Cheshire, Melbourne, 1957.

Pike, D. (ed.). *Australian Dictionary of Biography.* Vols. 1-4. Melbourne University Press, Melbourne, 1966-72.

Roberts, S. H. *The Squatting Age in Australia 1835-1847.* Melbourne University Press, Melbourne, 1935.

Roe, M. *Quest for Authority in Eastern Australia 1835-1851.* Melbourne University Press, Melbourne, 1965.

Steven, M. *Merchant Campbell 1769-1846: a Study of Colonial Trade.* Oxford University Press, Melbourne, 1965.

Suttor, T. L. *Heirarchy and Democracy in Australia 1788-1870: the Formation of Australian Catholicism.* Melbourne University Press, Melbourne, 1965.

Turner, N. *Sinews of Sectarian Warfare? State Aid in New South Wales 1836-1862.* Australian National University Press, Canberra, 1972.

Ward, J. M. 'Australia's First Governor-General' (M.L.).

——*Earl Grey and the Australian Colonies 1846-1857: a Study of Self-government and Self-interest.* Melbourne University Press, Melbourne, 1958.

——*Empire in the Antipodes.* Edward Arnold Ltd, London, 1966.

Waldersee, J. *Catholic Society in New South Wales 1788-1860.* Sydney University Press, Sydney, 1974.

Theses

Cleverley, J. F. 'The Administration of State-assisted Elementary Education in Mainland New South Wales 1789-1855'. Ph.D., University of Sydney, 1967.

Doyle, F. M. 'The Political Career of Sir James Martin'. B. A., University of Sydney, 1950.

Graham, N. I. 'The Role of the Governor of New South Wales under Responsible Government 1861-1890'. Ph.D., Macquarie University, 1972.

Irving, T. H. 'The Development of Liberal Politics in New South Wales 1843-1855'. Ph.D., University of Sydney, 1967.

Loveday, P. 'The Development of Parliamentary Government in New South Wales 1856-1870'. Ph.D., University of Sydney, 1962.

Molony, J. N. 'John Hubert Plunkett in New South Wales 1832-1869'. Ph.D., Australian National University, 1971.

Turney, C. 'A History of Education in New South Wales 1788-1900'. Ph.D., University of Sydney, 1962.

Articles

Abbott, G. J. 'The Introduction of Railways into New South Wales 1846-1855', *J.R.A.H.S.,* vol. 52, pt 1 (March 1966).

Baker, D. W. A. 'The Origins of Robertson's Land Acts', *Historical Studies, Selected Articles,* First series, edited J. J. Eastwood and F. B. Smith, Melbourne University Press, 1967.

Barrett, J. 'The Gipps-Broughton Alliance 1844', *Historical Studies, Australia and New Zealand,* vol. 2, no. 41 (November 1963).

Birch, A. 'The Sydney Railway Company 1848-1855', *J.R.A.H.S.,* vol. 43, pt 2 (1957).

Bland, F. A. 'City Government by Commission', *J.R.A.H.S.,* vol. 14, pt 3 (1928).

Buckley, K. 'Gipps and the Graziers of New South Wales 1841-1846', *Historical Studies, Selected Articles,* First series, J. J. Eastwood and F. B. Smith, Melbourne University Press, 1967.

Cable, K. J. 'Religious Controversies in New South Wales in the Mid-Nineteenth Century—1. Aspects of Anglicanism', *J.R.A.H.S.,* vol. 49, pt 1 (1963).

Carrington, D. L. 'Riots at Lambing Flat 1860-1861', *J.R.A.H.S.,* vol. 46, pt 4 (October 1960)

Currey, C. H. 'The First Proposed Swamping of the Legislative Council of New South Wales', *J.R.A.H.S.,* vol. 15, pt. 5 (1929).

Dickey, B. 'The Establishment of Industrial Schools and Reformatories in New South Wales 1850-1875', *J.R.A.H.S.,* vol. 54, pt 2 (June 1968).

Dowd, B. T. 'Daniel Henry Deniehy', *J.R.A.H.S.,* vol. 33, pt 2 (1947).

Dyster, B. 'Support for the Squatters 1844', *J.R.A.H.S.,* vol. 51, pt 1 (March 1965).

———'The Fate of Colonial Conservatism on the Eve of the Gold-Rush', *J.R.A.H.S.,* vol. 54, pt 4 (December 1868).

Forrest, J. 'Political Divisions in the New South Wales Legislative Council 1847-53', *J.R.A.H.S.,* vol. 50, pt 6 (December 1964).

Grose, K. '1847: the Education Compromise of the Lord Bishop of Australia', *Journal of Religious History,* vol. 1, 1960-1.

Houison, A. 'The Venerable Archdeacon Cowper', *The Australian Historical Society, Journal and Proceedings,* vol. 3, pt 8 (1916).

Irving, T. H. 'The Idea of Responsible Government in New South Wales before 1856', *Historical Studies, Australia and New Zealand,* vol. 2 no. 42 (April 1964).

Lamb, P. N. 'Crown Land Policy and Government Finance in New South Wales 1856-1900', *Australian Economic History Review,* vol. 7, no. 1 (March 1967).

———'Early Overseas Borrowing by the New South Wales Government', *Business Archives and History,* vol. 4, no. 1 (February 1964).

Loveday, P. ' "Democracy" in New South Wales: the Constitution Committee of 1853', *J.R.A.H.S.,* vol. 42, pt 4 (1956).

———'The Legislative Council in New South Wales 1856-1870', *Historical Studies,* vol. 2, no. 44 (April 1965).

———'The Member and his Constituents in New South Wales in the Mid-nineteenth Century', *Australian Journal of Politics and History,* vol. 5, no. 2 (November 1959).

MacMillan, D. S. 'The Australians in London', *J.R.A.H.S.,* vol. 44, pt 3 (1959).

Main, J. 'Making Constitutions in New South Wales and Victoria

1853-1854', *Historical Studies, Selected Articles,* Second series, Melbourne University Press, 1967.

Martin, A. W. 'A Note on the Attempted Assassination of the Duke of Edinburgh, Sydney 1868', *La Trobe Historical Studies,* vol. 1, no. 1 (April 1971).

McDonald, D. I. 'Gladesville Hospital, the Formative Years 1838-1850', *J.R.A.H.S.,* vol. 51, pt 4 (December 1965).

Nairn, N. B. 'The Political Mastery of Sir Henry Parkes,' *J.R.A.H.S.,* vol. 53, pt 1 (March 1967).

Ryan, J. A. 'Faction Politics: a Problem in Historical Interpretation', *Australian Economic History Review,* vol. 8, no. 1 (March 1968).

Walker, R. B. 'Another Look at the Lambing Flat Riots 1860-1861', *J.R.A.H.S.* vol. 56, pt 3 (September 1970).

_____'Bushranging in Fact and Legend', *Historical Studies,* vol. 2, no. 42 (April 1964).

_____'David Buchanan: Chartist, Radical, Republican', *J.R.A.H.S.,* vol. 53, pt 2 (June 1967).

_____'The Abolition of State Aid to Religion in New South Wales', *Historical Studies, Australia and New Zealand,* vol. 10. no. 38 (May 1962).

_____'The Later History of the Church and School Lands', *J.R.A.H.S.,* vol. 47, pt 4 (August 1961).

Ward, J. M. 'Charles Gavan Duffy and the Australian Federation Movement 1856-70', *J.R.A.H.S.,* vol. 47, pt 1 (1961).

_____'The Australian Policy of the Duke of Newcastle, 1852-1854', *J.R.A.H.S.,* vol. 50, pt 5 (November 1964).

Windeyer, J. B. 'Richard Windeyer: Aspects of His work in New South Wales 1835-47', *J.R.A.H.S.,* vol. 50, pt 2 (July 1964).

Windeyer, W. J. V. 'Responsible Government—Highlights, Sidelights and Reflections', *J.R.A.H.S.,* vol. 42, pt 6 (1957).

Withycombe, R. 'Church of England Attituders to Social Questions in the Diocese of Sydney, c. 1856-1866', *J.R.A.H.S.,* vol. 47, pt 2 (1961).

Index

Aaron, Dr Isaac, 44-5
Adelaide (S.A.), 49
Albury (N.S.W.), 8, 10, 128
Allen, George, 37
Allen, W. B., 96, 130
Allwood, Rev. Robert, 26
Anti-Transportation Committee, *see* New South Wales Anti-Transportation Committee
Arnold, W. M., 72, 105, 108-10, 121, 139, 141-3, 146; and Legislative Council reconstruction, 90; and patronage, 131-3; and railway construction, 124, 128-9
Atlas, 25, 30, 39
Austin, A. G., 2
Australasian Anti-Transportation League, 46-7
Australasian Chronicle, 13, 17, 42
Australian (newspaper), 12-13, 35, 42
Australian Colonies Government Act (1850), 50
Australian Gas Light Company, 50
Australian Mutual Provident Society, 50
Australian Patriotic Association, 9

Baker, D. W. A., 2
Bank of New South Wales, 145
Barcan, A., 8
Barker, Frederick (Bishop of Sydney), 100-2, 106, 108, 113, 150
Barrett, John, 2
Bayley, L. H., 106, 123
Bells Life in Sydney, 51
Belmore, Earl of, 154-6
'Berrima incident', 57
Berry, Alexander, 19
Bigge, J. T., 6
Billyard, W., 118
Birch, A., 160
Blake, I. J., 111, 131
Bland, Dr William, 17, 35, 80
Bligh, J. W., 55, 66
Blondin, 113

Border Post, 133
Bourke, Sir Richard, 5, 7, 9, 101
Bowman, James, 23
Bowman, William, 31-2, 35
Boyd, Ben, 27, 30, 33, 34-5, 42-3
Bradley, William, 48
Brenan, J. R., 17, 75
Brisbane, Sir Thomas, 6, 21
British and Foreign Schools system, 23
Broughton, William Grant, 4-5, 9, 12, 16, 25-7, 28, 52, 101, 113; and Church of England Lay Association, 25; and church schools, 23-5 *passim*
'Brownlow Hill', *see* Macleay family
Buchanan, David, 78, 80, 96, 131-2, 144, 153
Buchanan, James, 136
Buckley, K., 2
'Bunch', the, *see* elections (N.S.W.), Legislative Assembly (1856, 1857)
'bunyip aristocracy', 54
Burdekin, Marshall, 148-9
Burrangong goldfields, 126-7
Burton, William, 94, 117
bushranging: N.S.W., 137, 141, 143-4
Butler, Edward, 145
Byrnes, James, 71, 75

Caldwell, John, 111
Camden, electorate of, 11-17
'Camden Park', *see* Macarthur, James, and Macarthur, William
Campbell, John, 71, 84, 88
Campbell, Robert (Snr), 4
Campbell, Robert (son of Robert Snr), 5, 18, 25, 43, 55, 61, 70, 73, 76, 84, 85, 103, 130-1; and constitutional change, 54-5, 61; and electoral politics, 64-6, 69, 72-3, 86; and Legislative Council reform, 90; personal qualities, 55, 120-1; and religion, 60, 101, 107; and transportation, 45-6, 56
Campbell, William, 152
Chambers, Joseph, 131

187